Politics of the Untouchables

Politics of the Untouchables

Congress and the Bhangis: A Socio-Political Analysis

SHYAM LAL

RAWAT PUBLICATIONS
Jaipur • New Delhi • Bangalore • Guwahati • Kolkata

ISBN 978-81-316-0768-8

Published by
Prem Rawat for **Rawat Publications**
Satyam Apts, Sector 3, Jawahar Nagar, Jaipur 302 004 (India)
Phone: 0141 265 1748 / 7006 Fax: 0141 265 1748
E-mail: info@rawatbooks.com
Website: www.rawatbooks.com

New Delhi Office
4858/24, Ansari Road, Daryaganj, New Delhi 110 002
Phone: 011 2326 3290

Also at *Bangalore, Guwahati* and *Kolkata*

Typeset by Rawat Computers, Jaipur
Printed at Chaman Enterprises, New Delhi

To

Baba Saheb Dr Bhim Rao Ambedkar
on his 125th Birthday Anniversary Year.

Who else, but Ambedkar, 'The Only One', 'The Unique' and 'Matchless/Incomparable', 'Historical Figure' and 'Versatile Intellectual Indian' amongst his contemporaries.

But, who understood or neglected Ambedkar, or took advantage of him for the fulfilment of one's own selfish motives?

Though there's a competitive spirit pertaining to planning, but where is India of his dreams?

This book is my humble and heartfelt tribute for Baba Saheb Ambedkar.

Contents

Preface

It is well known that sweepers and scavengers remain an utterly neglected section of the society even after 67 years of independence. Due to what is traditionally regarded as a degraded and defiled occupation, the society has always kept them at a distance. The work of sweepers entails hazardous task of clearing waste material including human excreta and garbage.

Much has been spoken and written about India's untouchables. Unfortunately, very little has been written or spoken about Rajasthan's dalits in general and the Bhangis in particular, the lowest of the low untouchables. Therefore, I think it is an important issue to address the latter.

To begin with, the Bhangi – untouchables amongst untouchables and the lowest of the low will be an example for all political parties to contemplate their pitiable conditions and do some serious *chintan* (thinking). Even Congress supporters would feel disgusted by the Congress rule. Congress and Bhangi became synonymous – a reality the entire state and nation could see except Congressmen. The Bhangi community is fed up with negative and betraying attitude of Congress.

Today, the common perception is that too many caste Hindus still believe that the Congress did lot for Scheduled Castes (SCs) in general and Bhangis in particular, and empowered them. Dalits empowerment have been the key slogan for Congress since independence but field data reports show that Bhangis still lag way behind other SCs in having a say in decision-making process. Of course, it is not totally true. Despite having supported Congress over six decades, Bhangis still distrust the Congress. The blame lies partly with Congress who have not paid attention to Bhangis as they did for other SCs/STs. Partly, they themselves are responsible for their backwardness. Had they socially and politically united they would have benefitted more and led to empowerment in politics and could have taken advantage of the protective discrimination policy. This is the root cause of their troubles. There is also an irony here. Bhangis think Congress is their 'Mai-Baap' (Mother-Father) 'माई–बाप' (someone who is the only source of help) because of their support to it, but politically Congress used them as a 'Vote Bank'.

Congress leadership has repeatedly said that the government has been doing welfare programmes for them. We need to talk about Bhangi – the lowest of low. That is for sure. But we also need to keep some touch with historical veracity, for their pre-independent to post-independent support. Yet, in the past 67 years the Congress has flagrantly failed its potential. Consequently, 2013 State Assembly Election and 2014 Parliamentary polls provide an excellent window to demolish the myth, once and for all, about Congress's contribution to Dalits in general and Bhangis in particular.

When Congress sit on the opposition benches, just one question should haunt them, i.e. how to regain the scheduled castes' goodwill that the party has lost. Some cronies could tell Congress leadership that the question will sort out itself as time passes by; Congress leadership should show the door to such cronies. It is these gentlemen who have brought Congress party to this sorry state of affairs.

This book is an outcome of my constant interaction with community fellows, netas, social activists and social workers, who kept telling me in a variety of ways about their culture, economy, education, jobs and politics. What I have done is to put their views in a systematic manner.

Apart from my personal experiences, all the facts in this book have been picked up from illiterate, semi-literate Bhangis and also from a few formally educated persons.

I have met most Bhangis who feel they were betrayed by the Congress leadership. A very relevant issue raised by almost all Bhangi leaders, netas and social activists is the actual improvement in the condition of the Bhangi in post-Independence India in general and Rajasthan in particular, after years of positive discrimination and law banishing untouchability and discrimination against Bhangis. This is the theme of the book. In fact, one of the critical points raised by me is the 'invisibility' of the questions of marginality in sociological discourse on Bhangi caste. The author is particularly critical of the stance taken by most prominent Congress leaders to ignore the grass-roots realities of caste negligence which are ignored by government organizations.

On several occasions, my upper caste colleagues/friends have discussed the socio-economic and educational conditions of the community, caste fellows and their families with me. Such discussions were of immense use in building critique of their socio-economic and educational conditions, from the point of view of staunch supporters and followers of Congress and Congress patronage. I thank all those colleagues.

Since independence, Bhangis have not progressed – but actually regressed. Surely something went wrong somewhere. The Bhangis themselves are quite amused. They are feeling regressed when others (upper caste Hindus) are not feeling so. The Bhangis are weak. They are not capable of defending themselves. So, let us just discuss the reality. During the last few years, we have not seen any small/big protests, rallies, dharnas, demonstrations, strikes, etc. in the capital by the Bhangis, as other castes/communities have done against the government for ignoring their interest. In this book I have tried to reflect the reality as I saw and experienced. I have not taken any sides. I am an objective observer. I am trying to present the reality, how a common Bhangi got sucked into that and its consequences. I can understand the pain of lakhs of Bhangis who were denied their legitimate rights. Their reality needs a book on its own.

From 1990 onwards, a number of sociologists, viz. Shyam Lal, Bindeshwar Pathak, Stephen Fuchs, B.V. Pandya, S.N. Chaudhary, B.N. Srivastava, Sachchidananda and few others had reported, through their research studies, the change in the social and economic conditions and mobility pattern in the various regions of the country. However, they never focused on their social and economic backwardness. Politically, they are marginalized.

During the national movement/agitation, the Bhangis whole-heartedly supported the Gandhi Congress. Even after the independence of the country in 1947, till today, Bhangis remained with Congress. Yet they are socially neglected, economically backward and politically they are nowhere. I, therefore, decided to discuss all these issues in this book. In fact, these issues do not figure in any other studies. Over a period of 67 years, what Congress has done to Bhangi community, particularly in Rajasthan, to liberate them from caste and class exploitation and oppression finds detailed discussion in this work.

There is no doubt that the Bhangi's problems must be tackled, but I am afraid that the problems of the Bhangis may again be forgotten as it has been so far. For the ills which the Bhangis are suffering, though they are not as much advertised as those of the corruption, inflation and jobs, these are not less in reality.

The centre and state governments owe a duty to the Bhangis, as it does to all oppressed and suppressed people, to break their shackles and set them free. I have written this book because I feel that there is a need to draw the attention of political leadership to this problem. I hope the publication of this book will attract the attention of political leaders, social reformers, sociologists and all those who are interested in the emancipation of the downtrodden.

First of all, I sincerely express my deep sense of gratitude to my respected teacher Professor Gopal Bhardwaj, Department of Sociology, JNV University, Jodhpur, who has been kind enough to write the Focus Setting for the book.

Many organizations and individuals have lent their support and cooperation in various ways at different stages in this work. I am grateful to them for supplying valuable material for historical study of the various aspects of the Bhangi community.

I have had a very fruitful discussion on various parts of the work with Indu Mathur, Department of Sociology, University of Rajasthan, Shyam Lal Verma, Department of Political Science, University of Rajasthan and K.S. Saxena, former Director, (UGC) Academic Staff College, JNV University Jodhpur. I am grateful to them for their valuable comments and encouragement.

Finally, I would like to thank my friends Jagdish Roy and Daulal Mathur for helpful suggestions and pertinent comments on earlier version of this study.

SHYAM LAL

Focus Setting

Prof. Shyam Lal, a sociologist, a devoted researcher and a prolific writer, having written over twenty books by now has come out with this interesting book – *Politics of the Untouchables: Congress and the Bhangis – A Socio-Political Analysis*. This is a book raising challenging questions, what has the political party, Congress done for the Bhangis, except for keeping it captivated on false hopes and exploiting it as a vote bank. This is also suggestively so clear from the title of the book and is what the reader will find from the content's inside the book.

If there is any one sociologist nearing the age of seventy and could non-stop do so much of research and writing work, it is Prof. Shyam Lal. It is he who alone could take up studies of leftover or not so exclusively covered castes of SC, along with those of ST, OBC and minority identity, more from Rajasthan. It is he who could also, simultaneously and commendably work in credit worthy and contributing academic positions including Vice-Chancellorship at Jodhpur, Jaipur and Patna. It is he, all self-made by himself, almost as an ignored or isolated one, without patronage of any positioned high priest or subjective support base. It is he, one and alone, who himself by caste is a 'Bhangi', with birth and upbringing in a hard to subsist family .... and yet Shyam Lal could so grow, could do so much and get and set such an example of himself, by his sheer diligence and perseverance. Shyam Lal and Ambedkar have a common caste identity, though no match to him and yet Ambedkar all through remained with Shyam Lal as an inspiring mentor. Shyam Lal could even write frankly and uniquily about himself and his even and odd relations, in one of his books *Autobiography of a Bhangi Vice-Chancellor* (at Jodhpur), and a similar one about his Patna tenure. Few of Prof. Shyam Lal's books have also been translated in Hindi.

I am one who has remained so proximal to Shyam Lal right from his sociology student days, and could see how he has been performing and progressing till now. What one is by birth also determines one's acquisitions, favoured or hindered, but how Shyam Lal could overcome so much of it by dare, dedication and doership. I could also be the reader of almost all that is coming from his pen, his sociology writings. One distinctiveness in all these is richness and genuineness of data, so effortfully and painstakingly collected, and its elaborate descriptiveness which is certainly substantive, valuable and usable for his readers, not only of Sociology or Social Sciences, but also of many other orientation and interests.

Apart from its narrow academics, if sociology and social sciences must also have wider scope, relevance and public following, Shyam Lal's writings so well fulfils such a purpose and possibly many may be its users, of whatsoever interest or intent. I might also prefer to consider Shyam Lal's sociology, his intense concern for his own caste Bhangi along with those at lowly socio-economic level in Indian society as his personal protest or passive activism. If Srinivas's birth as a Brahaman was somehow at the source of his 'Sanskritization', so also Shyam Lal's own caste Bhangi could condition him for such a persuasion and assertion through many of his writings, so unconcealed. Thus he only could also detect 'Asparshikaran' (when and how one of higher caster becoming untouchable) as a reverse process of Sanskritization. Here one may express concern for 'objective' ... oh, this objective ... can any human thinking and action be and remain 'objective', to what extent, yet for the sake of prevalent pretension in social sciences?

This book of Shyam Lal's and many other writings of his cannot properly be understood if Bhangi caste's position in the entire caste system and in comparison to other castes is not taken note of. Caste system is a very complex phenomena, in many ways and for multiple reasons, for its very long history, for internal variations and contradictions, for perceptions about it so much removed from the reality, and so grossly and subjectively politicized. A tropic situation thus emerges about castes ... (1) In 'Reality' (2) In 'Perceptions' (3) As a recently 'Politicized'.

Each caste as an endogamous unit is a discrete and independent entity in comparison to other castes. The problem arises because of the lumping up of the castes, historically and traditionally in the 'Varna' groupings and after India's independence in the newly formulated SC, ST, OBC like generics. In both type of cases, individual castes lumped into such grouping were never on the equal footing and because of this, whereas 'Varna' identity of each and all castes hardly mattered for them, but caste reservations after independence did materially help or harm individual caste among SC, ST and OBC due to who benefitted most and who remained as a left out or deprived caste or castes? Bhangi is one such caste, the caste, which got the least amongst SC and even could not get that much life peanut shells or bones.

Bhangi is exclusively the only caste which is known all over India for its most filthy scavenger's occupation, marked untouchable reckoning and lowest stigmatized statuslessness. No other occupations or openings were ever available or possible for Bhangis, which was not the case with all other castes. Therefore, historically and socially if any single caste deserved to be taken up first and separately for welfare, with materially to benefit and change, this caste must have been Bhangi, which may even now be taken up, better late than never.

Sociological study of caste is a recent approach, otherwise caste has been in focus for Indian classical writers, reformers and many others, all through our long history, and more so during our freedom movement, on the part of many leaders, lately including Gandhi, Ambedkar, Lohiya, etc. whereas Indian sociologists ignored all such interests and references and were almost entirely under the influence of Western sociology;

Western sociologists on the other hand were having their own perceptions and distortion about India, either being ignorant or making deliberate inferences.

This is no place to point out all these here, but at least to question if caste system was really 'Hierarchy' or not, and what an ethnocentrity as if Western Society ever was 'Equivalous'? castes were Higher and Lower, but classes were by classification Higher-Middle-Lower, etc.; and whether authority (archy) of higher upon lower was more a reality or perception and distortion in case of castes? Where and when was West that equal or liberal towards it lower and racially Black class? Westerners also failed to see that ritually though caste units were separated economically and occupationally, castes were also mutually cooperating and interdependent – to put it locally as 'Algav' and Sahgav, like 'you' and 'we', both were simultaneously existential and self-sustaining. Yes India yet did have its social problems; but West too had theirs, which were much more serious and inhuman.

Reservations for select castes and tribes were certainly needed but their wholesale clustering or lumping into SC, ST, OBC must have been done based upon factual survey and scrutiny. Due to assertive pressure and vote bank politics, these 'Schedules' were kept on expanding mostly by underserved inclusions, even until now. There was also need for periodic and continuous 'Social Impact Study' which was also never done. It could have revealed that which castes and tribes and who among them benefitted the most, and those who were staggered and left out. In due course, even within reservation availing castes and so-called tribes, these benefits were getting blocked by counted rich and resourceful families, as becoming vested interest of the few at the cost of exclusion and deprivation of a huge bulk of their own commoners. 'Social Impact Study' could have prompted for needed amendments and to do away with such blockings and many anomalies. Then perhaps the water will reach up to the tail, the locale of Bhangis and real tribals.

It was Mahatma Gandhi who did unprecedented and a lot for Bhangis, not only in words but also by his works, and brought them in focus before all, in and outside India. Gandhi even used for Bhangis a renewed and fulfilling identity 'Harijan'. On Bhangi or Harijan matters the so-called conflict between Gandhi and Ambedkar was also more misunderstood and misused, even after the lifetime of both, more for ulterior than fair reasons. After India's independence and in the process of the execution of caste reservations, the cause and topmost deserved social justice for Bhangis got damaged and lost when their identity was submerged in newly lumped SC and further into what came in parlance a new term and formation of a ubiquitous and nefarious 'Dalits', constituted by those of reserved groupings and their outside ideologue supporters. The vociferous among Dalits were even demanding a ban and to consider offensive if 'Bhangi' or 'Harijan' term is anymore used for caste Bhangis. Somewhere, if Bhangis were using 'Valmiki' identity for themselves, this was also considered unduly 'Sankritizing' by Dalitizing dictates. Who could realize that Dalit usage was a disguise on the part of those other than Bhangis, and a loss of identity for Bhangis.

It is not out of place here if we refer Lohiya's commendation for Ambedkar for his scholarship and social activism, for his radical as well as rational persona, and over and above, for his 'like himself alone' historic contribution for what independent India must likely to be. Lohiya was more supportfully sensitive for Bhangis and was repentant as to why liberal and rationally so fair and objective Ambedkar was hesitant; otherwise a very special constitutional provision or a exclusive separate reservation for Bhangis could have been provided from the very beginning, with full support and acclaim from all. Of course, Lohiya's prime objective was 'Samta Samaj' and casteless free India, though, contrary to it, there emerged trends of turning India's 'Jantantra' into Jatitantra' ... Democracy into Casteocary. How shocking it could have been for Lohiya, and also for Ambedkar, if only in few years to come, Ambedkar's name was hijacked by those having no concern with him, for their caste's reservation, or for caste politics? In due course, it was as if there was noone to care or bother for Bhangis.

I wish that Shyam Lal may now discern and detect another fast emerging disturbing and encroaching trend of self-seeking interest on part of a micro section of Indian society, who are hardly sparing opportunities of quality education at all levels, including professional education, which has been fast becoming privatized and exorbitantly expensive. Rich and resourceful high-ups only can afford such expenses and payments for their sons and daughters, who even if are not deserving, with innate talent, they may even succeed for degrees and jobs through huge spendings and if needed through corrupt give and take practices. Not only General Category Castes's parents are so availing or indulging in such ill-gotten gains, but now there are enough of such seekers from SC, ST, OBC, new rich and resourcefulls. A huge bulk of youth and hopefuls belonging to these reserved categories may now expect not much of opportunities from reservations, left for them by their own once benefitted or so benefitting caste fellows. Bhangis are not only worst affected, but even the 'Safai Karmachari' (scavenging) jobs which were exclusive for them, not only in Municipalities and Panchayats but also in government offices, Railway, Defense, etc. are now being sought after by candidates from all other castes, even including Brahmans, because of paucity of jobs and charms of government jobs. Poor Bhangis even with educational degrees, have nowhere to go and know what to do? To put it in the generalized way, now, India is perhaps only for those who can anyway make enough money and, with increasing requirements of all and shrinking resources, much of that needed for life and living is becoming out of reach for over half of our people. India's 'Freedom' ... 'Democracy' ... 'Constitution' ... and its Socialists could hardly provide enough to our commoner countrymen including those from lowly castes and Bhangis and real tribals.

Though it is somewhat sensitive that is why Shyam Lal wrote this book; there are understandable and unavoidable reasons at the source of it. It was because of Gandhi and some reformist Congress leaders of our freedom movement that the curse removing cause of Bhangis and our much needed commitment for them could come into projection and prominence, and what was also needed to be taken up for them in independent India, at the very first instance. During those days no other caste had that much Congress following and in Congress colour, all over India. This happened because of Ambedkar too, more for Bhangis as a very special case for support and upliftment on the part of the State and Govt. After independence, although Gandhi's cause for serving and strongest support for Bhangis was not there and Ambedkar also had bitter experience with Congress, Bhangis yet remained with Congress as sure supporters and assured vote bank. Other political parties could hardly try or trust if Bhangis would go with them, as is the case even now.

Putting Bhangis among SC was a shocking rebuff and loss of hope and justice for the Bhangis themselves. They were certainly historically, socio-economically and public image-wise exclusive and much different from other Scheduled Castes, and were not in a position to compete with all other castes among the Scheduled cluster. Added to this, for many long years, Congress was the ruling party at the centre and in the States. Congress PMs, CMs and ministers all through ignored and were apathetic towards what was most essentially needed to be done for the Bhangis. Bhangis were also without their own caste leaders of any influence, eminence and position, and if there were any here and there, they were the uncertain and entangled ones, even finding their own existence rough and tough. This was very much so in the State of Rajasthan and during the long tenure of last Congress CM. Shyam Lal cites in this and other books a good number of such cases, even with names of Bhangi leaders, expectants, etc. that how they were ignored or suffered in the hands of Congress. Prof. Shyam Lal himself, though more than deserving and experienced, there was Congress CM's conscious 'No and Never' for his progressive appointment. Yet Shyam Lal was made Vice-Chancellor at Jodhpur and Jaipur by BJP CMs and it was even CM of Bihar, Nitish Kumar, who could pick up Shyam Lal as Vice-Chancellor for his Patna University, a very rare case for any outsider to get entry in Bihar. Shyam Lal is not alone but there are many more Bhangi claimants and potentials who persistently stood distanced and dejected during Congress rule in Rajasthan. Such Bhangi youths are also a huge count.

Shyam Lal could yet do so much in the academic field of sociology and also perform commendably and set his record and example as three times Vice-Chancellor of three different universities. Had it not coincided, two such offers at a time, BJP CM Madam Raje in Rajasthan even entrusted Shyam Lal the task of planning and setting Ambedkar Foundation, an Institution of Higher Learning, Research and Excellence in Rajasthan, with offer of its founder Chairman or Director. It is not out of any grudge or expectation that Shyam Lal has written this book, but to show how Congress missed and failed, and even betrayed to fulfil the just and deserving cause of Bhangis. This book also exposes what happened to the caste reservations and what amendments are now to be taken up as urgent task, to do justice with all those, among SC and ST, who could get almost nothing and, now, nothing is likely to be left for them, by unevenly maximum benefitting castes of the SC, ST identity and rich and resourceful from within such castes. This book thus stands as a reminder, a testimony, and outspoken call for correction and adhering commitment, though late but now in favour of Bhangis and the real tribals. Sociology must also not only remain academic, but must also equip its practitioners to assume activist roles, to serve society and humanity in pronounced and praxised ways.

Gopal Bhardwaj
Department of Sociology
JNV University, Jodhpur

1

Introduction

National Freedom Movement opened the doors for socio-educational and religious reforms for all untouchable communities in general, and Bhangis in particular. The Reform Movement, a landmark in the history of India, is attributed to Gandhi-Ambedkar pact of 1932 and to the galaxy of vernacular social reformers. The single greatest gift of these exalted personalities of India was bringing the untouchable communities into the main stream of the society.

The main purpose of socio-religious movement advocated several methods of bringing the changes amongst the untouchables – such as inculcating in them *sanskaras* and good habits. It outlined the need for acquainting them with the value and importance of education. There was also greater emphasis on their social and religious content. The principles of socio-religious reforms are said to be gradually diminishing in each succeeding decades of the post-independence period. Though, there are several reasons, yet three reasons are most important – as to why Bhangis particularly have been neglected in the post-independence era.

First, the Bhangis are not politically so united and conscious as other scheduled castes/communities, such as Chamars and Jatavas in Uttar Pradesh; Meghwals, Chamars, Bairwas and Raigars in Rajasthan and Mahars in Maharashtra. The Bhangis are not aware of their socio-political importance and are not set to ensure that they get the maximum mileage from it.

Second, so far, Bhangi politics has mainly been an appendage of Congress strategy. The numerous Dalit groups in the country did not perceive themselves as representing one electorally collective block with their own say in national affairs. Instead, they linked their fate to what the major political parties then decided was good for them.

Third, Bhangi neta does not represent the community. It is known to mortgage their voice to Congress. They urged Bhangi voters to vote for Congress.

Finally, Bhangi leadership was headed by numerous factions. They are divided on the basis of the regions and sub-castes and they constantly formed and reformed themselves as they sought maximum advantage individually. Congress was always the mediator through which they took part in the state and national politics and the Congress was the ultimate beneficiary as well as the final arbiter of their destiny.

Issues of Bhangis

The Bhangi issues must be seen in an isolated manner from the rest of the scheduled castes/communities. There are issues relating to occupational change leading to socio-economic mobility, low identity, dismal representation in state assembly, parliament and other public bodies, urge for self-respect, movement towards viable and sustainable communities, reservation and discrimination as well as issues relating to manual scavenging, separate reservation and formation of commission for safai karamcharis. Clubbing the problems of Bhangis with other untouchables is not proper, since the Bhangi's problems are more basic, more complex and more urgent, calling for greater attention and action. I would give an overview of Bhangi visions, illusions and fourfold discriminations they face today. The problems of Bhangis are not only social but also economic and political.

Congress the Only Choice: The Bhangi's Viewpoint

When Pandit Jawahar Lal Nehru was speaking to a huge gathering of sweepers at Ram Lila ground, New Delhi, on 2

January 1964, he had expressed his concern in these memorable words:

> I cannot refuse to meet you. So, I have to come here. I do not know what I should tell you as I feel ashamed of long back I had a chance to visit your basties where you live. On seeing the most pitiable conditions, I was very much shocked. I realized that even after independence of the country, you have been suffering in the same way as you had been before independence. All this worries me and therefore, I was hesitating to be in your midst.[1]

Unfortunately, except giving them some sort of facilities, Nehru's successors have done little for ameliorating the suffering of the sweeper community. As a result, even today after 67 years of the independence of the country, 7.5 lakh sweepers in India clean service latrines in the country.

Since independence, SC's were considered a 'committed' vote bank of the Congress. The Gandhi Congress during the pre-independence period, did provide them political space to participate in the freedom struggle. This is not to deny the role of power, hegemony and dominance exercised by the upper castes who dominated the upper layer of the Congress leadership. SCs voters remained loyal to the Congress in the troubled times of 1967 and even during 1977, the Congress was not totally deserted. However, sign of decline in its SCs vote share became the order during elections held in the late 1980 and the early 1990s. The 1996 Lok Sabha elections finally presented a changed electoral landscape, when SCs deserted Congress in many states.

So far as the Bhangis are concerned, other political parties had failed to make an inroad among them. Thus, they remained with Congress during this critical period. It should be noted here that even prior to independence some Bhangis were actively working in the party. It is also significant to mention that Yashwant Rai, the then first President of 'All India Safai Mazdoor Congress' (henceforth called Safai Mazdoor Congress) and others who supported the Congress since its inception (1965), attempted to mobilize the Bhangis enbloc throughout the country for the Congress party.[2] They told the Bhangis that it was their dharma to support the Congress.[3] The Safai Mazdoor Congress did remain active and also survived beyond 2000.

The Bhangi's tilt toward Congress is the outcome of pre-independence relations arising out of Congress sympathy with them. For instance, Congress under the leadership of Mahatma Gandhi, Pandit Jawahar Lal Nehru, Smt Indira Gandhi, Rajiv Gandhi, P.V. Narasimha Rao and others fortunately encouraged pro-Bhangi feelings by accepting them in the party and doing something for their socio-economic betterment. Bhangis since then tend to see Congress as their patron. Thus, an objective analysis shows that Bhangis and Congress party were once inseparable.

From pre-independence to post-independence, Bhangi's across the country actively participated in Gandhi's movement/agitation and supported Gandhi Congress whole-heartedly. Shyam Lal in his book 'सामाजिक न्याय एवं दलित राजनीति'[4] described his view, thus:

> जहां तक भंगियों का प्रश्न है, दूसरे राजनीतिक दल उनका समर्थन प्राप्त कर सकने में असमर्थ रहे थे। इस प्रकार इस कठिन समय में भी भंगी समुदाय कांग्रेस के साथ रहा। इस बात को ध्यान में रखा जाना चाहिए कि स्वतन्त्रता प्राप्ति से पूर्व भी भंगी समुदाय के कुछ लोग कांग्रेस पार्टी में सक्रिय रूप से कार्यरत थे।
>
> मेहतर समाज तो धन, धरती और धन्धे से भी वंचित है। गुलामी, बेरोजगारी तथा रात दिन की कड़ी मेहनत के बाद दो–चार आने की मजदूरी पर अपने बाल बच्चों के साथ जीवन निर्वाह करता है। स्वतन्त्रता संग्राम में सहयोग देने के लिए उसके पास भला क्या था? यातना के लिए जर्जर शरीर, आहूति के लिए प्राण। यही था उसका देश के प्रति सच्चा स्नेह और बलिदान। फिर भी मेहतर समाज ने यथा सम्भव अपनी दयनीय स्थिति में भी गांधी और कांग्रेस को आजादी की लड़ाई के लिए आर्थिक सहयोग दिया।
>
> भारतीय वार्षिक रजिस्टर के अनुसार 22 जुलाई 1931 को कानपुर नगर पालिका के सफाई मजदूरों द्वारा सार्वजनिक सभा में गांधी को 11,000 रू. की थैली भेंट की गई। उसी दिन संध्याकाल प्रार्थना सभा में 51 रुपये 13 आना और दिया। 23 जुलाई 1931 को मेहतर सभा ने पुनः संग्रह करके 3,242 रुपए सवा 15 आने और भी दिये। 25 जुलाई 1931 को उन्नाव रेल्वे सफाई कर्मचारियों ने गांधी को रेल्वे स्टेशन पर 282 रुपए की थैली भेंट की। 25 जुलाई 1934 को गांधी के लखनऊ आने पर मेहतरों ने 3495 रुपए

पौने 12 आने की थैली भेंट की। इटावा से 732 रुपए, फरूखाबाद से 645 रुपए, मुरादाबाद से 32 रुपए 8 आना, जालोन से 601 रुपए, आगरा से 9 रुपए साढ़े 5 आने, सीतापुर से 301 रुपए सवा 9 आने, बांद्रा से 185 रुपए 2 आने की थैलियां भेंट की। इसके अलावा अलग–अलग व्यक्तिगत रूप से उस दिन मेहतर समाज के लोगों ने गांधी को 10,943 रुपए साढ़े 7 आने भी दिये। 26 जुलाई 1934 को कानपुर में 3,592 रुपए 13 आने भेंट किये। 27 जुलाई 1934 को कानपुर में 3,592 रुपए 13 आने भेंट किये। 28 जुलाई 1934 को गोरखपुर के मेहतर समाज ने 951 रुपए की थैली भेंट की। 31 जुलाई 1934 को काशी के हरिजन विद्यार्थियो ने सार्वजनिक सभा में अपने अध्ययन के पैसों से बचत करके गांधी को 5,000 रुपए की थैली भेंट की। 1 अगस्त को शेष छात्रो ने 37 रुपए 9 आने 4 पाई की राशि और भेंट की। उडीसा के फटे हाल मेहतरो ने पाई–पाई जोड़कर गांधी और कांग्रेस को चंदा दिया। इस प्रकार सम्पूर्ण अखण्ड पाठ भाारत के सफाई मजदूरो ने आजादी के आन्दोलन में आम जनता के साथ–साथ धन दिया। इसी प्रकार बाद में 'कस्तूरबा राष्ट्रीय फण्ड' एवं 'भारतीय राष्ट्रीय कांग्रेस फण्ड' में भी इस मेहतर समाज ने धन का सहयोग दिया।

इसी प्रकार सरकारी अभिलेख सूचना विभाग, उत्तर प्रदेश लखनऊ के अनुसार 29 जुलाई 1934 को काशी की एक सभा में गांधी ने मेहतरों की प्रशंसा करते हुए कहा 'मेरी दृष्टि' में एक पाई देने वाला 10 से 50 हजार देने वाला घनश्याम दास बिड़ला से भी उस 1 पाई की कीमत अधिक है। हजारों रूपयों की अपेक्षा मुझे तो गरीब की गांठ की कोड़ी पाकर ही अधिक आशा और प्रसन्नता हुई। इसी प्रकार मेहतर समाज ने गांधी और कांग्रेस को अपनी शक्ति से भी अधिक धन सहयोग दिया।

जहां तक राष्ट्रीय आन्दोलन में, राजपूताना और विशेषकर मारवाड़ के भंगियों के आर्थिक सहयोग का सवाल है, यह कहा जा सकता है कि 6 जुलाई 1934 को जब महात्मा गांधी अपनी हरिजन यात्रा के दौरान अपने दल बल सहित अजमेर व ब्यावर होते हुए लूनी रेल्वे जंक्शन पहुंचे तब स्वतन्त्रता सैनानी जयनारायण व्यास के नेतृत्व में भंगियों के एक प्रतिनिधि मण्डल ने उनका रेल्वे स्टेशन पर गर्म जोशी के साथ स्वागत किया। लखारों के बास के भंगियों ने इस अवसर पर गांधीजी को रेल्वे स्टेशन पर रुपए 993 की थैली भेंट की।

वैसे तो आजादी के बाद 56 वर्षो में अधिकांश समय तक केन्द्र और राज्यों में कांग्रेस ही सत्तासीन रही। परन्तु न तो गांधी के उत्तराधिकारियों ने और न ही कांग्रेसजनों ने मेहतर समाज की सुध ली। आज भंगी सामाजिक, आर्थिक और राजनीति में हाशिए पर जा रहे हैं।

इस बात का भी उल्लेख करना महत्वपूर्ण है कि यशवन्त राय जो कि उस समय 'कांग्रेस अखिल भारतीय सफाई मजदूर कांग्रेस' (जिसे बाद में सफाई मजदूर कांग्रेस के नाम से जाना गया) के सर्वप्रथम अध्यक्ष थे तथा अन्य लोगों, जिन्होंने 1965 में कांग्रेस का समर्थन किया, सम्पूर्ण देश में भंगियों को कांग्रेस पार्टी में संगठित करने का प्रयास किया। उन्होने भंगियो से कहा कि यह तो उनका धर्म (कर्तव्य) है कि वे कांगेस का समर्थन करें। सफाई मजदूर कांग्रेस सकिय बनी रही तथा आज भी अस्तित्व में है।

भंगियों का कांग्रेस के प्रति झुकाव स्वतन्त्रता प्राप्ति से पूर्व के सम्बन्धों तथा कांग्रेस की उनके साथ संवेदना का परिणाम था। उदाहरण के तौर पर, महात्मा गांधी, पण्डित जवाहरलाल नेहरू, श्रीमती इन्दिरा गांधी, राजीव गांधी, पी.वी. नरसिंम्हा राव आदि के नेतृत्व में कांग्रेस ने भंगियों को पार्टी में उचित स्थान प्रदान कर तथा उनके सामाजिक आर्थिक उत्थान हेतु कार्य कर उनके प्रति सकारात्मक दृष्टिकोण का उदाहरण प्रस्तुत किया। तभी से भंगी समुदाय कांग्रेस को अपने संरक्षक (Patron) के रूप में मानता है। इस प्रकार एक वस्तुनिष्ठ विश्लेषण इस बात की ओर संकेत करता है कि एक समय में भंगी तथा कांग्रेस एक दूसरे से घनिष्ठ रूप से जुड़े हुए थे।

फरवरी 1979 में पश्चिमी बंगाल के बैरकपुर जिला, चौबीस परगना में वाल्मिकी मन्दिर में सफाई मजदूर कांग्रेस का 12वां अधिवेशन सम्पन्न हुआ। इस अधिवेशन में इन्दिरा गांधी मन्त्रिमडल के भूतपर्वू रेल उपमन्त्री बूटा सिंह, सफाई मजदूर कांग्रेस के अध्यक्ष पद पर निर्वाचित हुए।

अध्यक्ष पद पर अन्य उम्मीदवारों के बनिस्पत बूटा सिंह का चयन दो बातों पर आधारित था। प्रथम, बूटा सिंह प्रधानमन्त्री इन्दिरा गांधी के निकट सहयोगी थे। द्वितीय, बूटा सिंह भंगियों को सरकार में तथा कांग्रेस संगठन में कुछ पद प्रदान करा सकने में सक्षम थे। अतीत में बूटा सिंह के प्रति भंगियों का यह अनुभव रहा कि बूटासिंह का नेतृत्व उनके लिए लाभकारी सिद्ध होगा।

स्वर्गीय इन्दिरा गांधी तथा राजीव गांधी के प्रधान मंत्रित्व काल में बूटा सिंह के रूप में सत्ताधारी दल के भीतर एक शक्तिशाली भंगी नेता के रूप में उभरे। उन्होने दिल्ली, बम्बई, कलकत्ता, गुजरात, राजस्थान, पंजाब तथा अन्य राज्यों में भंगियो की अनेक बडी रैलियां तथा सम्मेलन आयोजित किये। तथापि स्वर्गीय राजीव गांधी की हत्या के पश्चात बूटासिंह के राजनीतिक स्तर में धीरे– धीरे गिरावट आई तथा तत्पश्चात उन्हें कठिन समय का सामना करना पड़ा।

जब बूटा सिंह देश के समस्त भंगी समाज के नेतृत्व की महत्वकांक्षा रख रहे थे, उसे 1998 के संसदीय चुनाव में कांग्रेस ने टिकट तक नहीं दिया। बाद में कांग्रेस छोड़ने के

बाद बूटासिंह ने राजस्थान में जालौर के सुरक्षित निर्वाचन क्षेत्र से एक स्वतन्त्र उम्मीदवार के रूप में चुनाव लड़ने का साहसिक निर्णय भी लिया।

अधिकांश भंगी कांग्रेस कार्यकर्ता तथा नेताओं का मानना है कि 1998 के चुनावों के समय बूटासिंह को कांग्रेस का टिकट न देने का निर्णय, कांग्रेस पार्टी द्वारा भंगी नेतृत्व की उपेक्षा करने का एक भाग था।

राजस्थान में कांग्रेस पार्टी के पर्याप्त संख्या में विधायक तथा निगम के सदस्य जैसे– मेघवाल, रैगर, बैरवा, चमार, बलाई तथा खटीक जाति के हैं तथा राजनीतिक शक्ति इन्हीं अनुसूचित जाति के लोगों के हाथों में रही है।

अखिल भारतीय सफाई मजदूर कांग्रेस के अध्यक्ष बूटासिंह तथा अन्य कार्यकारी अध्यक्ष मांगीलाल आर्य के द्वारा भंगियो में राजनीतिक चेतना जागृत करने के लिए आन्दोलन चलाया गया। यहां तक कि भंगी जाति के सरकारी अधिकारी भी कांग्रेस पार्टी की सभाओ में जाने में नहीं हिचकिचाये। इसके बावजूद भी भंगी समुदाय के लोगों का कांग्रेस पार्टी से अलगाव बना हुआ है। राजस्थान सरकार के भूतपूर्व मन्त्री मांगीलाल आर्य का कहना था कि कांग्रेस पार्टी को भंगियों का समर्थन हासिल करने के लिए कुछ ठोस कदम उठाने चाहिए। उसे भंगी समाज तथा उसके नेताओं के विरुद्व उत्पन्न उन पूर्वाग्रहों को समाप्त करने का प्रयास करना चाहिए जो कि अन्य अनुसूचित जातियों, समुदायों तथा उच्च जातियों के द्वारा उत्पन्न किये गये हैं। मांगीलाल आर्य ने भंगी समाज में यह प्रकाशित किया है कि भंगियों के द्वारा कांग्रेस को सम्पूर्ण समर्थन देने के बावजूद उसने सम्पूर्ण देश में तथा विशेष तौर पर राजस्थान में भंगियों को दर किनार कर दिया है।

1998 के 12वें आम चुनावों के परिणाम बूटासिंह के राजनीतिक जीवन के लिए निर्णायक साबित हुए। लोकसभा चुनाव में विजयी होने के तुरन्त पश्चात भारतीय जनता पार्टी समेत अनेक राजनीतिक दलों ने बूटासिंह से समर्थन हेतु सम्पर्क स्थापित किया। इस प्रकार 7 वर्ष के दीर्घ अन्तराल के पश्चात बूटासिंह ने 19 मार्च 1998 को 74 वर्षीय भाजपा नेता श्री अटल बिहारी वाजपेयी के नेतृत्व में मन्त्रिमण्डल की सदस्यता ग्रहण की तथा दूरसंचार मंत्री का पद ग्रहण किया।

कुछ समय पश्चात 20 अप्रेल 1998 को प्रधानमंत्री वाजपेयी ने झारखंड मुक्ति मोर्चा रिश्वत काण्ड में लिप्त होने के फलस्वरूप बूटा सिंह को मंत्रीमण्डल से हटा दिया। इस प्रकार भारतीय जनता पार्टी से कुछ प्राप्त कर सकने में असफल होने के पश्चात बूटासिंह ने कांग्रेस में पुनः प्रवेश के प्रयास आरम्भ कर दिये। कांग्रेस पार्टी में पुनः प्रवेश हेतु बूटा सिंह कांग्रेस अध्यक्ष सोनिया गांधी से मिले। परिणाम स्वरूप 3 मई 1989 को जयपुर में राज्य कांग्रेस की अध्यक्षा एवं सांसद गिरिजा व्यास की उपस्थिति में उन्हें कांग्रेस में पुनः शामिल किया गया।

Notes

1. For studies of Akhil Bharatiya Safai Mazdoor Congress, policy and its inclination towards Congress, see, Shyam Lal. *The Changing Bhangis of India: A Study of Caste Association*, Jaipur, Sublime Publications, 1999.
2. Ibid., p. 100. Also see, p. 181.
3. Ibid., p. 181.
4. Shyam Lal, *Samajik Niyay Avam Dalit Rajneeti*, Jaipur, Sublime Publications, 2004, pp. 33–35.

2

The Bhangi

An Untouchable Caste

The Bhangi: Names and Titles

A caste of the removers of night soil and the cleaners of latrines belongs to a well-defined group in the Indian social order. All such workers in India are, today included under the general nomenclature 'The Bhangi'. For this occupational group there are various names and titles in use in different parts of the country but the better known term is 'The Bhangi'. Thus they are known in South India as 'hela'[1] meaning 'cry' and that they were called so because they had to cry out to demonstrate their identity while moving on the roads. According to another theory it is derived from the word hilna meaning 'be domesticated'; another source of derivation is from hela meaning basket load or hel or hil meaning filth mud.

The title for them in Gujarati is Halalkhor[2] – One who eats what is lawful, one whose earnings are legitimate. This euphemistic title is said to have been introduced by Emperor Akbar. 'Khakrob'[3] is from Persian words 'khak' meaning earth and 'rob' meaning sweeping. In the Punjab the Bhangis are known as Chuhra[4] and this name has been derived from their work of collecting and sweeping up scraps *(Chura-harna)*. Similarly, in Bombay (now Mumbai) they are known as *Ghare*[5] and 'Bhangi'. The Bengali name 'Hari'[6] is supposed to have come from haddi – bone. The Hari was the bone gatherer and was familiar to the early settlers of Calcutta (now Kolkata) under the quaint designation of harry-wench. In Rajasthan they are called *Mehtar*[7] and this name has been derived from Persian Mehtar-prince, said to have been applied to them in derision. The Bhangis might have adopted gratifying appellations as prefixes to their caste name. Thus, the Bhangies of Uttar Pradesh call themselves 'Valmiki'[8] who are followers of Valmiki Rishi, the first Sanskrit poet and the famous author of the Ramayana. Though this caste is known by different names, the sweeper community in most states appears to have had the same stock of traditions and legends. The title Bhangi is now generally employed and has, therefore, been taken as the designation of the caste. Details regarding names have been given in the following table.

Table 2.1

Various Names of the Bhangi Caste in Different States

States/Union Territory	*Names*
Bengal[9]	Hari, Hadi
Uttar Pradesh	Valmiki, Dhanuk
Madhya Pradesh	Mehtar, Bhangi
Assam	Mehtar, Bhangi
Orissa (Odisha)	Mehtar, Bhangi, Valmiki, Madiga,,
Bihar[10]	Mehtar
Tamil Nadu	Thoti
Andhra Pradesh	Madiga
Punjab	Mira, Lalbegis, Chuhra, Balashahi, Valmiki**
Maharashtra[11]	Ghare, Bhangi
Gujarat	Halalkhor, Hela, Barwashia
Delhi[12]	Bhangi, Valmiki
Karnataka[13]	Madiga
Kerala[14]	Madiga
Rajasthan[15]	Bhangi, Mehtar, Chuhra, Valmiki

In the country the scavenging castes, are known by different names in different regions. Thus, according to Sachchidananda they are known as 'Bhangi, Valmiki, Chuhra,

Mehtar, Mazhabi, Lalbegi, Halalkhor, etc. in North India, Hari, Hela, Dom, Senei, etc. in Eastern India; Mukhiyar, Thoti, Chachati, Pakay, Relli, etc. in South India and Mehtar, Bhangi, Halalkhor, Ghasi, Olangna, Zadmalli, Barvashia, Metariya, Jamphoda, Mela, etc. in Western and Central India. In 1911 census, some of them started returning as Adi Dharmi, Adi Dravida, Adi Karnataka and Adi Andhra'.[16]

From vedic period to present day, sweepers/scavengers of India were/are called by different names in different periods. Altogether 18 different names of caste were given by S.P. Sumanakshar. According to him, they are 'Chandal, Mehtar, Bhangi, Chuhra, Hela, Lal Begi, Lal posh, Shekha, Halal khor, Bhakhiyar, Malkala, Khar rob, Berwah, Mazbi, Valmiki, Harijan, Naval-Dharmi and Adi-Dharmi'.[17]

Earlier Literature and Origin of Bhangi

Indians mainly live in villages. Even today, more than 70 per cent of the country's population is rural. In ancient days the percentage was much higher. Being bereft of an enclosed place for defecation inside the house, people generally defecated in open fields, their women using secluded places either surrounded by trees or partly covered with crops or hidden by a raised grassy mound. The same situation is still prevalent. The people living in the town needed specified places for defecation and, hence, there was need for disposal of night soil. In this way scavenging was not unknown even in ancient days in India. The scavenging work was done by a particular section of society constituting a caste or a sub-caste.[18]

The sacred scriptures throw some light on the existence of a system for the disposal of night soil. Bindeshwar Pathak writes in his, *Road to Freedom …*

> (1991) that according to the contents of sacred scriptures and other literatures, scavenging specially the disposal of night soil by a particular caste or castes of Indian society, has been in existence since the beginning of civilization.[19] One of the 15 duties for slaves enumerated in the Naradiya Samhita, was to dispose of human excreta.[20] In Vajasneyi Samhita the Chandals and Paulkasa have been referred to as slaves for the disposal of night-soil.[21]

He further writes that during the Maurya period Patliputra (now known as Patna in Bihar State, India) was one of the five ancient towns where the city mayor as Nagrak was the head of the organization entrusted with the task of looking after the civic affairs of the town. The scavengers and sweepers cleaned the city and disposed of night soil.[22]

There is a reference in the Kautalya's *Arthashastra* that during the Maurya period, the sanitary condition of towns was very much improved. Chanakya, known as Mantri (Principal adviser) to the Emperor, has mentioned that every house should have a kitchen and a bathroom. He had suggested that one, who defecated in the open space must be fined. However, those who defecated due to illness or any disability, must be forgiven.[23]

Pathak has pointed out that after the advent of the Muslims in India that 'Sweeping and Scavenging' seems to have taken the form of a formal profession. According to him:

> The Muslims had brought with them some women who used the Burqua (veils) to cover their faces and they did not like to defecate in the open. The bucket privies were, therefore, designed and constructed for their defecation in Purdah. Those made captives were forced to clean latrines like bucket privies and throw the night soil at distant places. After those captives were released, they were not accepted by their caste men and, hence, they formed a separate caste of Bhangi who were renamed as Mehtar by Emperor Akbar.[24]

Similarly, Malkani (1966) and other eminent scholars have sought to establish that the Bhangis (scavengers) of today are those people who were warriors made captives after they fell to the enemy.[25]

During British period, we witnessed the growth of the Bhangis. This is evident from Srivastava's book, *Manual Scavenging in India*. Srivastava has pointed out that,

> during the British period with setting up of army cantonments and Municipalities, a large number of people were perhaps required to do these services on the regular basis.[26]

Thus, according to Srivastava,

> the names of scavenging castes suggest that they are a functional community recruited from many different racial and social groups.[27]

The following extract from, *Road to Freedom* sheds adequate light on this fact.

> Therefore, not only Kshatriyas, but also those who were engaged in cleaning night soil since ancient time, such as Chandals, Paulkasa and also those who were made captives in wars either in India or in Jerusalem or other parts of the world, are Bhangis and Mehtars of today. According to the 1931 Census, the total number of the Bhangis was estimated at 19,57,460; 10,38,678 males and 9,18,782 females in India.[28]

The foregoing account reveals that historical developments led to the emergence of a special class of scavengers in India, known as Bhangis or Mehtars. This class became a hereditary occupational group with a fixed role and status in the Indian society. The unalterable role and status and the hereditary system made this class immobile and it developed into a caste or a sub-caste occupying the lowest stratum of society. With the allocation of hereditary occupation of scavenging and an immobile position, the caste or sub-caste of Bhangis became an integral part of the Indian social structure. This development was not possible without social sanctions.

The scavengers (Bhangis) were placed at the lowest rung of the caste ladder. The nature of the job or work traditionally associated with them, or imposed upon them, pushed them to the lowest stratum of the social hierarchy of exterior castes. The task of cleaning night soil was the most inferior job because this involved the touching of human excreta by the Bhangis. Consequently, they did not get social justice nor the human treatment. Being economically poor and socially backward, they could not revolt against the unjust sanctions nor could they rid themselves of the scavenging work.

The Possible Origin of the Bhangis and their Ethnic Relationships: A New Hypothesis

How did these persons come to be known as Bhangis? Were they declared to be outcastes first and then forced to do the filthy work or were they from the very beginning doing this work and were subsequently declared to be the lowest one. If the answer is that they were not doing this filthy work from the very beginning, but later on were compelled to do so, there arises a further question namely, what can be the reasons for it. For this we suggest the following possible reasons.

Mythological Tenet

As the question of the origin of the Bhangis has never been raised before, naturally, there exists no theory as to how the Bhangi group started performing this filthy work. There are of course the views of Hindu Dharma Shastras. The most relevant and frequently quoted story of the origin of the Bhangi caste in Dharma Shastras and the Smrities, can be referred to as 'Chandala'. According to Manu:

> Chandala is declared to be born from a Brahmani mother and a Sudra father, whose occupation was conveyance of corpses and task of acting as Public Executioner.[29] Other reports give him a less respectable pedigree, for he is said also to be the offspring of Musalia father (Sudra who pounds the Brahman called Musalia) by a woman fisherman, whose occupation is to clean the street every morning and evening, remove the night soil, and receive the corpses.[30] And again he is said to be the son of Dom, one of the most despised of the groups having Nisad as his father and Sudra as his mother.[31] According to Osnash Smiriti, he is declared to be the offspring of Chandala father and Vaishya mother.[32]

One cannot draw any definite conclusion from these statements of Dharma Shastras. According to N. Prasad:

> It is abundantly evident that these sacred books contain no uniform or consistent account of the origin of the castes, but on the contrary, present the greatest varieties of speculation on this subject.[33]

Historical Tenet

The next question that arises is whether the caste indicated by the term Chandala is the same as that indicated by the term 'Bhangi' which socially means scavengers, the lowest in the caste hierarchy. In other words, are they only different names for the same class of the people? It is a fact that Dharma Shastras do not answer this question. For this we must go to the Chinese travellers who visited India and placed on a record what they observed in the form of modes and manners of the Indian people. Of these Chinese travellers, Fah-Hien came in AD 400 during the reign of Chandra Gupta II and has left an authentic record of the people of this country. Unfortunately he has noted very little about the untouchables of India. Still whatever little he says about the life of the untouchables is of value. Referring to the social life Beal, quoting Fah-Hien, writes:

> The people are very well off, without poll tax or official restrictions. Only those who till the royal lands return a portion of profit of the land. If they desire to go, they go, if they like to stop they stop. The kings govern without corporal punishment; criminals are fined, according to the circumstances, lightly or heavily. Even in cases of repeated rebellion they only cut off the right hand. The king's personal attendants, who guard him on the right and left have fixed salaries. Throughout the country the people kill no living thing nor drink wine, nor do they eat garlic or onion with the exception of Chandalas only. The Chandalas are named 'evil men' and dwell apart from others, if they enter a town or market, they sound a piece of word in order to separate themselves, then men knowing they are, avoid coming in contact with them. In this country they do not keep swine nor fowls and do not deal in cattle, they have no shambles or wine shops in their market places. In selling they use cowrie shells. The Chandalas only hunt and sell flesh.[34]

On reading this brief description of Chandalas we can say with some confidence that the term Bhangi was not in existence at the time of Fah Hien. It gives us some idea of untouchability prevailing at the time of Fai-Hien. Here, the observations of Dr Ambedkar are worth mentioning.

> Certain parts of this description of the treatment given to Chandalas do seem to lend support to the conclusions, that is, a case of untouchability.[35] But there is no indication in this passage whether they (Chandalas) even if they formed untouchable caste, were at all the Bhangis. In all probability, it was the name given to those people who were living on the outside of the villages.

The next Chinese traveller, who came to India was Yuan Chwang. He came to India in AD 629. He stayed in India for 16 years and has left a most accurate record of his journeys up and down the country and of the manners and customs of the people. About the general characters of the cities and buildings of India, Walter, quoting Yuan Chwang writes:

> As to their inhabited towns and cities the quadrangular walls of the cities (or according to one text, of the various regions) are broad and high, while the thoroughfares are narrow tortuous passage. The shops are on the highways and booths or (inns) line the roads. Butchers, fishermen, public performers, executioners and scavengers have their habitations marked by a distinguishing sign. They are forced to live outside the city and they sneak along on the left when going about in the hamlets.[36]

This description is too short and too brief for drawing a definite conclusion thereon. There is, however, one point which deserves our attention in Fah-Hien's description. We find the reference to Chandalas only in Fai-Hien's description while the description given by Yuan Chwang applies to different communities other than the Chandalas. This is a point of great importance. It is, therefore, just possible that when Yuan Chwang came to India untouchable groups and untouchability had emerged. The following extract from Dr Ambedkar may be quoted in support of this conclusion:

> We can conclude that while untouchability did not exist in 200 AD, it had emerged by 600 AD.[37]

We may now turn to the question as to who the Bhangis are and how the Bhangi caste originated in India. These are the main issues which we would like to investigate. Unfortunately, no such study has so far been attempted; the result is that though people are aware of the existence of the Bhangis among the Hindus yet they do not know the causes of their origin. A definite idea of this unique feature is, however, essential not merely for a real understanding of the Bhangis, but also as the best means of emphasizing the need of investigating about the origin of this caste.

True, the origin of the Bhangi caste appears to be a complex problem. Races and invasions, institutions and government of different periods in the history of India have left their imprint on the caste. Hence, there is a need for a historical perspective for understanding the origin of the Bhangis in India.

The first thing to be noted is that this caste group is predominantly 'Non Aryan or Dravidian in character'.[38] The reason for this is explained by Crook in the following terms:

> Non-Aryan or Dravidian races were at an early time reduced to servitude and compelled to perform the vilest functions of the Aryan Common Wealth.[39] It is therefore, obvious that they did the work of the scavengers which is the filthiest of the filthy occupation.

But today, this caste is a very large one and it would be difficult to account for it merely on this ground. As now constituted, the caste is made up of a 'heterogeneous' or of 'different elements'[40] of the people. There are few salient points on which reliance is placed. With these presumptions, we enter the other tenets of the hypothesis.

Anthropological Tenet

With some confidence, it can be said that the original caste group (which was of aboriginal origin) may be the ancestors of the present Bhangis and other untouchables of India. For this there are two tests we can apply to find the truth. One is anthropometric test and the other is ethnological.

Considered in the light of the anthropometric characteristics of Indian people, Ghurye has something very striking to say in his volume on *Caste and Class in India,* from which the following extract is reproduced:

> Taking the Brahmin of the United Provinces as the typical representative of the ancient Aryans we shall start comparisons with him. If we turn to the table of differential indices we find that he shows smaller differential index as compared with the Chuhra and the Khatri of the Punjab than with any caste from the United Provinces except the Khatri. The differential index between the Khatri and the Chuhra is only slightly less than that between that the Brahmin of the United Provinces and the Chuhra. This means that the Brahmin of the United Provinces has closer physical affinities with the Chuhra and the Khatri of Punjab than with any caste from his own province except the very high caste of the

> Khatri. The Brahmin is as much akin to the Chuhra as the latter is to the Khatri of the Punjab.[41]

With this evidence, it cannot be doubted that there was a time when both the Brahmins and Chuhra (Bhangi) were one and the same people.

When Aryans came here as conquerors, they retained themselves the religious and military functions of the social order. So as the time went on, they held the functions of priests and nobles and became the great landed proprietors and ranch men.

The conquered people were kept in subjection. They performed the most lowly task of life and that lowest task was scavenging only. This is what Stanley Rice has said:

> Thus the Dravidians applied to the Paraiyans the same test which the Aryans are assumed to have applied to the conquered inhabitants. They reduced them to the position of serfs and assigned to them those duties which it was thought beneath their own dignity to perform.[42] Therefore he further adds: 'There is strong probability that the outcastes were the survivors of the conquered peoples, who, as castes tendered to coincide with occupation, became the drum-beating, leather working and farm labouring classes to which as serfs they had been relegated from early times'.[43]

Again there are some variations in the features of the members of the caste. This may be illustrated from the Bhangi caste of Northern India. Some idea of this may be obtained from the following summary given by Crook:

> Some Bhangis have dark complexion, stunted figures and peculiar dark flashing eyes which is so characteristics of Dom. Others again are of a much taller form and fairer complexion.[44]

The reasons for this racial mixture are explained again by Crook in the following terms:

> Partly by the fact that their admittance as servants into high class families facilitates illicit connection with superior class and partly that tribe habitually recruits itself by admission of outcaste from superior tribes.[45]

Ethnological Tenet

There is yet another section of ethnological scholars who believe that certain classes were unable to maintain their identity and prestige with changing order and that consequently they have sunk to the lowest level. Perhaps these contentions are borne out by many Got (Gotras) names: for instance. Chouhan, Solanki, Gehlot, Parihar, Rathore, Pandit, Kalla. These are the names of Rajput and Brahmin gotras and are also found in the Bhangis. But they suggest dependency. Let us see what authorities have to say on this subject. This is what Dr Ambedkar has to say on the subject in his book, *The Untouchables:*

> As I have said if totem, kul and Gotra have significance it means that those who have the same totem must have been kindred. If they were kindred they could not be persons of different race.[46] Prof. Atal says 'that these Jatis (Gots or Gotras) suggest the past affiliation of these groups (Untouchables) with Rajputs.[47]

Descent of Kshatriyas and Bhangis from the same sources has been justified on the basis of similarities by D.S. Chaturvedi. Quoting Chaturvedi, Bindeshwar Pathak[48] writes ...

Kshatriyas and Bhangis have descended from the same source. For, he says, one notices a marked similarity between them. He has cited the following similarities:

Bhangi : Vas, Vasvar, Bir Gujar, Bhadwaria, Bisen
Mehtar : Bundelia, Chandal, Chauhan, Nado, Yaduvanshi, Kachhwaha, Kinwar, Thakur.
Rajput : (99) Bundela (48) Bargujar Panna (222) Panna Dajoha or Yaduvanshi Gujar Panna (248) Rout.

The people belonging to the Chandal caste requested the census officer in 1911, to accord them the status of the Brahmins as they had the Brahmin origin. In that respect their customs, rituals and other sacramental roles are identical with those of Brahmins. There is no doubt that the Chandals were made to dispose of sullage. These Chandals took the initiative to enrol themselves as Brahmin only after they became affluent. Obviously, the castes engaged in the disposal of human excreta were not at all divergent of a single caste.[49]

If the above mentioned analogies are correct then it would be quite logical (from ethnological point of view) to say that the Bhangis at one time did belong to a high social status.

Conversion and Ex-communication Tenets

Besides all this, however, there are other links connecting the Bhangis of Northern India with higher castes. Direct evidence on this issue could be had if higher castes converted as Bhangis had been studied. Unfortunately, the study of converted Bhangis has not yet been undertaken either by the students of sociology or of anthropology. When such data is collected it would enable us to give a decisive opinion on the possibility that the Bhangis were high caste men. For the present, we are satisfied in this regard from the information we have collected from the high caste converted Bhangis from different districts of Rajasthan.

In this, connected reference may be made to the tradition current among the Hindu society, according to which breach of established social norms and usages was a social crime. Any one who violated these approved social laws was guilty and was forcibly declared an outcaste. This means that the position of the ex-communicated had been lowered and they were treated as untouchables and were also prohibited from following their traditional occupation. Now they were with no means of livelihood. Without it they would starve. It would be natural in these circumstances for these outcastes to agree to give to others their services as sweepers. In Hindu society this often happened from the early times. This process is still going on. As a consequence there always existed in early times a floating population consisting of persons of different castes. Risley's following thesis can be accepted in case of the Bhangi's origin:

> 'Almost every caste professes to have traditional occupation, though many of its members have abandoned it, but that the adoption of new occupation or of changes in the original occupation may have given rise to sub-division of the castes which ultimately developed into separate and distinct castes'.[50]

This can be clearly supported from the following observations of B.N. Srivastava:[51]

> The names of scavenging castes suggest that they are a functional community recruited from many different racial and social groups. It is very likely that people belonging to the lowest strata were compelled to take on this profession especially in the urban areas due to economic necessity. The great variations in the physical features of the different sections of this community, but also the varied recruitment from higher castes of 'broken men' – outcastes destitute, etc. shows that the members of various castes have joined this profession at different points of time obviously due to economic compulsions as this occupation was regarded as unpleasant by the economically better off sections. This only proves that the members of different castes and communities have taken upto this vocation mainly due to economic constraints.

Invasion Tenet

From the ancient Indian history, we also know, that subjugation of a tribe after tribe has been a recurring phenomenon in India. The subjugation occurred over wide areas. Indian history fully illustrates this fact and we may observe rising and falling of tribes and castes under repeated foreign and local waves of conquest. But then what were the social consequences? History has recorded very useful information. As N. Prasad points out:

> '... the force of class struggle always determined the status of a class or its ossified form, caste'.[52] This can be clearly supported from the following observations of H.P. Shastri:[53]

The people of Bengal who, after the downfall of the Hindu rule, did not accept either Brahmanism or Islam but stuck to their old mode of worship, became the untouchables of today. History is not without such examples.

In the case of the Bhangis, the same principle was at work. Malkani, who has made a general study of the Bhangi caste says:[54]

> The Bhangi is essentially a recent product of urban life, first created as an occupation by Muslims and later on in British rule, made into hereditary caste.

Traditions Regarding Origin of the Term 'Bhangi'

In the absence of any authentic, written record about the origin of the Bhangis, one has to depend necessarily on the oral traditions. In following pages, an attempt is made to use information collected and references available in the history, and the meaning and origin of their community names.

As Descendants of Valmiki Rishi[55]

According to narrative handed down from generation to generation and at present current in the older generation of the Bhangis, they are descendants of Valmiki Rishi the first Sanskrit poet and famous author of the Hindu epic, Ramayana. Their supposed connection with Valmiki rests on occupational and not on racial occupational and not on racial identity. Valmiki's story, as it prevails among the Bhangi's, represents him as a low caste and as such as having taken to the living of a robber. Owing to this abhorrent activity of Valmiki, he was designated as a sweeper. The relics of this mythological narrative are still prevalent among the Bhangis.

In the *Tribes and Castes of Central Provinces of India*, there is a detailed reference as to the origin of Bhangis. It runs as follows:[56]

> The religion of the sweepers ... centres round the worship of two Saints Lal Beg or Bale Shah and Balnek or Balmik, who is really the huntsman Valmiki, the reputed author of the Ramayana. Balmiki was originally a low caste hunter called Ratnakar, and when he could not get game, he was accustomed to rob and kill travellers. But one day he met Brahma and wished to kill him, but he could not raise his club against Brahma, and the God spoke and convinced him of his sins, directing him to repeat the name of Rama until he should be purified of them. But the hunter's heart was so evil that he could not pronounce the divine name and instead he repeated 'Mara Mara' (Struck, Struck) but in the end by repetition this came to the same thing. As a small spark of fire burneth up a heap of cotton, so the word Rama cleaneth a man of all his sins. So the words 'Rama' 'Rama' were taught unto Ratnakar who ever repeated them for sixty thousand years at the self-same spot with a heart sincere. All his skin was eaten up by the white ants. Only the skeleton remained. Mud had been heaped over the body and grass had grown up, yet within the mound of mud Saint was still repeating the name of Rama.

'After sixty thousand years Brahma returned. No man could he see, yet he heard the voice of Rama, Rama, rising from the mound of mud. Then Brahma bethought that the saint was beneath. He sought Indra to pour down rain and to wash away the mud. Indra complied with his request and rain washed away the mud. The saint came forth. Naught save bones remained. Brahma called loud to the saint. When the saint beheld him, he prostrated himself and spoke. 'Thou hast taught me the words "Rama" "Rama" which have cleaned away all my sins'. Then spoke Brahma 'hitherto thou wast Ratnakar. From today thy name shall be valmiki (from Valmik, an ant hill). Now do thou compose a Ramayana in seven parts, containing the deeds and exploits of Rama'. Valmiki had been or afterwards became a sweeper and was known as 'Cooker of Dog's food (Swapach), a name applied to sweepers, who have adopted him as their eponymous ancestor and patron Saint.'

The following is the text in English of Bhangis origin from Marwar Census 1891.[57]

> One day God Brahma (Creator of the world) was passing through a street. There, God Brahma saw a dump of refuse. To get it removed, God Brahma immediately rubbed his skin and from its greasy material (the layer form on the skin by sand, perspiration and other skin discharge) produced a man and named him 'Matrak'. Matran removed the refuse from Mahi earth. Since then he was known as 'Mahithar' and later on it turned into Mehtar. They were called the Bhangis because the children of the Matrak ate the flesh of the dead animals and entered into the temple of the Goddess Matangi without bathing. Upon this, the Goddess was shocked and cursed them that they will always sweep and remove the night soil. Therefore they are known as Bhangis.

In the first volume of his book entitled *Tribes and Castes of N.W.P and Oudh*[58] Crook has dealt with all castes found in the Hindu society. There are 18 legends dealing with the origin of the Bhangis. Out of 18, one important runs as follows:

> ... The Holy Prophet (Hazrat Paighambar), Saint (Mehtar) Ilias, or the prophet Elias, attended the court of the Almighty God, where many prophets were sitting. Mehtar Ilias coughed and finding no room to spit in, he spat upwards and his spittle fell upon the prophets. They all felt disgusted and complained to Almighty God, who directed that he should serve throughout the world as a sweeper. Mehtar Ilias begged that some prophet should be created in the world to intercede for him, and it was ordered that

such a one should be born. According to the order of the God of Mercy he came into the world and took to sweeping and passed many days in the hope of forgiveness. One day the great Saint Bare Pir Sahib, Pir-I-Dastagir or Sayyid Abdul Qadir jilani. took his coat (Chola) off and gave it to Mehtar Ilias to wear. Mehtar Illias put it into an earthen pitcher (Matka) and intended to wear it at some auspicious time. One day the great Saint asked him why he did not wear the coat. He answered 'My work is to sweep and it would become dirty. I will wear it on some lucky day.' The great Saint said 'wear it today and come to me'. He agreed and went to open the pitcher, but it was shut so fast that he could not open it. He came to the Saint and said that the pitcher would not open. The Saint said 'Take my name and say to the pitcher that the Pir Sahib calls you'. Mehtar Ilias went and did as he was bidden, and putting the pitcher on his head brought it to the Saint. The Saint said Nikalao, Lal Beg, 'come out quickly my boy' (Lal is My dear boy, Beg means quickly). Immediately out of the pitcher came a fair man wearing red clothes, and the Saint said to Lal Beg. 'This was the order of Almighty God that you should be the prophet of the sweepers and interecede for them at the day of Judgment'. Mehtar Ilias took him home, and placing him under a nim tree filled his pipe for him (a custom of the sweepers to the present day towards their religious teachers) and worshipped him. Lal Beg became at once invisible, and Mehtar Ilias went to the great Saint and told him the story. The great Saint said that Lal Beg had disappeared because he did not approve of his religion. 'However, worship him, and he will interecede for you'. He then ordered Mehtar Illias to do penance, and said 'In the first age the ghatmat (vessels worshipped to represent Lal Beg) will be golden, in the second, they will be of silver, in the third, copper, in the fourth earthen'. This is why the sweepers now worship vessels of earth, and believe in Lal Beg as their prophet.

These traditions, both ancient and modern, do not however, account for the origin of the Bhangis. They merely show how some persons were degraded into sweeper working group.

Etymological Meaning and Definition of Bhangi

The word Bhangi is originally derived from Sanskrit root Bhang – Hemp and Bhangi meaning 'hemp addict'.[59] Crook in support of this derivation advances the Buria custom of calling their leader Bhangi or hemp addict as title of honour.[60] Sir H.M.

Elliot[61] also derives the term 'Bhangi' from the same word in the sense of their drinking habits. Editors[62] Gove and Webster further confirm Crook's and Elliot's findings and indicate that Bhangi is one 'addicted to Bhang'. The Bhangi are to be regarded as a group of hemp drinkers.

A much wider connotation of the term 'Bhangi' has been put forward by an eminent economist and sociologist, D.R. Gadgil. According to him Mehtar Bhangis are castes traditionally confined to the business of removing night soil. They are on this account considered among the most degraded in Hindu society. Moving out of the caste occupation is, therefore, extremely difficult for them.[63] Sahay supports these views in his article 'Eradication of Untouchability and the Caste System'. According to him[64] Bhangi means 'Those who are associated with filthy work like carrying of night soil, cleaning of drains and the like'.

Harold R. Issacs[65] while defining the term Bhangi writes 'Night soil ... has traditionally been the task of the untouchables at the bottom of even the untouchable's scale. This kind of scavenger is known as Bhangi and Bhangis are a people apart from even among people apart'. Again, editors James, Brodly, Craigle and Onion[66] say that Bhangi means 'a person engaged in sweeping a room, chimney, etc. and in India would apply it particularly for a person of lowest caste'. Lynch also used the term 'Bhangi' in this limited sense.[67]

Bhangi according to Chauhan,[68] are 'Those who have broken away from society and it is, therefore, derogatory in meaning'. Ghurye[69] quoting Enthoven writes 'Bhangi is one who performs the useful functions of removing night soil. It is a term probably applied to the caste simply as a token of contempt for those who are broken or out caste'. Occupationally, today the Bhangi corresponds to the remover of night soil.

Position of the Bhangis in Caste System

Because of their low caste status the Bhangis are in some sense less a part of the community of Jodhpur than are most of the other higher castes. But the community also incorporates them in a particular way because it could not survive without them.

Caste and Social Status

The status of the Bhangi caste has openly been described as untouchables. In Jodhpur they are often dubbed with vernacular term 'Bhangi' which means just that. Elsewhere too, their status has been actually that of the untouchable. It is true that social graduation among the untouchables follows pattern which are basically similar to those prevalent among the upper castes. Blunt, has drawn attention to such a factor operating in the past 'eleven caste will not touch a Bhangi'. He further adds that '... being touched by such an untouchable required a good Hindu to bathe himself and wash his clothes'.[70] Dumont's[71] study also indicates that out of a total 25 untouchables there are twelve castes which do not touch the Bhangi. Hutton places the Bhangi caste in the lowest grade of Hindu social system. According to him:[72]

> Occupation again is also in part at any rate, the reasons for low standing of ... Khateek, who is a butcher or the Chamar who tans hides, and works in leather. Below all these are the scavenging castes, the various grades of the Bhangis or sweepers.

The position of the Bhangis differs vitally from that found in various parts of India. Bhangi accept food at the hands of any other castes but do not accept it from Dhobis and Dholis. Gupta[73] supports this statement in his discussion of the leather workers and untouchable group of the village of Awan. He writes 'The Bhangis accept scraps of food from the plates of the eaters ranked above the Balai, save the Dhobi, the Dholi and the Mogya'.

This is further proved by the following extract from Marwar Census Report, 1984.[74] We (Bhangis) consider ourselves polluted by the touch of Dhobi and Dholi. In that case we have to take off our clothes, sprinkle *Gangajal* (water of Ganga) over ourselves and bathe. 'Everywhere Dhobi and Dholi rank higher than Bhangis but they are regarded as untouchables and their status is superior to Bhangis. This superiority has been shown very clearly also by Gangrade.[75] in a study of Dhobis in a village near Delhi. Even Bhangis refuse food touched by them and it is only in recent years that the Bhangis have started to eat from their hands. The Bhangis of Delhi who work in Dhobis' houses are also paid for their services in cash and are given food at the time of marriage.[76] Similarly, butchers (Khateek) are higher caste (as mentioned earlier) yet Bhangis of Kishan Garhi (UP) do not accept food from them. This is proved by the following extract from McKim Marriott's[77] publication titled *Castes Ranking and Community Structure in Five Regions of India and Pakistan.*

> Butchers locally claim to be Rajput. In support of this claim, they give themselves famous Rajput clan names and cite their external ties of marriage and descent with other groups of equally illustrious Rajput nomenclature elsewhere. At the same time members of the sweeper (Bhangi) caste in Kishan Garhi regard Butchers as too low in rank to receive sweeping services and too low to be able to give inferior bread as payment to sweepers or to any other caste.

> When Bhangis walk along a street or road, wrote L.S.S.O. Molley[78]... they (Bhangis) have to give warning of their presence by calling out, Payse or Paraysa (Keep at distance) and sweeper was required to wear a crow's feather on his turban to show his unclean caste.

When high caste persons refer to a Bhangi as untouchable they mean only that they cannot take food or water from him and that his touch will pollute food, water and utensils used for food and water. The Bhangis are regarded as defiled especially because of their repugnant traditional occupation of removing night soil and tanning and because of their eating carrion beef and meat of other dead animals.

Since the name 'Bhangi' has acquired abusive connection as on the phrases. 'Dirty as Bhangi' 'Son of Bhangis' the Bhangis of Jodhpur prefer to designate themselves by other names. some Bhangis call themselves Valmiki taking the name of their most famous Saint Valmiki. Other Bhangis of whom there are many from different districts, style themselves 'Harijan'. The word 'Harijan' means the 'Children of God' and was first coined by Mahatma Gandhi. A few call themselves Arya. But the Bhangis of Jodhpur prefer to be called by name of Harijan.

Old Bhangis extended some kinship terminology and behaviour to higher castes persons. Some address higher caste persons as 'Mai-Baap' (Mother-Father). Older Bhangis feel that *jajmans* (patrons) should receive the same respect as mother or father. Older member of higher castes often address their Bhangis as their children. Now very few persons use those terms and their use in general is resented by the Bhangis. The Bhangi caste's status relation with Brahmin and castes below Brahmin are clearly structured. Food, water and vessels are kept strictly separate and the Bhangi is never permitted to enter the house of higher caste. If a man of higher or lower than Bhangi caste works at Bhangi's house for construction or repair of the house, etc. he will have his own vessel for water or will go somewhere else for water.

There is a potential bond among the Bhangis and all other low caste people, no matter what their relative status is. They are all low in caste in relation to members of higher castes. All are somehow or the other economically dependent upon the members of the higher castes.

Ceremonial Status

The Bhangis occupy an isolated position in the ceremonial life of Jodhpur. Although they follow the customs and rituals of the members of the higher castes, they worship Gods, Goddesses separately in their own houses or Bustees (hamlets). Similarly, they do not join with members of the higher castes in any ritual. As traditional workers for all higher castes, the Bhangis receive food and other domestic things at important festivals, such as Holi, Diwali, Sheetla Ashtami. Rakhi, etc. but they do not celebrate these festivals on equal terms with the members of the other higher castes.

Economical Status

Bhangis are economically tied to the city, especially to members of higher castes as traditional workers and labourers. The Bhangi's traditional work is sweeping and removing refuse in the city. For this purpose the city was divided among different Bhangi families. Each family has been divided among different Bhangi families. Each family has been serving a certain number of houses (Jajman families) from generation to generation. The Jajman compensates his Bhangi for his work through periodic payment in cash or/and kind made throughout the year, mainly on monthly basis. Bhangis may also receive gifts such as free clothing, food, raw materials, etc. on festivals like Holi, Diwali and other important occasions like marriage, birth and death.

It is an unwritten law that if a Bhangi wants to move out of the city or is ill, he would have to find a substitute in his place. In this matter the high castes have no choice as to who would work for them. If they want to sell the work of a street in which they are working, they could do so to another family of their own caste. This sale is only effective on the condition that in that particular area no other Bhangi has any claim and also that people who bought it are satisfied. The price would be fixed according to the income of the area. We can have a clear picture of this practice from an autobiography of a Bhangi.[79]

The Purchaser: How many landlords have you and what is the size of each of their families?

The Seller: I have six Muslim households. One landlord is the Subedar Major in the King Emperor's service and other five are landowners, their land has been covering ten villages outside the town.

Purchaser: How much cash per year do you receive from each house? How much grain, oil and sugar do you receive and what is the average number of marriages?

On this depends the sale, but no one ever thinks of asking how much work there is to do, because it is understood that once the purchaser takes over the responsibilities he would do whatever there is to be done. Besides, if there is any extra work, the jajman always compensates his Bhangi. But the sale of this nature takes place very rarely as it means the losing of one's birthright and family reputation. Also, this is the only means of livelihood open to Bhangis and the richer the jajmans they serve the higher the prestige and honour they get, not only among neighbours but also in the District itself, and that means a lot to them, because this is the only basis on which depends their status in the community.

Outside employment is a recent phenomenon among the Bhangis of this region. Some of the Bhangis[80] joined the Army and fought in the Second World War in Burma, Afghanistan and other places. Others have been noted as servants of British Residents. The trend of outside employment has been further accelerated in recent years as non-traditional occupation has become possible, in and outside Jodhpur. Jodhpur is one of the most rapidly growing city in Rajasthan. Its economy is highly diversified, employment being provided by the University and other educational units, the Government Medical College, Hospital and other Medical Centres, several small scale industries and State Government offices; location of the Rajasthan High Court has added to the population and resumption of non-traditional occupation by the Bhangis has helped to improve steadily the economic position for them within Jodhpur.

Outside employment has gradually increased. Until 1976, there were few Bhangis of Jodhpur residing and working outside the region. With the exception of a few families which have sufficient economic sources, majority of the Bhangi families have still been doing the work of removing night soil. Although there is temporary mobility of the Bhangis from this city to other places over the last two generations, only a countable number of Bhangis from Jodhpur are known to have settled permanently in other place.

Political Status

Until the middle of the twentieth century, the Gujarati Gotra Bhangi,[81] the scavengers (Kamin) of His Highness of Jodhpur State, were judges and arbitrators for Bhangis and for three other untouchable castes namely Kuchbandia, Satia and Sansi of the whole Jodhpur state. This was told to us when we approached one of the oldest living eminent persons of Gujarati Gotra Bhangi. The chief of Gujarati Gotra Bhangi met at the Panchayat to discuss matters of interest to the Bhangis themselves and to the other untouchables, and to arbitrate disputes of every nature that might arise within or between the three untouchable castes of Jodhpur state. The members of the Panchayat who know the castes and caste members intimately and pride themselves on their own integrity, could find out the facts, arrive at a decision and enforce it too. They were empowered by His Highness of Jodhpur State to impose penalties like fine, punishment, ex-communication from the caste and also imprisonment for six months. The decisions of Panchayat Chief were not subject to appeal before any higher authority. Through fear, the Bhangis and other lower caste people were peaceful and followed the political leadership of their Gujarati Gotra Bhangi.

Notes

1. Crook, W., The Tribes and Castes of NWP and Oudh, Vol. 1 Calcutta: Office of the Superintendent of Government Printing India, 1896, 260.
2. Ibid., p. 260.
3. Marwar Census Report. Report on the Census of 1891, Vol. 11, Jodhpur, Jodhpur Press, 1894, p. 179.
4. Russell, R.V., *The Tribes and Castes of Central Provinces of India*, Vol. IV London: Mac Millan, 1916, p. 215.
5. Gunarthi, R.C., *Rajasthani Jatio-ki-Khoj*, Ajmer Vedic Yantralaya, 1950, p. 278.
6. Russwell, op. cit., p. 215.
7. Marwar Census Report 1894, op. cit., p. 179.
8. N.R. Malkani, Report of the Committee on Customary Rights to Scavenging. Delhi, Ministry of Home Affairs, Government of India, 1966, p. 131.
9. Based upon the list given in the Order in Council, issued under the Government of India Act of 1935 and the same was reproduced by Dr B.R. Ambedkar. *The Untouchables*, Balrampur. Jetavan Mahavihar Shravasti, 1969, pp. 17, 18, 20, 23 and 24.
10. Malkani, op. cit., pp. 6, 130 and 131, Ambedkar, ibid., p. 19.
11. Gunarthi, op. cit., pp. 278–279.
12. Ram Ratan, ibid., p. 179.
13. Ishwaran, K., *Tradition and Economy in Village India*, Bombay, Allied Publishers, 1966, p. 70.
14. Dass, Bhagwan, *Valmiki, Jyanti Aur Bhangi Jati*, Jullundur, Bheem Patrika Publication, 1973, p. 15.
15. Ethnographic Atlas of Rajasthan, 1969 with reference to Scheduled Castes and Scheduled Tribes, Delhi: The Manager of Publications, 1969, pp. 24–30.

16. Sachchidananda, *People at the Bottom: A Portrait of the Scavengers.* New Delhi, Concept Publishing Company 2001, p. 15.
17. Sumanakshar, S.P. Prachin, *Adimjati Valmiki Dharm Sanskriti and Itihas* (Hindi), Delhi, Bharatiya Dalit Sahitya Academy, 2008, p. 3.
18. Pathak, Bindeshwar, *Road to Freedom: A Sociological Study on the Abolition of Scavenging in India*, Delhi, Motilal Banarasi Dass Publishers Private Limited, 1991 p. 37.
19. Ibid., p. 37.
20. Ibid., p. 37.
21. Ibid., p. 37.
22. Ibid., p. 37.
23. Ibid., p. 37–38.
24. Ibid., p. 38.
25. Ibid., p. 38.
26. Srivastava, B.N., *Manual Scavenging in India: A Disgrace to the County.* New Delhi, Concept Publishing Company, 1997, p. 17.
27. Ibid., p. 17.
28. Pathak, Bindeshwar, op. cit., p. 38–39.
29. Crook, op. cit., p. 261.
30. Gunarthi, op. cit., p. 275.
31. Ibid., p. 274.
32. Ibid.
33. Prasad, N., *The Myth of Caste System*, Patna: Sanjana Prakashan, 1957, pp. 18–19.
34. Beal, quoted by Ambedkar, ibid., p. 190.
35. Ibid., p. 190.
36. Walter, quoted by Ambedkar, ibid., p. 198.
37. Ambedkar, op. cit., p. 199.
38. Crook, op. cit., p. 261.
39. Ibid., p. 261.
40. Ibid.
41. Ghurye, G.S., *Caste and Class in India*, Bombay. Popular Book Depot, 1957. pp. 120–121.
42. Rice, Stanley quoted by Ambedkar, op. cit., p. 56.

43. Ibid., p. 55.
44. Crook, op. cit., p. 261.
45. Ibid., p. 261.
46. Ambedkar, op. cit., p. 82.
47. Atal, Yogesh, *The Changing Frontier of Caste*, National Publishing House, 1968, p. 261.
48. Pathak, Bindeshwar, 1991, op. cit., p. 38.
49. Ibid., p. 38.
50. Risley quoted by Prasad, op. cit., p. 24.
51. Srivastava, B.N. 1997, op. cit., p. 17.
52. Ibid., p. 46.
53. Shastri, quoted by Prasad, op. cit., p. 46.
54. Malkani, op. cit., p. 137.
55. Story as narrated by the Bhangis.
56. Russell, op. cit., pp. 225–226.
57. Marwar Census Report 1894, op. cit., p. 179.
58. Crook, op. cit., pp. 262–267.
59. Crook, ibid., p. 260.
60. Ibid.
61. Ibid.
62. Gove, P.B. and Webster, W. (ed.) *International Dictionary of English Language*, Unabridged, Vol. I, USA. Gand C. Marriam Com. 1966, p. 210. See also Dube, G.S. A.K., *Harijan Bustee*, Varanasi Navchetna Prakashan, 1970, p. 7 and 9.
63. Gadgil, D.R., Poona: A Socio-Economic Survey, Part II Publication No. 25, Poona, Gokhale Institute of Politics and Economics, 1952, p. 94.
64. Sahay, K.N. 'Eradication of Untouchability and Caste System', Ranchi: *Journal of Social Research*, Vol. XVIII No. 2, 1975, p. 4.
65. Issacs, ibid., p. 53.
66. James, A.M. Brodly, M.H. Craigle, W.A., and Onion, C. I, (ed.) *The Oxford English Dictionary*, Vol. X Sale X. U.K. The Clarendon Press, 1961, p. 306.
67. Lynch, Owen, M, *The Politics of Untouchability: Social Mobility and Social Change in a City of India*, New Delhi. National Publishing House, 1974, p. 131.

68. Chauhan, B.R., *A Rajasthan Village*, Delhi. Vir Publishing House, 1967 p. 18. These characteristics have been drawn from writings of some other writers. More particularly reference is made to the following in addition to Chauhan and Ghurye. Gunarthi, ibid., p. 21, Dube, ibid., p. 5. Verma, R.C., *Manak Sabdha Kosh Vol.* IV, Prayag Sahitya Sammelan, 1965, p. 164. Mehant, Nagarmal, Mehtar Mimansa, Bikaner: Harijan Sewak Sangh, Vikram Samvat 2004, p. 8.
69. Ghurye, G.S., *Caste, Class and Occupation*, Bombay, Popular Book Depot, 1961, p. 32.
70. Blunt, op. cit., p. 99 and 102.
71. Dumont, Louis, *Homo Hierarchicus*: *The Caste System and its Implication*, Delhi: Vikas Publishing House, 1970, p. 136.
72. Hutton, op. cit., p. 34.
73. Gupta, op. cit., p. 39.
74. Marwar Census Report, 1894, op. cit., p. 180.
75. Gangrade, K.D. 'Panchayat Election of 1959 and 1963: Ranchi' *Man in India*, Vol. XIVI, No. 11 p. 138.
76. Chanana, Subhadra, 'The Cultural Relation of Occupation: A Dhobi Case'. Ranchi. *Man in India*, Vol. IV, No IV, p. 319.
77. Marriott, McKim, *Caste Ranking and Community Structure in Five Regions of India and Pakistan*, Poona: Gokhale Institute of Politics and Economics, 1965, p. 27.
78. Molley, L.S.S.O., *Indian Caste Custom*, Delhi. Vikas Publishing House, 1974, p. 150.
79. Hazari, ibid., p. 6.
80. Talk with Tudji and Bhera. Inhabitants of Hanumanji ki Bhakri, who fought in II World War.
81. Talk with Mangi Ram Gujarati.

3

Akhil Bharatiya Safai Mazdoor Congress

Formation and Organization

The formation and growth of the Bhangi Sabha like other social organizations cannot be attributed to a single factor. The need for such an organization was felt differently by different leaders and at different times. It was in early 1965 that the Bhangis of Maharashtra held many meetings of castemen and conceived the idea of convening an all-India Sammelan. These major promoters had different motivations for forming the caste organizations. The term, Safai Mazdoor was used in the deliberations as a blanket one to include all those castes whose traditional occupation is scavenging and sweeping. In this chapter, all endeavour has been made to analyse their explanations for the necessity of the caste organizations which may enlighten us about their problems and perceptions of their organizations.

The four different caste organizations[1] namely Akhil Bharatiya Valmiki Sabha, Uttar Bharatiya Valmiki Harijan Sangh, Valmiki Sewa Samaj and Harijan Sewa Samiti, were formed with the urbanite Bhangis of Bombay, Maharashtra, in the early 1960s. These very small organizations were functioning independently from each other under the presidentship of Surtaram Valmiki, Ratablal Karotia, Bhuralal

Jedia and Ambalal Solanki respectively. A major concern of such an organization was to promote social reforms, education and liberal democratic ideas among the Bhangis community. These organizations remained ineffective in the social sphere. However, in the post-independence period they remained somewhat active in politics. Leaders of various organizations soon discovered that it was not good to work independently. The need was to create a social consciousness among the fragmented and disorganized masses of Bhangis. They felt if all these organizations work as one entity then they could start a Maharashtra level Bhangi Association. In order to do this, for the first time, the political leaders and social workers of these organizations of Maharashtra assembled in 1963 at Bombay (now Mumbai)[2] to chalk out the details. The meeting was presided over by Sukla, the foremost constructive worker of Maharashtra whose influence on the Bhangi movement had been remarkable. At this meeting all the leaders and worker emphasized the necessity of finding out the ways and means of caste upliftment and welfare. It was mentioned in this connection that this was possible through horizontal caste solidarity. The need for caste organization at the state level was also felt. The main idea was to unite various caste organizations by making them conscious of their common Bhangi heritage. The meeting was a great success. Having realized the significance of caste in social and the political spheres, the Bhangis of Maharashtra at this meeting united under the new banner called 'Rashtriya Safai Mazdoor Congress'[3], Maharashtra (RSMCM), with Bhagwan Dass Kandara, the then MLA Maharashtra, as President and Vasudev Changra as Mahamantri. For the Bhangi masses, this was a great achievement. Thus, RSMCM came into existence on 27 May 1964. Though subsequently enlarged, it essentially remained local in the sense that it was an association of the Bhangis of Maharashtra. The aim, however, was to serve the interest of the Bhangis in the whole of Maharashtra. Therefore, the RSMCM remained active for full two years. There were also other noted Bhangi leaders who wished to promote various activities among the Bhangis. A fresh impetus for the RSMCM came in 1966. We shall discuss this subsequently.

As stated above the present RSMCM in Maharashtra was a local organization. The local leaders felt that if they could merge all such organizations functioning in various states into one, they could start an all-India level Bhangi Sabha. Following an exchange of ideas sometime in April 1966. Bhangi Bhagwan Dass Kandara[4] President of the RSMCM issued an appeal to the caste people in the country. Its agenda was to bring together the various small organizations by merging them into single organization at all-India level. People belonging to this caste assembled at labour camp in Matunga, Bombay (now Mumbai), from Rajasthan, Punjab, Haryana, Uttar Pradesh, Maharashtra, Gujarat, Madhya Pradesh and Delhi. Some caste leaders from Bombay raised an objection over this Sammelan and some of them wanted to sabotage the Sammelan. The leaders admonished the assembled Bhangis by revealing the strategy of the Congressmen who wanted to use them as tools for their interests. However, in spite of the initial obstacles, the Sammelan was convened and enthusiastically attended by the caste men. A few traditional caste elites boycotted the Sammelan and some preferred to be neutral under the growing influence of the Congress leaders. But their opinion of the opposition was not heeded and the Sammelan was held. It was the first time in the history of the Caste that Bhangis from more than eight states assembled and held the meeting.

Besides the common masses, the Sammelan was also attended by some noted leaders and workers. Mention may be made of Shri Manohar Lal Bige and Jamnalal Jawa (Pune) Bhuralal Jedia and Nathmal Kandara (Bombay), Kanhailal Valmiki, MP, Narayandeen Kalyan Chand Valmiki, ex MP (Uttar Pradesh), Yashwant Rai (Punjab) Vashu Dev Changra (Kalyan, Bombay), Roshanlal Chauhan and Ratan Lal Valmiki (Delhi), Mangilal Arya, N.D. Gujarati, Channulal Jedia and the author himself (Rajasthan). In all, it was estimated that the total number of persons including women and children must have been about five hundred.[5] Most of them were from Maharashtra and a few from other states.

On 21 May 1966, the Sammelan was inaugurated by Shri V.K. Krishna Menon, the then Defence Minister of India and presided over by Yashwant Rai. In his welcome address Rai, Chairman of the Reception Committee, elaborating almost inhuman social, economic and political conditions of the Bhangis prevailing in the country, urged the Sammelan to come forward and join in against the social evils.

The Sammelan was addressed by Ratan Lal Valmiki, Roshan Lal Chauhan, Narayandeen, Bhagwandeen, Mangilal Arya, N.D. Gujarati and many others. Struggle to unite for freedom campaign to eradicate untouchability, call for unity and sense of solidarity among the Bhangis, etc. were the most common themes of speeches delivered by the leaders and worker.[6]

The meeting ground of the Sammelan was full of posters and banners having various slogans. It would be in the fitness of things to mention some of these slogans which reflect the spirit and objectives of the Sammelan (1) Mahatma Gandhi-ki-Jai-Ho, (2) Bharat Mata ki Jai Ho (3) Inqulab Jindabad. It should be noted here that N.D. Gujarati and Mangilal Arya from Rajasthan had a greater influence over the Bhangis than others because both were efficient organizers. They appealed to their fellow brothers to pass a resolution for the constitution of an all-India organizations. All the Bhangis, who had made an effort to attend the Sammelan to observe the proceedings and if required to protest against any pro-Government decision, supported the appeal. They said that the formation of an all-India organization would mean that they were really conscious of the plight of the Samaj. Their views were supported and the proposal was passed. At last, Gujarati's and Arya's dream became a reality.

As a result of all this, on 23 May 1966. Akhil Bharatiya Safai Mazdoor Congress (ABSMC) was constituted in Bombay[7], 'Yashwant Rai was made the first President of the newly constituted Congress. N.D. Gujarati from Jodhpur, Rajasthan was elected Vice-President. Other office-bearers were:

1.	Mahamantris	(i)	Shri Vashu Dev Changra (Bombay)
		(ii)	Shri Shanker Roy (Lucknow)
2.	Mantri	(i)	Shri Mangilal Arya, Pali (Rajasthan)
3.	Treasurer	(i)	Dada Sahib Surat Ramji Valmiki (Bombay)

The provisional Executive Committee of the following 29 members was formed for carrying out the functioning:

1.	Shri Bhuralal Jedia	16.	Shri Ratanlal Karotia
2.	Shri Omprakash Chhabra	17.	Shri Prashadi Lal
3.	Shri Ambalal Solanki	18.	Shri Jai Singh Bhai Solanki
4.	Sh. Shemul Charan Adiwal	19.	Shri Sohanpal Valmiki
5.	Shri Banvari Lal	20.	Shri Jugal Lal Bagdri
6.	Shri Ramji Lal Chauhan	21.	Shri Pritam Singh
7.	Shri Murari Lal	22.	Shri Gordhan Dass Kandara
8.	Shri Mashi Charan	23.	Shri Chhjan Paharia
9.	Shri Pandit Guljaṛi Lal	24.	Shri Nanak Chand
10.	Shri Dulan Punjabi	25.	Shri Srinivas Dakolia
11.	Shri Mahasya Har Jyan Ji	26.	Shri Mohan Lal
12.	Shri Khached Ram Chaudhary	27.	Shri Mukdam Ratanlal Tak
13.	Shri Bankelal	28.	Shri Shiv Charan Mehtab
14.	Shri Chaudhary Roshan Lal	29.	Shri Rishal Hanshi Hans
15.	Shri Nahru Bhai Chauhan		

The aim of the Caste Sabha was to promote and spread socio-educational awakening among the Bhangis. In order to attain the goals, the Caste Sabha laid down the following line of action:

1. To create consciousness – 'We' feeling among the Bhangis.
2. To improve social, economic and political conditions of the Bhangis.
3. To work for social, economic and political benefits of Bhangis.

Yashwant Rai was born in a well-to-do family. Though he had lost his father at an early age, he was a protected child and passed his childhood in the family of Lala Lajpat Rai. He had his education in Punjab and in London. Thus, his early socialization occurred in a group of Rai family members and he received protection from them. Formation of a caste organization to him, in the first instance, was a tribute to late Lala Lajpat Rai who often advocated socio-economic betterment of the Bhangi community. Lala Lajpat Rai believed that by educational and economic development and with caste unity, Bhangis could assert their political importance.

ABSMC is a Caste Sabha representing caste and lineage groups drawn from the scavenging and sweeper communities of India. It is largely responsible for spreading the 'Safai Mazdoor' label and the consciousness that goes with it to many caste groups ranging from the Mazbi, who are high in the Bhangi hierarchy, to the Bhangis who are the lowest, with Hella (Muslim caste) and Gancha Bhangi in the middle. Socially, there is great distance among the various caste groups in the Bhangi hierarchy. Hella and Gancha Bhangis do not marry in Bhangi families. Economically and educationally, most of these castes are poor. Most of the Hella and Gancha families are as destitute as the Bhangis, if not more; common socio-economic interests and a growing secular identity partly due to past folklore but more due to the common resentment against the upper castes have brought these different castes together. With a few exceptions, however, Hella Bhangis have in the past generally kept away from the caste organization. Thus, for the vertical extension of the organization Mazbi, Hella, Gancha and such other minor sub-jatis of the Bhangis were recognized by the leaders as Safai Kamgar and they were also enrolled as members of the Sabha after 1966. Such activities brought about consciousness and generated a rather strong desire for the betterment of community.

In this process of assimilation, which is still going on, the economic factor was supplemented by the Safai Mazdoor Congress's constant efforts to upgrade the position of the Bhangi caste in the social hierarchy of India. This was in fact a strong uniting force in the Safai Congress. There was a conscious and deliberate attempt on the part of the leaders of the movement to break with tradition. Symbols of caste pollution were deliberately discarded. One of the first to go was the eating restriction wherewith the high and the low were made to eat/sit together in common feasts. The Safai Congress has proved to be great levelling force for its various constituents. During this period, the Bhangis were involved in socio-religious reforms, but their political participation was limited. Due to their backward socio-economic conditions, most of the Bhangis were politically inactive. Only well-to-do were active in politics. Among the Bhangis a large number were with the Congress and they expressed their loyalty to Congress Party. The following explanation can be given for their support to the Congress.

First, Yashwant Rai, the founding member of the Caste Sabha, was active in public life since 1947 with the Congress Party. He, as the President of the Safai Congress and having access to well-placed Congress leaders made efforts, to bring about a rapprochement between the Bhangi caste and the Congress Party in different states. Himself a staunch Congressman and supporter of the Congress Party, Rai emphasized that the Congress was the only party capable of representing all sections of the weaker society.

Second, the existence of the Congress was long and from the very beginning; it had supported and protected the interests of the untouchable communities in general, and the Bhangis in particular.

Third, being the party in power, the Congress alone could help the Bhangis. Rai made an open attempt at mobilizing the Bhangis as supporters of the Congress. An example of this is summarized below. In the General Elections held in the country from time to time Rai and his lieutenants openly advocated the Congress Party. The Bhangi leaders and workers in their unofficial meetings advocated support to the Congress Party. Many welcomed the views. Some anti-Congress Bhangi leaders, on the other hand, also strongly opposed it. This brought great polarization in the ranks of the Bhangis, who moved nearer to the Congress Party.

The long-term efforts at building up a wider organization for the Bhangis covering their divergent interests brought out not only the important fact that a viable caste federation could be created only on the basis of an identity of social and economic interests, but also brought to surface pertinent problems of political articulation that the Safai Congress had to face. To what extent should the Safai Congress take active interest in politics? And to the extent it had, how far should it identify with the Indian National Congress? Both these issues cropped up again and again causing controversy between those who emphasized political action and those who urged concentration on educational and reform activities.

During the general elections, as stated earlier, directions were given to the Bhangis of different states by their leaders to work for the Congress.[8] A few of these leaders were themselves elected on Congress nomination. But social and educational activities suffered throughout this period of involvement in politics. On 29 July 1977, the Safai Congress was registered at Bombay (now Mumbai) as Akhil Bharatiya Safai Mazdoor Congress under Registration No 7282. A constitution for the Congress was drawn up and the movement was placed on an organized and universal footing.

The annual session of the Safai Congress was held regularly for full thirteen years till 1979. The Safai Congress did remain active and also survived beyond 1980. During this period, efforts were made to launch the various socio-economic and political activities.

The twelfth session of the Safai Congress held in February, 1979 at Valmiki Mandir in Berakpur, Calcutta (West Bengal) and was presided over by Shri Rai, who had been actively associated with the Safai Congress and had held the office of the President of the Safai Congress since 1966. This session of the Safai Congress was in many respects a departure from the earlier ones. This time, Shri Buta Singh, former Deputy Railway Minister in the Indira Gandhi Cabinet was elected President and Shri Rai was nominated Chairman of the Safai Congress.[9] Similarly, Mangilal Arya was elected Working President and Vasudev Changra was again elected Mahamantri of the Safai Congress. With this change, many leaders felt it necessary to revive the socio-educational programme of the Safai Congress. The unit of operation was decentralized. Meetings were organized for these workers and Congress leaders were invited to speak at the meetings.

The choice of Shri Buta Singh as compared to any other candidate was conditioned by two considerations. First, being a close associate of the then Prime Minister Indira Gandhi, Buta Singh would provide an opportunity for the Bhangis to capture some position in the government as well as in the Congress organizations. The Bhangi's experience with Buta Singh in the past had made this a prime consideration for its leaders.

Secondly, Buta Singh provided financial and other resource necessary to build up the organization and mobilize the great mass of the Bhangis spread over a large area.[10]

Soon after this, Buta Singh popularized the National Congress policies through the Safai Congress. But its response was poor. However, the Congress took some steps towards accommodating and recognizing the Safai Congress as it had done with other backward, tribal and Harijan organizations and placed some important Bhangi leaders in positions in the ministries of various states. In this regard, Buta Singh took up the matter personally with the Prime Minister, Indira Gandhi and Rajiv Gandhi and requested that the Safai Congress, being a social organization could be protected by the Congress.

This encouraged the Bhangi leaders and promoted pro-Congress feelings, although the social programmes of the Safai Congress and political involvement of its leaders always caused stress and strain in its organizations. The emphasis on the political side kept increasing with the Buta Singh driving the organization towards the Congress, and he advocated complete identification with the Congress.

Since the very inception of the Safai Congress in 1966, the Safai Congress leaders and workers had succeeded in approaching some of the noted Congress leaders, such as V.K. Krishna Menon, Mirkasim, Devkant Barua, Mrs Indira Gandhi, Rajiv Gandhi, Sanjay Gandhi, etc.

The National Congress leaders had presided over some sessions of the Safai Congress and also expressed their concern about miserable economic condition of the Bhangis in the country. Mrs Indira Gandhi and Rajiv Gandhi took keen interest in the Safai Congress. It was through their inspiration that a few caste persons were given tickets in various States for Assembly and Parliamentary elections.

Resolutions passed at the various sessions of the Safai Congress were mainly directed towards the socio-economic plight of the Bhangis. The resolution passed at the rally attended by Safai Karamcharis from all over India on 21 September 1990, at the Boat Club[11] lawns in New Delhi are as follows:

Resolution I

1. Safai services should be nationalized.
2. Declare Safai Pesha (Scavenging occupation) as technical services.
3. Fix the wages at par with the wages paid for technical jobs in workshops.
4. Pay and service conditions be fixed by law passed by the Parliament. The law should be listed in the Union list.
5. Special drive for the education of the children of Safaiwalas be launched on a national level.
6. Physical handling of the human excreta by the Safai Karamcharis including the headload be banned by law. Modern equipment should be provided to the Safai Karamcharis.
7. Special Medical Care cover like the ESI should be extended by the government of India at all-India level.
8. Arrangement for transportation from the bustees to the work sites be provided at government cost by the local authorities.
9. The Industrial Disputes Act, 1947 may mean 240 days 'aggregate service instead of 240 days' continuous service.
10. As per the Public Health Manual 1928, the Safai Karamchari should be appointed on the basis of the population of the areas.
11. The Contract System for appointing Safai Karamcharis under the Contract System Abolition Act, 1971 must be banned.
12. Free of cost accommodation may be provided to the Safai Karamcharis to enable them to live respectfully and peacefully.
13. Employment may be provided to the dependants of the medically unfit, death-in-service and retired personnel.
14. A minimum wage may be fixed for the Safai Karamcharis working in private houses.

Since the occupations of sweepers or scavengers is looked down upon and the Safaiwalas are treated as degraded persons in our social culture, all those who are engaged in this profession should be given full facilities of Scheduled Castes irrespective of their caste, creed or religion.

Resolution II

This massive Harijan rally assembled in the Centenary Year of Dr Baba Sahib Bhim Rao Ambedkar from all over India on the lawns of historic Boat Club facing the India Gate reiterated its full adherence to Shrimati Indira Gandhi's ideology and her special endeavour for the amelioration of the Scheduled Castes, Scheduled Tribes and Weaker Sections.[12] This Rally places on record its appreciation of the great services rendered to the country by our respected leader, Shri Buta Singh and places its full trust in his leadership.

Resolution III

This massive Harijan Rally having taken serious note of the widespread caste and communal tensions, fanned by the fundamentalist and separatist forces in India, declares its resolve to fight this menace with all its strength in the country and calls upon all progressive and secular organizations to join hands against this evil.

Resolution IV

This rally resolved that the birthday of Maharishi Valmiki should be declared as a public holiday to be published in the gazette by the Government of India.

Though the Caste Sabha has a written constitution which prescribe objectives, functions, organizational set-up, procedures, membership, etc. yet the leaders hardly take it seriously. The important thing is that except a few leaders and workers, most of the members do not know the specific aims of the Sabha as mentioned in its Constitution.

According to the constitution,[13] the organization is divided into State, district and city units with an elected Executive Committee, have President, Working President, Vice President, Mantri, Sangathan Mantri, Pracharak Mantri and Treasures at each level. State, District and City units have been formed in the States of Maharashtra, Uttar Pradesh, Bihar, Orissa, Andhra Pradesh, Goa, Karnatak, Madhya Pradesh, Himachal Pradesh, Gujarat, Rajasthan, Punjab, Delhi, Haryana and West Bengal. However, they hardly meet even once a year except on the occasions when the Sabha's Sammelans are held. Except a few

State leaders who have State level positions, none has cared to enrol members or to send reports of the Units regarding their activities to the Central Officer. A regular office with well-maintained records is run only by the Rajasthan State unit. Even at the State level, office records are not kept properly.

Year-wise detailed figures of the membership are not available for all years. The only available figures furnished by the Sabha Working President related to the year 1997–98 and are given below:

Year	1997–98
Members	66,419

This does not provide enough data to arrive at any generalization regarding the Sabha's membership. It only indicates that a large number of Safai Mazdoors are not interested in getting themselves enrolled as members of the Congress. Sometimes, the Sabha could hardly register even three hundred members. In order to know more about the nature of the membership, the author collected data through a personal talk with Mangilal Arya,[14] Working President of the Sabha. From this, the following two points emerged:

1. Membership of the Sabha is not constant both in terms of the numbers and individuals. Sometimes it enrolled more than five thousand members and at other times, it hardly registered two hundred members. Similarly, the same individual usually did not continue membership from year to year. This is so because the Bhangis take their membership very casually. They pay membership fee only when approached by a leader. The membership fee is nominal. It is ₹ 12 per annum. Occasionally, office bearers of the Sabha have to contribute some amount in addition to the ordinary membership.
2. Several of the leaders and workers do not see any difference between the traditional Caste Council and the Sabha. According to them having been born Bhangis, they ipso facto become members of the Sabha. Several leaders occupied positions in the Sabha even without paying the

annual subscription participating in any activities of the Sabha for years. Similarly, a lay Bhangi considered himself as its member. Thus, to many Bhangis what mattered is the sentiment of belonging to the Sabha rather than the 'Conscious act of membership' as understood by some scholars.

Decision-making and executive power of the Sabha are highly concentrated in the President, the Working President and the Secretary – the core positions. These omnipotent offices have so far been occupied by three leaders, viz. Sardar Buta Singh, Mangilal Arya and Vashudev Changra. They are popularly known as the trio who decide the policies and carry out the activities of the Sabha in close cooperation with each other.

Buta Singh,[15] a tall and handsome Mazbi Sikh, with a pleasing personality, had retained the Presidentship of the Sabha since 1979. His public life began with the Akali Dal. In 1962, he was elected to the Lok Sabha from Punjab as an Akali candidate. But in 1964, he joined the Congress Party. His association with Indira Gandhi, Sanjay Gandhi, Rajiv Gandhi and with many noted Congress leaders and his emotional appeals for the socio-economic improvement brought the Bhangi masses around him. He earned glory, became an idol of the Bhangi masses and capitalized his influence both within and outside the Sabha. In 1991, due to the assassination of the Rajiv Gandhi and Narasimha Rao becoming the Prime Minister of India, Buta Singh remained out-of power. Owing to his declining influence in the ruling Congress Party, on the one hand, and his leadership conflict with others, office of the President was criticized by some. His influence on the Sabha sharply declined after 1991.

Vashudev Changra[16] an economically well-off man and active worker stepped into the Secretary's position in 1966 and continued in that office until 1997. Changra participated in the Sabha with a sense of doing something for the community. He was also interested in politics. He believed that it is the duty of well-to do persons to help their kin and caste mates. In 1966, he assisted the Maharashtra leaders in arranging the Matunga meeting. Similarly, being the Secretary of the Sabha, he organized a few Sammelans in different states. He entered public life sometime in 1960 and became an MLA in Maharashtra. He was also primarily interested in politics rather than caste. Though he was close to Buta Singh, he successfully worked as a mediator between Buta Singh and Yashwant Rai and kept them together till Rai died. It is the General Secretary who is the key man among the Sabha officials.

Mangilal Arya[17] who believed in action rather than position, enjoyed the defacto power for nearly fifteen years. He preferred the working President position, the real locus of power. He entered public life in the 1980 elections by becoming an MLA and Deputy Minister in 1980. Again, in the 1985 general election he was elected to the Rajasthan Legislative Assembly he became State Minister for Sheep and Wool. Similarly, in the year 1989, again he became the State Minister for Law. He is primarily interested in politics rather than caste. He had love for the organization and also had a political purpose. He assisted Buta Singh, but the major decisions and their execution were left to the President himself. Buta Singh, owing to his preoccupation with the Congress party, could not spare much time for the Sabha's activities. Therefore, Buta Singh wanted Arya, who could devote his time, as the working President of the Sabha. The working President looks after the day-to-day affairs of the Sabha.

The other officials of the Sabha at the state level are the President, one working President, six Vice Presidents, one Mahamantri, six Mantris, six Sanghathan Mantris, six Prachar Mantris and one Treasurer. Besides these, there shall be an Executive Committee of 51 members for carrying out the functions. These are only ornamental positions. We may call them 'Secondary', in which certain leaders are accommodated. It needs to be noted that most of the Bhangis leaders aspire to the positions merely as status symbols. Elections for any of these positions so far have rarely taken place. In the beginning the trio and later the President himself decided the allotment of most of the offices to leaders and their decisions were endorsed by the Working Committee. Thus, these offices are often distributed as symbols of status only. They do not have any functional value in the working of the Sabha. In other words, the office bearers neither have any responsibility nor do they perform any duties of the caste organization.

The Working Committee of the Sabha is a huge gathering, whose number in 1983 was about thirty. Tables 3.1 and 3.2 show the Statewise office bearers and ordinary members in the Working Committee.

Most of the office bearers at all the three levels are Bhangis. They drive the largest support for the Sabha's activities from the Bhangis. The Sabha Presidents office is run from a room in the bungalow of Sardar Buta Singh in New Delhi and daily meetings are held there. The office of the Sabha is located in Maharshi Valmiki Sadan B. Flat, Govinji Keni Marg, Naigaon, Bombay, Maharashtra.

The Young and educated Bhangis are not very keen on associating themselves with the caste organizations. Most of the recruits are mainly interested in politics. They become members of the Sabha either because they have got Congress Party tickets through the Sabha or having got elected as MLAs/MPs. They are offered positions in the Sabha. This indicates the future trend of the caste organizations.

Table 3.1

Statewise Distribution of the Office Bearers and Members of the All India Safai Mazdoor Congress Working Committee, 1983

S. No.	*Office Bearer's Name*	*Designation*	*State*
1.	Shri Buta Singh	President	Punjab
2.	Shri Mangilal Arya	Working President	Rajasthan
3.	Shri Charan Singh Kandara	Vice President	Delhi
4.	Shri Ram Dhari Valmiki	- do -	Haryana
5.	Shri Kalu Ram Valmiki	- do -	West Bengal
6.	Shri Chiman Lal Buthadia	- do -	Gujarat
7.	Shri Sonpal Valmiki	- do -	Uttar Pradesh
8.	Shri Vashu Changra	General Secretary	Maharashtra
9.	Shri Ralal Jawa	- do	Madhya Pradesh
10.	Shri Kapileshwar Keshri	Secretary	Bihar
11.	Shri Bishan Lal Tak	- do-	Haryana
12.	Shri Firoz Meena	Secretary	Madhya Pradesh
13.	Shri Ramanlal Valmiki	- do -	West Bengal

Cont'd...

...Cont'd

14.	Shri Kishanlal Lahora	- do -	Rajasthan
15.	Shri Madanlal Gangahedi	- do -	Delhi
16.	Shri Dada Sahed Surta Ram	Treasurer	Maharashtra
17.	Shri Mohanlal Jakhami	Organizing Mantri	Punjab
18.	Shri Vishambhar Singh	- do -	Delhi
19.	Shri Tulsi Ram Valmiki	- do -	Uttar Pradesh
20.	Shri Rameshwar	- do -	Maharashtra
21.	Shri Dharam Singh Valmiki	- do -	Andhra Pradesh
22.	Shri Bhupat Bhai Datia	- do -	Gujarat
23.	Shri Arjun Prasad Priyadarshi	Propaganda Mantri	Mantri
24.	Shri Kamal Chand Chanwaria	- do -	Rajasthan
25.	Shri Govind Bhai Bagela	- do -	Gujarat
26.	Shri Pyarelal Bhatia	- do -	Punjab
27.	Shri Hari Kumar Chauhan	- do -	Uttar Pradesh
28.	Shri Chatur Singh Parcha	- do -	Haryana
29.	Shri Jodhraj Valmiki	- do -	Bihar

Source: Mangilal Arya, Working President, All India Safai Mazdoor Congress.

Table 3.2

Statewise Distribution of Members of the All India Safai Mazdoor Congress Working Committee, 1983

S. No.	*State*	*Number of Ordinary Members*
1.	Assam	1
2.	Andhra Pradesh	4
3.	Bihar	3
4.	West Bengal	1
5.	Delhi	7
6.	Gujarat	5
7.	Goa	1
8.	Haryana	2
9.	Madhya Pradesh	5
10.	Maharashtra	8
11.	Punjab	3
12.	Karnataka	2
13.	Rajasthan	13
14.	Uttar Pradesh	6
	Total	61

Source: Mangilal Arya, Working President, All India Safai Mazdoor Congress.

Notes

1. Letter dated 9.3.1993 from Mangilal Arya, Working President All India Safai Mazdoor Congress (AISMC), addressed to the author.
2. Ibid.
3. Ibid.
4 Ibid.
5. Ibid.
6. Ibid.
7. Ibid.
8. For more details, see Shyam Lal, 1981, *Caste and Political Mobilization: The Bhangis'*, Jaipur, Panchsheel Prakashan.
9. Letter dated 9.3. 1993 from Mangilal Arya, Working President All India Safai Mazdoor Congress (AISMC), addressed to the author.
10. Talk with Mangilal Arya.
11. For details, see, particularly pamphlet 'Resolutions passed at the rally assembled from all over India on 21 September 1990 at Boat Club, New Delhi', published and circulated by All India Safai Mazdoor Congress, dated 21.9.1990.
12. Ibid.
13. All India Safai Mazdoor Congress (Regd). Registration No 7282 published by Vashudev Changra, Mahamantri, All India Safai Mazdoor Congress, 333, Railway Quarters, Kalyan Distt. Thane, Maharashtra.
14. Talk with Mangilal Arya.
15. Talk with Buta Singh.
16. Talk with Mangilal Arya.
17. Talk with Mangilal Arya.

4

Rise and Fall of Buta Singh

The twelfth session of the Safai Mazdoor Congress was held in February 1979 at Barakpur District Chobis Pargana, Valmiki Mandir, Calcutta (now Kolkata) in West Bengal. In this session Buta Singh, former Deputy Railway Minister in Smt Indira Gandhi's cabinet was elected President of Safai Mazdoor Congress.[1]

The choice of Buta Singh as compared to any other candidate was conditioned by two considerations. First, being a close associate of the then Prime Minister, Indira Gandhi. Second, Buta Singh would provide an opportunity for the Bhangis to capture some positions in the government as well as in the then Congress organisation. The Bhangis experience with Buta Singh in the past had made them think that Buta Singh's leadership will deliver the fruit for them.

During late Indira Gandhi and Rajiv Gandhi's Prime Ministership, the then Home Minister Buta Singh had emerged as a prominent Bhangi leader in the ruling party. He had organized several big rallies and Sammelans of the Bhangis at Delhi, Mumbai, Kolkata, Gujarat, Punjab, Rajasthan and other places. However, Buta Singh's political stature gradually diminished after the assassination of the late Prime Minister Rajiv Gandhi and had to pass difficult years since then.

Buta Singh, who was aspiring to speak on behalf of the whole Bhangi community in the country was not even given the ticket by the Congress party for Parliamentary elections in the year 1998. Later when he fell out with Congress, he made a bold decision to contest the election as an independent candidate from the Jalore reserved Parliamentary constituency, Rajasthan and won the election.[2]

Most of the Bhangi Congress workers and leaders say that the denial of the Congress ticket to Buta Singh on the eve of 1998 polls, was part of an effort to neglect the Bhangi leadership in the Congress party. The Congress is the only political party to give top level position to a few prominent, Scheduled castes candidates. For instance, Ms Meira Kumar, former General Secretary of All India Congress Committee, who represents the Chamars, long back, had resigned from the Congress party. The former Chief Minister of Rajasthan, Jagannath Pahadia belonged to Khatik community. Though Congress derives its support exclusively from the Bhangis, it had also given little representation to the Bhangis in its higher echelons. A large number of Congress legislators and corporators belong to the Bairwas, Chamars, Balahis, Meghwals and Khatiks in Rajasthan and political power remained in the hands of these scheduled castes/communities.

The campaign launched by Buta Singh and Mangi Lal Arya both President and Working President of All India Safai Mazdoor Congress respectively and others had spurred political awareness amongst the Bhangis. Even government officials from the Bhangi caste hesitate to attend meetings of the Congress party. Despite this, the Bhangis continue to be alienated from the Congress. Mangi Lal Arya, the former Minister, Government of Rajasthan said that the Congress party should take concrete steps to win over the Bhangis. It should also make an attempt to neutralize the prejudices against the community and their leaders, which have been fostered by the other scheduled castes/communities and upper castes. Arya had been telling the Bhangi masses that despite their total support to the Congress, it was the Congress that had marginalized the whole community in the country and Rajasthan in particular.

The result of the 12th General Elections of 1998 marked a turning point in the political career of Buta Singh. Immediately after winning the MP election, the political parties including BJP contacted Singh for his support. Thus, Buta Singh once again, after a long interval (nearly 7 years), joined the Ministry headed by 74-year old BJP leader, Atal Behari Vajpayee on 19 March 1998. He took the oath as Cabinet Minister for Tele-communications.[3]

In no time, the tension became acute when Prime Minister Vajpayee on Monday 20 April 1998 dropped Communication Minister, Buta Singh from his Council of Ministers in the wake of the Supreme Court observation including him in the Jharkhand Mukti Morcha bribery caste.[4] Thus, having failed to get anything from BJP, he again started his efforts for the re-entry into the Congress. In order to get re-entry in Congress party, Buta Singh met Congress President Ms Sonia Gandhi. Consequently, on 3 May 1999, he was re-admitted in the Congress party in the presence of Congress President of the state unit Ms Girija Vyas, MP at Jaipur.[5]

Blow for Buta Singh: Congress Denied Ticket, 2014

In December 2013, after losing badly in four states (Rajasthan, Madhya Pradesh, Delhi and Chhattisgarh), the Congress revoked the expulsion of Buta Singh after many years, Buta Singh, once a trusted man of both Indira Gandhi and Rajiv Gandhi was not only brought back to the party's fold considering to his old loyalty, but was also assigned the task[6] of holding back channel discussions with the two mighty women of politics – Tamil Nadu Chief Minister, J. Jayalalita and BSP Supremo, Mayawati. Then it was thought that he would be put up as a Congress candidate from Jalore-Sirohi seat that he had won five times or would be fielded from, the Ganganagar (SC) seat. But the party denied him ticket from the two constituencies.[7] The Congress opted for Uday Lal Aanjana from the Jalore-Sirohi and a former Minister, Bhanwar Lal Meghwal from the Ganganagar reserved seat.[8]

However, having been denied Congress ticket. Buta Singh with a distinguished record of being Agriculture and Home Minister at the centre, former Governor of Bihar, former Chairman of the National Commission for scheduled castes and eight time MP, four times from Jalore, constituency, was said to be in talks with Chief Minister Vasundhara Raje[9] and was likely to join BJP.

Hurt by the denial of BJP, Buta Singh, 79 years old stalwart approached the Samajwadi party. He will contest the Lok Sabha election 2014, on a Samajwadi party ticket[10] from Jalore-Sirohi constituency in Rajasthan. Samajwadi party spokesperson, Ram Gopal Yadav said that Buta Singh would be the party's authorized candidate for Jalore-Sirohi.

But actually Buta Singh[11] contested as an Independent from Jalore and put in much efforts to make the contest a triangular fight. But for BJP candidate Devji Patel, it was almost like a cake walk. He took away 53.94 per cent of votes and defeated his nearest rival and Congress candidate Udai Lal Anjana by a margin of 3.81 lakh votes. Buta Singh was nowhere near to make it a triangular fight.

Notes

1. For studies of Akhil Bharatiya Safai Mazdoor Congress Policy and its inclination towards Congress, see Shyam Lal, *The Changing Bhangis of India: A study of Caste Association*, Jaipur, Sublime Publications, 1999. pp. 100–101.
2. Ibid., p. 184.
3. 'Vajpayee, 42 others take oath' in *The Times of India*, New Delhi, 20 March 1998.
4. 'Buta Singh sacked from Cabinet', in *The Times of India*, New Delhi, 21 April 1998.
5. 'बूटासिंह कांग्रस में लौटे' दैनिक भास्कर, जयपुर, 4 मई 1999.
6. See, 'Will Buta Singh contest as an Independent from Jalore' in *The Times of India*, Jaipur, Thursday, 20 March 2014.
7. Ibid.
8. Ibid.
9. See, 'Sonaram, Harish Meena joins BJP', in *The Times of India* Jaipur, Wednesday, 19 March 2014.
10. See, 'Buta joins S.P. Gets Raj Ticket' in *The Times of India*, Jaipur, Saturday, 22 March 2014. Also see, 'बूटासिंह सपा में' दैनिक भास्कर, जयपुर, शनिवार, 22 मार्च 2014.
11. See, 'Triangular fight non-existent in state LS election' in the *Times of India*, Jaipur, Monday, 19 May 2014.

5

Discrimination of Bhangis by Political Parties and Caste Hindus

During the last 20 years and more there has been some sociological literature generated on the Bhangis in India. These studies indicate that there has been cultural, but hardly any socio-economic changes among the Bhangi masses, while a few, especially in the urban areas who have surfaced among the Bhangis, may be those to be educated first, moved to the various government centres in search of jobs got stabilized there. However, my Jodhpur study on Bhangis (1992) has shown that Bhangis, after independence of the country, have achieved some material change but not upward mobility. They have achieved some educational mobility.[1] But despite change of the education mobility, they continue to remain in the lower segment of Hindu society as they were in pre-independence period. Of course, the severity of the untouchability in urban areas in the Rajasthan is missing but rigidity of caste-symptoms persist even in both the untouchables and caste Hindus. These impressions were gathered in early 1978. Data collected in 2000 shows that picture of Bhangis today is not much different from that in 1978. But the framework of general conclusions is fairly discernible. It is the sociologists views which are relevant in understanding the Bhangi caste but which, however have been lost sight of in the midst of political din and fury. Some of the data and insights garnered by them are now brought before the public gaze. The studies confirm that Bhangis suffer from four types of discrimination:

1. From Political Parties
2. From Caste Hindus
3. From Government, and
4. From other Untouchables.

Discrimination of Bhangis by Political Parties

The Bhangis are divided into various factions and parties. The Bhangi social workers and political leaders who are loyal to Congress, are feeling neglected today. They are also demanding that they should be given Congress tickets for the constituencies reserved for the scheduled castes. They feel that the worst victims had been the Bhangis. For instance, from 1952 to 1972, in the State Assembly elections held in Rajasthan, all the time only one Bhangi was elected,[2] which was negligible in comparison to the other scheduled castes. However, after 1977 the number had already increased to 2.[3] This also presents a dismal position of the Bhangis in the assembly. The most shocking fact is that since 1985 assembly elections held in the state, there was not a single sweeper representative. Thus, during the last more than two decades no tickets were given by the Congress to the Bhangi candidates, out of 33 reserved seats in the state. However, in the state assembly elections of 1998, Madan Maharaja was given ticket from Kota district, Rajasthan to appease the Bhangis but he was defeated. Madan Maharaja accused Urban Development Minister, Shanti Kumar Dhariwal (Congress Minister from Kota) for engineering his defeat.[4] More or less the same conditions remain in other states too.

It could also be noted here that there are Meghwal, Bairwa, Jatav, Koli, Raigar, Gingar, etc. MLAs in the state assembly 2013, and MPs in Parliament, 2014, but no Bhangi MLA, no MP and no RPSC member in Rajasthan. Congress has not paid much attention in the same degree as it has concentrated on other dominant Dalit Castes/Communities. Similarly, Congress has allotted land for the hostels to many castes/communities including SCs, but Bhangis have almost no land for Valmiki hostel, Valmiki Bhawan and Valmiki Dharamsala in the state.

When such matters came up before the government, the bureaucracy created so many hurdles. This tells us more about the Bhangis caste than other dominant SCs.

All of this leads to unavoidable conclusion that Congress government was actually an ungenerous, small minded, envy ridden and blinkered towards the welfare of the Bhangis. So, how can Bhangis trust the Congress?

Lok Sabha Elections Since 1952 to 2014

From pre-independence to post-independence, Congress and Bhangis remained inseparable (up to 1984). In 1952, the first popular Congress Ministry came into power. Pandit Jawaharlal Nehru was elected the first Prime Minister of free India.

It is also true that the Bhangi had made very little progress in the field of politics. The contrast is all the more obvious if one considered the progress made by Meghwal, Bairwa, Chamar and Raigar communities of Rajasthan in the field of politics. Thus, in 1998 Bhagwan Das, a leading Supreme Court Advocate and also a famous Bhangi writer, wrote a book *Baba Saheb Bhimrao Ambedkar Aur Bhangi Jaatiyan* which narrated the dismal scenario of Bhangi representation in Parliament. His book, which he had published first in 1996 and revised edition in 1998, carried the following pitiable story.[5]

> भंगी जातियों के बहुत कम लोग संसद में प्रवेश कर सके। कान्सटीट्यूएट असैम्बली में श्री कन्हैया लाल बाल्मिकी 'उत्तर प्रदेश' से चुनाव लड़कर आये और श्री यशवन्त राय पंजाब से हमेशा मनोनीत किये गये, वे कभी चुनाव में कामयाब नहीं हो सके। पहली लोक सभा में श्री कन्हैयालाल और भगवानदीन सांसद रहे। 1957 में श्री कन्हैयालाल और श्री नारायणदीन उत्तर प्रदेश से जीतकर आये। राज्य सभा में कल्याण चंद, श्री अच्छेलाल बाल्मिकी, लोक सभा में श्री गोपाल पचेरवाल, श्री शिवचरण, धन्नासिंह गुलशन मजहबी और सरदार बूटा सिंह, मंगलराम प्रेमी संसद में रहे। 1996 में बहुजन समाजवादी पार्टी के बढ़ते हुए प्रभाव को रोकने के लिए जिसकी लीडरशिप चमार जाति में जन्मे श्री काशीराम और कु. मायावती के हाथों में है, को भारतीय जनता पार्टी के गैर चमार जातियों को अपनाना शुरू किया है। भंगी जातियों में जन्मे चार सांसद भारतीय जनता पार्टी के टिकट पर जीत कर संसद में आए।

Not only in the state assembly polls, the data as gleaned from the eminent sweepers regarding the sweepers 'representation in the Lok Sabha, also revealed again a very dismal picture. In Lok Sabha elections held in the country from 1952 to

1989, the number of sweepers representatives was as meagre as 12 only.[6] In 1989 among 544 members of Lok Sabha, the sweepers had only 3 representatives. These figures were gathered in early 1989. Data gathered in 2002 show that the picture of Bhangi (MPs) Parliamentarians today is not much different from that in 1989. The data as gleaned from the eminent sweepers, regarding the sweeper's representation in 544 members of Lok Sabha (2014) also revealed again a very dismal picture. Parliamentary election held in April 2014 show that the picture of Bhangi (MPs) Parliamentarians today is only one. In 2014, Manohar Lal Utwal was elected from Devas reserved constituency, Madhya Pradesh to Lok Sabha as BJP candidate. Earlier, he was an active BJP worker and he was elected to state assembly three times as BJP candidate in Madhya Pradesh. He also became the first Bhangi Minister of Madhya Pradesh in 2008.

Despite more than six decades of affirmative action and various schemes launched by the Government, the plight of the sweepers by and large remained as hitherto earlier. They did not get the nominal share. This neglectful attitude taken by the Congress Party, particularly compelled a few dithering sweepers to start joining other political parties. It is interesting to note here that majority of sweepers are not interested in supporting other parties but feel perturbed over continuous indifferent attitudes of the Congress party towards them. For the State government that nominates a large number of persons from the different castes/communities (high and the low castes) in various bodies, the Bhangi nominees surprisingly lag behind.

Congress: Socio-Economic Background of the SC Members and Rajya Sabha Elections since 1952 to Present Day

Statistics shows that not a single person from this community was nominated for Rajya Sabha compared to nominees from the other scheduled castes and scheduled tribes. The figures themselves speak a volume of this. In 1965 and 1966, Jagannath Pahadia (Khatik) was elected from Rajasthan to the Rajya Sabha as the Congress candidate.[7] In 1972, Jamnalal (Bairwa) was elected to Rajya Sabha.[8] In 1980, Dhuleshwar Meena was not only elected to the Rajya Sabha for the first time from Rajasthan, but was also elected in 1986.[9] In 1982, Nathi Singh (Jatav)[10] and in 1984 Smt Shanti Pahadia (Khatik)[11] were elected as Rajya Sabha members. In 1992, Moolchand Meena[12] was not only elected to the Rajya Sabha for the first time, but was also elected second time in the year 2000 also. Similarly, Ms Jamna Barupal (Bairwa)[13] daughter of Panna Lal Barupal, five times MP from the Ganganagar Parliamentary Constituency, was elected to the Rajya Sabha in the year 2000. All were Congress nominees. Thus, for the period from 1952 to 2000, not a single Congress person from Bhangi community was elected to the Rajya Sabha. This indifferent attitude towards Bhangi community in the State has compelled them to rethink over it.

For the first time the Bhangi community has seen a Bhangi MP (Rajya Sabha) in 2005, since 1952. BJP had nominated just one candidate namely Kishan Kumar Valmiki – a resident of Sanganer, Jaipur from the community. In the past 62 years, despite secular message and promises to work for the dalits in general and Bhangis in particular, Congress has not nominated even once a candidate from this community. Thus, no Bhangi MP had been elected from Rajasthan, which have been staunch supporters of Congress since pre-independence days.

These are some of the experience of a large number of illiterate Bhangis in Rajasthan state who have been afforded an opportunity to enter the political arena following the enactment of quota basis for them in various bodies. Brandished by well entrenched cultural and social taboos, high castes' mindset and strong caste bias, these Bhangis are struggling against enormous odds to be effective in social life.

The entry of the Bhangis in the political field is yet to be accepted by the high caste Hindus and dominant scheduled castes/communities, who have been witnessing the death of their dominance within the political organizations/bodies. They have, therefore, been ignoring Bhangis. When nominated or elected, these Bhangis are expected to act as their puppets. There is a strong resistance against the Bhangi leadership. They are subjected to poor economic conditions questioning their base and influence. Lack of political leadership and social unity have fettered Bhangis potential who have to constantly struggle against attempts at co-option by powerful scheduled castes/communities. The medicine has proved worse than the disease.

The Bhangis have traditionally supported the Congress. But of late, the Congress base among the Bhangis has become somewhat shaky, with the continued neglect of the Bhangis by the Congress. Like State Assembly Elections, even in Municipal Corporations, Municipal Council and Municipalities Elections, 1999, again Bhangis were neglected by the Congress throughout the state and this has further lowered the image of the Congress among the Bhangis.

The older generation of the Bhangi caste workers had been associated with Congress for long and had participated in the Praja Mandal agitation and National movement; they had supported the Congress in the Assembly and Parliamentary Elections since the elections of 1952. This caste had little formal education, but had closer ties with Congress, particularly the urban dwelling Bhangis. The issues which this community saw as paramount was the demand for allocation of tickets to the Bhangis. In obtaining the tickets for Nagar Palika, Nagar Parishad and the Nagar Nigam, the Bhangi activists always approached the Congress leadership. During the Nagar Palika, Nagar Parishad and Nagar Nigam elections of 1999, the prominent leaders of the Bhangi caste workers were: Babu Lal Ghavri, Dinesh Tarvandi and Madan Kharadi (all from Udaipur), Vishnu Sarvate, Tara Chand Chanwaria, Ms Raj Kumari Kandara and Prem Chanwaria (all from Jodhpur), Kamal Chanwaria from Jaipur.[14] who had been party loyal lieutenants for the last two decades, attempted to secure the party tickets. They approached the local Congress leaders. The upper caste Congress leaders promised to take up the matter with appropriate authorities on their behalf. There were continued efforts to fight the elections of 1999 as party candidates. Despite their sincere efforts regarding party tickets the Congress refused the tickets. Later, Tarachand Chanwaria and Babu Lal Ghavri fought as independent candidates in Jodhpur and Udaipur respectively, but lost the elections.[15] However, in an attempt to emerge as independent victorious candidate Ghavri reached an understanding with BJP and also received the party support during the election in reserved constituency, Udaipur.

Despite the general refusal regarding the tickets to Bhangi caste social workers by Congress, however, two Bhangi activists were benefited by the tickets, but in the election they did not fare quite well. Out of two Congress candidates, Kamal Chanwaria lost election from Brahmpuri reserved constituency, Jaipur. Ms Raj Kumari Kandara was declared elected from the Nagauri Gate reserved constituency, Jodhpur[16] as the nomination form of BJP candidates was rejected by election officer. In addition, Pankaj Valmiki, a BJP candidate[17] won seat to Nagar Nigam, Jaipur from Sanganer reserved constituency, Jaipur.

The first year of Congress's rule (1999) had been an eventful one. It saw the adoption of policies which were to appease the Bhangi caste. It was at this juncture that it was decided to nominate a few Bhangi social workers in some Nagar Palikas, Nagar Parishad's and Nagar Nigams to represent the Bhangi community. According to Babu Lal Ghavri and Babu Lal Pandit,[18] Congress nominated Rampal Arya from Bhilwara, Madan Kharadia from the Udaipur, Tara Chand Chanwaria from Jodhpur and Kamal Chanwaria from Jaipur, in the local bodies. According to Ghavri and the others, even during the Chief Minister Bhairon Singh Shekhawat's rule in the state, BJP nominated Badri Parihar from Udaipur, Mrs Kalyani from Jaipur in the local urban bodies.

The Bhangi population is scattered throughout the Rajasthan. It does not have a majority anywhere to elect representatives on its own strength even in the reserved constituencies. To get elected a Bhangi candidate has to depend on substantial caste Hindu and other scheduled castes voters. Bhangi candidates who have poor economic conditions, have no chance of winning over caste Hindu and support of other untouchables. The scattered pockets of Bhangi population are also highly vulnerable to pressures from local elites. These, very effectively put into jeopardy the electoral fortunes of Bhangi candidates.

The Congress has traditionally been supported by the Bhangis. For the first time, the other parties are wooing the Bhangis, who constitute a good segment of voters. The Bharatiya Janta Party (BJP) and the Samata Party that do not have large base among the Bhangis, have won the support of the

'Akhil Rajasthan Valmiki Samaj', whose leaders argue that only a few influential Bhangis have been benefitted by the Congress. Many Bhangis, however, still identify themselves strongly with the Congress, though Congress was bitterly criticized by Gopal Pacherwal,[19] Samta Party President of the state unit and others at Akhil Rajasthan Valmiki Samaj Sanyukt Prantinidhi Sammelan held on 24 October 1999 at Kota.

Over the past few years, BJP gradually exerted its influence over the Bhangis. The BJP under the leadership of Shri Bhairon Singh Shekhawat had recently begun efforts to cover up new spheres of influence in the low untouchable castes.

The lack of interest shown by the Congress has forced the Bhangis to join other political parties on their own. The Bhangis who were staunch supporters of the Congress had been so dissatisfied with this party that it seems there is no ray of hope for the Congress to get them back to its fold at all. For Rajasthan, Bhangi netas demanded Congress, for the last 20 years to help innocent Bhangis running here and there for transfers and postings.

By continuous indifferent attitude towards the Bhangis in allocation of tickets for MLA, MP, Rajya Sabha members, Nagar Nigam, Nagar Parishads and depriving them of their nomination in various public bodies/organizations, both Congress and Government, have compelled the Bhangi leaders to vindicate the attitude of Congress for Bhangis in the last 67 year as 'Disappointing and belittling for them'.

Discrimination of Bhangis by Caste Hindus

In sociological literature, there have been three schools with a different views on so-called untouchables. One holds that they were not part of the Hindu caste system and were called out-castes. The second, hold that they were part of the Hindus caste system though they shared differentially in its traditions. The third, says that they were autonomous and had their own unique and separate traditions.

The first view suited the missionaries and second the caste Hindus for different reasons. The missionaries wanted conversion and caste Hindus did not want the untouchables to get away from their grip. The caste Hindus wanted them to remain in the Hindus fold for three reasons:

1. Untouchables in general, and Bhangis in particular, removed impurities so that caste Hindus could remain pure.
2. Most of the untouchables supplied cheap or unpaid labour to the upper castes and,
3. In the one man one vote political culture, retaining the untouchables' Vote Bank was a necessity for the dominant castes and classes. So they opposed the conversions not so much for religious reasons but for the socio-economic ones. If the so-called untouchables were delinked from the Hinduism or caste systems, then the dominant castes would be the losers.

In Rajasthan, the Bhangis are humiliated even today by the caste Hindus because of their social background. Socially, they are still treated as untouchable Bhangis by the caste Hindus. This pattern prevails in the rest of India.

According to the study conducted by 'Action aid' a human rights group on 'Valmiki Community' in 13 districts of Rajasthan as reported in the *Times of India*[20] on Tuesday, 9 September 2014 that

> Communities involved in manual scavenging, which is banned in the country, but still exists, is the worst performer in terms of literacy levels. These communities ... are discriminated against in schools and this is the main reason behind the highest dropout among them.[21]
>
> Action aid, a human rights group also found that those students who have cleared schools or any vocational training are unable to get into unconventional job or profession. The study was conducted in Ajmer, Alwar, Sikar, Nagaur, Bharatpur, Kota, Bikaner, Karauli, Sawai Madhopur, Jhunjhunu, Bhilwara, Dausa and Tonk.[22]

The study further says:

> That among scheduled castes/communities, Valmiki has the lowest literacy and enrolment level. In the gender parity Index, 92 girls enrolled for every 100 ST boys in Class I in 2012–13 academic session. In Valmiki community, 70 girls enrolled for

every 100 boys in schools. The difference becomes sharper in the higher classes.[23]

The starting revelation of survey says that even in Anganbadi centres, the children of Valmiki Community face discrimination which has left families no option, but to withdraw them out from these centres.

Mohammad Ameen,[24] Programme officer, Action Aid also attracted the attention of State government. Ameen said,

> This community required statewide immediate attention to raise their social and economic levels. The report also discussed that very few students have taken their admission under RTE in private schools.

Scavenging has been in existence in Indian society since ancient times. A particular sub-caste amongst the untouchables was obliged to perform the scavenging jobs. On account of their associations with the so-called 'Dirty Occupation' many restrictions were placed in respect of their social interaction with the people of the so-called caste Hindus. Since the sweepers had been engaged in the manual disposal of human excreta, they are looked down upon as a: Profane group, the contact with whose members is considered defiling. This led to their spatial segregation, requiring them to live in separate cluster outside the towns and villages. These people lived away from the reach of other respectable people and in earlier times had to sound 'Paiyas' 'Paiyas' (keep at distance) while walking on road or entering in the market in order to inform people of their coming and let them avoid contact. The traditional social order assigned them the lowest social position because of their occupation and other despicable habits. The hereditary occupation of the manual clearing of human excreta became a source of their exploitation by others. They were subject to various forms of discriminations and disabilities. The evil of untouchability hurt and haunted them most, they continued to remain down-trodden, both socially and economically. They were treated as the lowest amongst the low and suffered from extreme form of economic and social backwardness. The economic and educational backwardness has deprived many sweeper families from taking advantage of the constitutionally conferred privileges meant for the welfare of dispossessed. Politically too, sweepers are little organized as compared to other untouchable communities.

Well-entrenched caste prejudices which perpetuate caste hatred, remain the basis of the successful implementation of the reservation programme in the state. Despite some improvement, the socio-educational and job status of the Bhangis in almost all the states remain dismal. They have no say in the political areas and the limited access to government job facilities. In some cases the Bhangis are denied jobs by both upper caste Hindus and dominant scheduled castes and scheduled tribes, but in several other castes socio-cultural taboos and lack of access to political bosses and the appropriate approach are the reasons for the low recruitment rate in the government organizations.

The Bhangis are neither recruited nor their services are utilized as peons primarily because their services both at the office and home adversely affect their purity and pollution. Caste Hindus and those working in offices have problem in taking water and other things from Bhangi peons as well.

Whether it is the selection of the scheduled caste candidates (even at Class IV category), on promotion, transfer and posting of scheduled caste officials, caste selective servants at the upper caste official's residence, untouchability, humiliation, harassment and atrocities on scheduled castes, the worst victims of casteism are the Bhangis.

It is not that shift in the reservation policy had not taken place. The government had initiated the implementation of the protective discrimination policy which had benefitted dominant scheduled caste or communities only.

Growth of Elite

In the following pages we will discuss here the modern elite that emerged after independence, and the traditional elite. We have noted in other writings that there were a few influential illoms among the Bhangis of Jodhpur, Jaipur, Kota and Udaipur. There were individual and families who were the recipients of titles, such as 'Mehtar Shah' and 'Pradhanji' given to them by local Chief and Rajas. Such titles gave them certain privileges and legitimized their higher status within the caste. During the princely states, there were no channels of mobility opened to them. After Independence the value system and nature of authority changed. Hence, elites of different kinds emerged, playing different kinds of roles. The point is to treat the growth of different kinds of elite as an indicator of upward social mobility of the individuals.

The growth of differentiated modern elite reveals the diversity of individual talent and level of achievement, which have to be seen in relation to the level of deprivation, in the traditional structure on the one hand, and the general performance of so-called progressive castes, which are relevant as opposition-reference groups on the other.

The notion of an elite is a relative one. In a community like Bhangi which was denied opportunities of various kinds, the individuals with a certain level of achievement are considered to be in elite positions. By this standard the first generation graduates, schools and college teacher, advocates, doctors, engineers, police officers and administrators belong to the elite category. The Bhangis like other untouchables were denied modern education opportunities which they have acquired after a series of agitations. Thus, when a Bhangi was employed by the state as a teacher, it was a big event for the community. Similarly, when the Bhangi became a doctor or college lecturer, they were considered to be: 'Samaj Ratan' for their parents were mostly night soil removers. The Bhangis were also denied all kinds of political participation. After 1947, when they achieved representation through reservation, they were elected to the Legislature and thus the first generation of professional politicians emerged. The Bhangis were also kept out of state administration and when they graduated and passed RAS exams to fill administrative posts in state administration, an administrator elite came into existence. This is the rationale for treating those employed as doctors, lecturers, engineers, government officials, RAS officers and professional politicians as part of the elite.

The basis for a discussion on the growth of an elite is the information available regarding 73 Bhangis who were listed in a write-up by former and the first RAS officer, Gopal Das in 1999. Gopal Dass, resident of Jaipur, who was the first Bhangi to be selected and appointed as RAS officer in 1959 (now retired) pointed out that efforts were made in the state to improve the socio-economic and educational status of the scheduled castes but the Bhangis among the scheduled castes continue to be in the same sad and poor condition. On 24 October 1999, referring to the situation in Rajasthan, Gopal Das concluded in a Bhangis' Sammelan at Kota on 'अखिल राजस्थान वाल्मिकी समाज संयुक्त प्रतिनिधि सम्मेलन' that statistics, however represent only the tip of the iceberg. According to him,[25] they were as follows:

IAS – 1 (Promotee), IPS – 1, RAS – 4, Allied Services – 2, Tehsildars – 3, Assistant Police Commissioner – 1, Police Sub-Inspectors – 3, Senior Jail Superintendent – 1, Inspector – 2, College Lecturer – 12, College Principal – 1, University Professor – 1, Principal, Secondary and Higher Secondary Schools – 5, Doctor – 20 and Engineer – 14. Besides this, there is only one Zila Pramukh and five Parshads.

We may now consider the growth of different types of elite among the Bhangis over a period of more than six decades.

As stated earlier, they were not admitted to schools established by the then Princely State governments. The modern intellectual elite developed when Bhangis started acquiring education after Independence in 1947. Until 1970s, they were predominantly employed as primary/middle school teachers and a few college lecturers. Since then, they have been many lecturers who have achieved an even higher level of elite status by being promoted to higher positions. Thus, while Purushottam Gehlot, son of late Kishore Ji of Nathdwara did his MA (History) from MLS University, Udaipur in 1967, was appointed as Lecturer in Government College, Chittorgarh in 1970 and was promoted as Principal PG Government College Sikar in 1996 and later became Joint Director, at Directorate of College Education Rajasthan, Jaipur in 2000. In 2006 he retired as Principal PG Government College, Jaisalmer. Some of the well-known PG Principals were Hanuman Prasad Gujarati, B.P. Lot and Dr Ram Swaroop Narwal. Sushila Reel of Jodhpur got her MSc degree (Botany) from JNV University, Jodhpur in 1979. She was appointed as Lecturer at Government College, Kotputli, Jaipur in 1982 and was promoted as Principal of Bangur PG Government College, Pali in 2010. Another notable woman is

Vimla Arya, who is also Principal at PG Government College Balotra, Barmer. Nemi Chand Boyat got his MA degree (History) from JNV University Jodhpur in 1973. He also joined Government College, Barmer as a Lecturer in 1982 and promoted to the post of Principal of Government Girls College, Balotra, Barmer in 2010 and later retired in the same year (2010). Out of 251, one-third (89) are advocates.

One of the outstanding present academician is Dr Shyam Lal. Shyam Lal is the eminent sociologist who has been Professor and Head, Department of Sociology, University of Rajasthan, Jaipur and subsequently became the Vice-Chancellor of three Universities namely JNV University, Jodhpur, University of Rajasthan, Jaipur and Patna University, Patna.

Modern allopathic doctors made their debut with Dr J.C. Jawa, born in Jodhpur. Since then, there have been many doctors. Thus, while Dr J.C. Jawa son of Poona Ram of Lakharon Ka Bas, Jodhpur did his MBBS from SMS Medical College, Jaipur in 1967. A little later, in 1972, he did his MS (Ophthalmology) and became Civil Assistant Surgeon and soon rose to the Chief Medical and Health Officer and Senior Specialist (Oph). It was he who went abroad as Ophthalmic consultant to Government of Iran on deputation from February 1978 to February 1985. In March 1996, he became Additional Director (FW) Medical, Health and Family Welfare services, Rajasthan, Jaipur. Amritlal, another brilliant contemporary, passed MBBS in 1976 from Sampurnanand Medical College, Jodhpur and entered government services in 1978 and later on, got promotion to Senior Civil Surgeon in 1990 and Deputy CMHO. Since then, there have been a few doctors who have achieved an even higher level of elite status by being settled in the foreign countries. Thus Dr Madan Lal Kandara son of Gun Ji of Jodhpur did his MBBS from S.N. Medical College, Jodhpur in 1982 and later on, he went abroad on deputation and settled down there permanently. Some of the well-known CMHOs were Dr Radhe Shyam Boyat and Dr Rajendra Jawa, while Moksh Swaroop Pandit, (1980) Dr Prem Valmiki and Dr (Mrs) Prem Valmiki were known doctors.

Besides allopathic doctors, there are a few Ayurveda doctors, who made their debut in this profession. One of them is

Dr Naresh Lohia. Dr Naresh Lohia son of Mohan Lal Lohia of Bikaner who got his BAMS degree from National Institute of Ayurveda, Jaipur in 2008 and later in 2012 he was selected by RPSC, Ajmer and posted in Government Ayurvedic hospital, Kesher Desher, Bikaner. Another notable man is Dr Subhash Gharu, who also got BAMS degree from National Institute of Ayurveda, Jaipur in 2008 and is working on contract basis in Ajmer. The interesting point is that the Bhangis are able to achieve a breakthrough in a profession which involved touching caste Hindu patients, who still recognized touch-pollution.

While there are more doctors and engineers among the Bhangis, there are a few engineers, many of whom are employed by the state government. This happened in a progressive time scale.

In order to get an idea of the growth of elite over a period of time, the 251 persons were divided into nine categories on the basis of their status. Thus, the period covered more than five decades from 1962 to 2014.

Table 5.1 gives the distribution of different types of elite. It will be seen that all professional elite put together, account for 251 while the political elite occupy a low place with 8 persons, followed by advocates with 89, doctors 28, lecturers elite with 23, and administrative cadre with 13.

Another profession in which Bhangis achieved a level of excellence is Law. The modern legal profession came into existence with establishment of courts. But the untouchables including Bhangis were kept out of education for centuries and hence they joined the profession after independence. The first lawyer in the community was Desh Raj Kalla. Since independence, there has been a significant growth of lawyers. Out of 251 elites, there are 89 lawyers. They enrolled as advocates and began practice in Jodhpur. Since 1996, they dealt in all types of matter, be it civil, criminal or even revenue cases. In the lower judiciary, there is one Bhangi Judicial officer namely Kamal Lohia.

Desh Raj Kalla enrolled as an advocate in 1996 and began practice in Jodhpur. Later in 2014, Valmiki advocates in Jodhpur had organized themselves in an association called

Table 5.1

Districtwise Distribution of Elite In Rajasthan, 2014

S. No.	District	Lecturer	College Principal	Univ. Professor	Doctor	Vaidyan	Veterinary Doctor	Advocate	Engineer	Bank Officer	Police Officer	Jailor	IAS	IPS	RAS	Administrative Officer	Hotel Owner	Petrol Pump	Gas Agency	Piggery
		1			2			3	4	5	6		7			8	9			
1.	Alwar	1						3												6
2.	Ajmer	2	2		2	1		14	3	1		1			1			1		7
3.	Bhilwara	1											1							
4.	Bikaner	1			7	1	2	4	4	1					1					
5.	Barmer		2				1											2		
6.	Bharatpur				1															
7.	Banswara								1											
8.	Bundi								1											
9.	Chittorgarh	3	1		1				1								1			
10.	Churu								1											
11.	Dausa	2																1		2
12.	Hanumangarh				1								1			1				
13	Jodhpur	1			5			30	12	3	3		1			1				
14.	Jaisalmer	1																		

Cont'd...

...Cont'd

15. Jaipur			1	5			22	4	8	2	2	1			11	1			
16. Jalore	1											1							
17. Karauli																	1		1
18. Kota			1				1	1											
19. Nagaur	1																		
20. Pali		1					3	2							1		1		
21. Sawai Madhopur		1																	
22. Tonk				1			4									1			3
23. Udaipur	1			4			8	5									1	1	
Total	14	8	1	28	2	3	89	35	13	5	3	4	1	2	13	3	7	1	19

Source: 1. The above figures are not taken from Government official record, but have been gleaned from well-informed persons in the community and published materials. It is possible, however that a few elite in a district were left out inadvertently.

2. Gopal Das was first selected for RAS in 1959 and thereafter (till 2014) four candidate from the community were also selected for RAS. Except Gopal Das, all the three RAS officer were elevated to IAS and one was recently selected as IAS in 2012.

* Out of 33 districts, the number of elite from 10 districts, could not be ascertained.

'Valmiki Samaj Advocates Associates' for professional and welfare purpose. Desh Raj Kalla became its patron. The first office bearers are Bal Kishan Chanwaria (President), Sunil Chanwaria (Vice President), Vikas Jawa (General Secretary), Vikram Barasa Co-Secretary and Rajendra Goel (Treasurer). Some of the Valmiki advocates are on government panel and one such panelist is Bal Kishan Chanwaria.

Valmiki advocates of Jaipur have close organizational links with those in Jodhpur. There are approximately 22 advocates in Jaipur. The encouragement received from advocates of Jodhpur, led the Valmiki advocates of Jaipur to organize themselves at Jaipur level. Thus, in 2014, they organized a new association called 'Valmiki Adhivakta Parishad' and Mahendra Kumar Chauhan became the President.

Besides being school teachers, college lecturers and university professors, the Bhangis have also taken to the practice of composing 'devotional songs/kavita'. Bhangi poets made their debut with Roop Chand Chanwaria. He was popularly known as 'Roopchand Kavi' and was a Class IV employee in the then Northern Railway. These songs created a stir when he sung from the dais. The community fellows praised such songs in public meetings. Roop Chand Chanwaria had composed a good number of songs/*kavita* for which he was honoured by the Bhangi Samaj. Another notable poet was Chetan Das Pandit. He was the first Bhangi who published collection of his Bhajans, songs/*kavita*, Doha, Chhand, Kundalia, Savya, Shorta, Chopai, etc. The book titled *Chetan Kavya Suman* having 95 pages was first published in 1991 by Pandit Prakashan, Jodhpur. Dr Shaktidan Kavia of JNV University, Jodhpur wrote the Foreword and Abhimat by 'Hari Bhajan' Hans Raj. There were also some government school teachers and one of earliest known and recognized 'Kavi' (poet) was Ishwar Lal Gharu of Bhilwara. Besides Gharu, there is also Manak Chand Souda of Tonk another government school teacher and poet.

The category of government service includes mostly officers doing administrative jobs and a few are Collectors and Deputy Collectors. Of the notables, one was J.P. Chandelia. He was elevated to IAS in 2001–2002. From 2002 onwards, he served as Collector of Nagaur and Churu districts and Commissioner of Jodhpur division. He also performed in various capacities in the Rajasthan government. Gopal Das, the first RAS (1959) was Assistant Collector of Ajmer. From 1959 onwards, he served as SDP, ADM and Additional DDO. The other is P.R. Pandit. He was promoted to IAS in 2012. He is also performing in various capacities in Rajasthan Government. J.C. Desai was elevated to IAS in 2012. Another notable one is Priti Singh Panwar, She is the first woman RTS officer in Rajasthan (2001 Batch). She is recently elevated to RAS officer on 10 October 2014 and posted as Assistant Director at the Directorate of DLB Jaipur. Thus, she became the first woman RAS officer from this caste. Aashish Chauhan is the first IAS officer from Rajasthan (2012 batch) and SDO Nainital, Uttarakhand government. Similarly, Virendra Kumar Panwar was the first IPS and was posted in Madhya Pradesh. He also performed in various capacities in the Madhya Pradesh government. He was elevated to IGP and later retired.

It is obvious that the growth of the professional elite, with internal variation, is closely related to educational mobility. Table 5.1 gives the distribution of elite in Rajasthan who have achieved an elite status through educational status after independence. Thus, significant educational mobility occurred among the Bhangis from 1947.

The growth of the business elite calls for a different kind of talent, namely entrepreneur ability with regard to mobilization of capital and organization of other resources. The most important business activity of the Bhangis before and after independence was trade in piggery, as Bhangis had the monopoly of this trade. There were also some traders doing this for Delhi, Haryana and Punjab and one of the earliest known trader was Harnath Mahena of Tonk, who received a recognition of merit from the Bhangi Samaj. Besides Harnath Mahena there were also Sukhi, resident of Mandawari, Tehsil Lalsot District Dausa and Haredi, native of Bada Darbaja, Gangapur city, District Karauli another trader. Besides piggery, there are quite a few meat shop (pig, chicken and fish) owners who made a name for themselves. Some of the well-known meat shop owners are – Rajendra s/o Ram Kishore, Vishambhar Dayal s/o

Devi Sahay, Shantan s/o Kalu Ram and Suresh (all from Rajgarh, Alwar), Mohan Mahena and Naval Mahena (both from Tonk), Dwarka s/o Mangilal, Durga Das Pandit s/o Aapu Pandit, Babu Pandit s/o Dinkar Pandit, Jwala Prasad s/o Lalchand, Lakhan s/o Ashok Boyat, Mahesh Pandit s/o Mihi Pandit and Mukesh Goyar (all from Beawar, Ajmer), Tilak and Bhola Ram (both from Bharatpur), Ashok and Rajesh (both from Alwar) and Puran from Mahua, District Dausa.

Besides Tonk, Alwar, Ajmer, Bharatpur, there are also some meat shop owners in Jaipur and some of the known owners are Pappa Ram (Near Ankur cinema, Jaipur), Bala Ram (Nahargarh, Jaipur) Bhag Chand (Hida ki Mori, Jaipur) and Suresh (Jawahar Nagar, Jaipur). Similarly, three decades ago Raju s/o Babulal, and Mahendra s/o Kundan, both from Bharatpur, migrated to Delhi. Raju opened a meat shop at Govindpuri, Delhi. Meat supply is another business for Mahendra – a resident of Trilokpuri, Delhi.

Later, commercial and industrial entrepreneurs came into existence. They opened gas agencies, petrol pumps, Iron work-shops, hotels and printing press. R.D. Jawa, was the first Bhangi who started 'Mewar Jawa Gas Agency', at Udaipur. Opening of petrol pump is another big business for Bhangis and Sunil Joad and Anil Joad of Naval filling station, Padru, Tehsil Siwana, District Barmer and Rakesh Kumar Jawa of Nimaj petrol pump are the owners. Similarly, Shyam Lal Chanal of 'Chanal Filling Station' on Nasirabad bypass road, Ajmer is the owner of this petrol pump. Shyam Lal s/o Ramjilal Jaipuria opened 'Avinash petrol pump' at Nagal Rajavtan, Dausa. Another notable petrol pump owners are Kishan Gharu, who opened 'Gharu Petrol Pump' at Siwana Tehsil, District Barmer and Harisingh Sarvan who opened 'Sarvan Service' centre at Toda Bheem, Karauli. The Bhangis have also taken the lead in the trade of hotels. Mukesh Valmiki of Jaipur and Purushottam Gehlot of Chittorgarh are hotel owners. Another notable hotel owner is Raju lal Nakwal, who started 'Chopal Restaurant' at Banasthali Vidyapeeth turning, Niwai, District Tonk.

Similarly, some of the educated Bhangis opened the dairy. This is significant as an indicator of the upward social mobility of any community, for it means increasing access to and control of scarce resources of employment. One of the known dairy owner is Shyamlal Kalla s/o Surja Ram Kalla of Udai Mandir, Jodhpur, who opened the dairy farm on modern lines at Bhadwasia, Jodhpur. There are 60–70 cows and buffaloes.

The political elite consisting of professional politicians began to appear only around the turn of 20th century, with the growth of national movement. With independence and adult franchise, and introduction of the representative institutions at different levels, the number of professional politicians increased. They hold positions in the new structure of power at various levels at the Parliament, the State Assembly, the Municipality, the three tiers of Panchayat Raj. They are also office bearers of different political parties and active workers.

After independence, scheduled castes/communities including Bhangi politicians came to occupy such positions as members of Rajasthan Legislative Assembly through elections.

Some of the known professional politicians may be listed for the sake of illustration. Narsingh Deo Gujarati was an active Congress leader and he was a member of Harijan Sewak Sangh to remove untouchability in Jodhpur region. He was one of the active social worker who agitated for independence in the forties. He was jailed for few months for which Rajasthan Government recognized Gujarati as a freedom fighter. Mangilal Arya fought the election on Congress ticket from Jalore reserved seat in 1980 and was declared elected. Later, he became Deputy Minister in the Congress ministry headed by Jagannath Paharia in 1980. He became the first Chairman of the National Commission for Safai Karamcharis in 1994 and later in 2003, he also became the first Chairman of State Safai Karamchari Ayog. Earlier to this, he was also working President of Akhil Bharatiya Safai Mazdoor Congress. Dharmpal Panwar was also leader of Congress and became the first Bhangi MLA in 1952. Hari Ram Gharu, an active Congress leader was MLA during the Congress rule. Gopal Pacherwal was a Janta Party MLA in 1977 and 1980 and became the first Bhangi MP of 'Janta Dal' (Lok Sabha) in 1989. He was also General Secretary of Janta Dal in 1989. Krishan Lal Valmiki was also first Bhangi MP, BJP. (Rajya Sabha). Madan Maharaja was a Congress MLA of Rajasthan Assembly. Dungar Ram Panwar was a Janta Party MLA and later became Deputy Minister in Bhairon Singh Shekhawat Ministry.

Bhangi politicians are found distributed over different political parties. From 1952 to 1985 in Rajasthan Legislative Assembly, there were 6 Bhangis. The distribution by political parties was as follows: Congress–4 and Janta Party–2. Since 1990 till today (2014), there is not a single Bhangi MLA in the State Assembly. One Bhangi MP (Lok Sabha) was from Janta Dal and another was MP (Rajya Sabha) BJP.

Thus, the Bhangi political leaders represent a low level of achievement at the state level.

Table 5.2

Types of Elite Since 1962

S. No.	*Types of Elite*	*Distribution of Elite by Status*
1.	**Lecturer (College and University) including Principal**	
	A. Lecturer	14
	B. Principal	8
	C. University Professor	1
2.	**Doctor**	
	A Allopathic Doctor	28
	B. Vaidyan	2
	C. Veternary doctor	3
3.	Advocate	89
4.	Engineer	35
5.	Bank officer	13
6.	Police officer including Jailor	8
7.	IAS including promotees	4
	IPS	1
	RAS	2
8.	Administrative (Govt service) Officer	13
9.	Business	
	A. Hotel owner	3
	B. Petrol Pump	7
	C. Gas Agency	1
	D. Piggery/Pig meat shop/	1

Source: This table is abstracted from Table 5.1.

It is to be noted that the negatively stereotyped image of the Bhangis particularly, is generally retained by the upper caste Hindus throughout their career. It is also observed that one main reason for lack of objectivity on the part of the selection committee is the composition of the selection committee itself, which is heavily overweighed in favour of dominant scheduled caste communities.

Yes, biased Administrative action against Bhangis is not a new phenomenon. Unfortunately, even senior bureaucrats are not free from prejudices. Their biases match the environment that they are living in. Over the years, attitudes have hardened considerably.

The continuing partisan role of high castes has caused frustration among the Bhangis who in desperation tend to take recourse to the traditional jobs as surveyed by the author in the Jodhpur in 1972.[26] There is a strong case for encouraging the recruitment of the members of the Bhangi community and other weaker sections at various levels in government sectors.

Notes

1. For the most important studies of the Bhangi caste, see, Shyam Lal, *The Bhangi: A Sweeper Caste and its Socio-Economic Portrait*, Bombay, Popular Prakashan, 1992.
2. The most important sources for the early movement and situation of the Bhangis in Jodhpur is Shyam Lal, *Caste and Political Mobilisation: The Bhangis*, Jaipur, Panchsheel Prakashan, 1981, p. 104.
3. Ibid., p. 103.
4. Discussion with Madan Maharaja, Kota, 24 October 1999.
5. भगवान दास, बाबा साहेब भीमराव अम्बेडकर और भंगी जातियां, उत्तर प्रदेश, दलित टुडे प्रकाशन , इंदिरा नगर, लखनऊ , 1998, पृ. 20.
6. Shyam Lal, *The Changing Bhangis of India*, 1999, ibid., p. 144.
7. त्रैमासिक पत्रिका, विधान बोधनी, अक्टूबर 1997 , स्वर्ण जयन्ति विशेशांक जयपुर, राजस्थान विधान सभा सचिवालय, 1997, पृ. 297.
8. Ibid., p. 257.
9. Ibid., p. 258 and 259.
10. Ibid., p. 258.
11. Ibid.
12. Ibid., p. 259.

13. दैनिक भास्कर , जयपुर, 30 मार्च 2000.
14. Discussion with Babu Lal Ghavri, Udaipur, 5 May 2002. Also with Babulal Pandit, Jodhpur, 6 May 2002 and Mukesh Behari, Jaipur, 10 May 2002.
15. Babu Lal Ghavri, Udaipur, 5 May 2002 and Babu Lal Pandit, Jodhpur 6 May 2002.
16. Babu Lal Pandit, Jodhpur, 6 May 2002.
17. Mukesh Behari, Jaipur, 10 May 2002.
18. Babu Lal Ghavri, Udaipur, 5 May 2002 and Babu Lal Pandit, Jodhpur, 5 May 2002.
19. Speech delivered on 24 October 1999 at Kota, by Gopal Pacherwal.
20. For details, see, 'Dropout rate among some SC Communities high: Study' in *The Times of India*, Jaipur, Tuesday, 9 September 2014.
21. Ibid.
22. Ibid.
23. Ibid.
24. Ibid.
25. Paper for Sammelan on 'बाल्मिकी समाज एवं उसके विकास पर एक सोच' Gopal Das, 24 October 1999 at Kota. The most authoritative account and comparative castewise analysis of beneficiaries of Protective Discrimination in Rajasthan is given by Satyanarain Singh, IAS (Retd) and former Member Secretary, Rajasthan OBCs Commission. 'सामाजिक न्याय एवं आरक्षण' *Rajasthan Patrika*, Jodhpur, 9 May 2002 – According to it amongst OBCs, SCs and STs, the dominant caste such as Jats, Ahirs, Charans, Malis, Gujjars (all OBCs), Balais, Bairwas, Chamars, Khatiks, Kolis (all SCs) and Meenas (tribe) appear to have been more beneficiaries in RAS, RPS, RJS, RTS, Police Sub-Inspectors Service and Medical and Engineering College admission, than Bhangis; Bhils, Dhankas, Kumhars and many other castes/communities in Rajasthan. Also see, 'OBC quotas: Jats eat out the Lion's share' in *Hindustan Times*, New Delhi, 17 April 2002. The role of affirmative action for upliftment of weaker and lower castes has to be reassessed.
26. श्याम लाल , जोधपुर के भंगी 'हरिजन सेवा' दिल्ली, वर्ष 21, अंक 2, जनवरी 1972, पृ. 22.

6

Discrimination and Prejudices Against Bhangis by the Government and Other Untouchables

Discrimination of Bhangis by the Government

The Bhangi community which had no MLAs in the State Assembly since 1985 till date (2013) is upset with what it perceives as total apathy of the Congress Government towards the Bhangis of Rajasthan. The Bhangis have complained about the indifferent attitude of Congress due to the attention being given to other dominant scheduled castes/communities of Rajasthan and this has only made the contrast more glaring. At the Deewali festival (2000), Mangilal Arya, working President of All India Safai Mazdoor Congress said that we are planning to meet soon to work out how best, we can ventilate our feelings with regards to the State's apathy. The state government had been a mute spectator to their miseries. The Bhangis in Rajasthan had respect for the Chief Minister. Bhangis stressed that even the change at the government in Rajasthan (Congress replacing BJP in 1998), has made no difference in the state government's attitude.

Bhangi Samaj and Social Injustice Rajasthan Public Service Commission

Since the very inception of Rajasthan Public Service Commission (RPSC), the members of the RPSC were represented by SC/ST candidates by Meena, Bhil, Meghwal, Chamar and Raigar but no one from the caste Bhangi so far. The Bhangis, therefore, requested the present Congress government that this time a Bhangi candidate be considered for the membership, but no sympathetic consideration was given. Despite more than five decades of the affirmative action, the plight of the Bhangis by and large remained as hitherto before. They did not get a nominal share. This indifferent attitude of the Congress particularly, compelled a few dithering Bhangis to join other political parties. Referring to the appointment of Bairwas, Meghwals, Chamars, Damamis, Bhils and Meenas as members and Chairman of Rajasthan Public Service Commission, it is evident that this community has practically no representation in this body from its inception. Prominent amongst those who served the Commission are:[1]

	Name	*From*	*To*
1.	Dhuleshwar Meena	1 January 1972 to	2 January 1978
2.	Dr D.D. Chauhan	8 November 1979 to	26 March 1985
3.	Sugan Chand Singhadia	28 May 1986 to	27 May 1992
4.	Hanuman Prasad	31 October 1992 to	6 October 1995
5.	Smt Kamla Bhil	28 July 1993 to	27 July 1999
6.	M.L. Parihar	14 December 1999 to	14 March 2001
7.	H.N. Meena	25 February 2002 to	19 September 2006
8.	H.L. Meena	18 April 2008 to	31 January 2012
9.	K.L. Berwal	18 April 2008 to	17 April 2014
	(all members)		
1.	Dr D.D. Chauhan	27 March 1985 to	7 November 1985
2.	Sugan Chand Singhadia	28 November 1989 to	4 September 1990
	(both Adhoc Chairman)		
1.	Hanuman Prasad, IAS	6 October 1995 to	30 September 1997
2.	N.K. Bairwa, IAS	30 December 2000 to	23 March 2004
3.	Dr Lalit K. Panwar IAS (R) (All Regular Chairman)	10 August 2015	Continuing

Why Can't a Bhangi be RPSC Member?

Bhangi netas and social workers say, if Bairwa and Chamar could become member of RPSC and also Bhil and Meena, why cannot a Bhangi become member of RPSC?

Since 1949, very often RPSC had a Muslim member and Chairman of RPSC. They also cited the example of current chairman Habib Khan Gauran (2012), who is a Muslim and rose to the top position. His appointment was made by the previous Congress government headed by Ashok Gehlot.

If Congress is secular and does not discriminate anyone on the basis of caste, creed and religion, then what is the problem if a Bhangi is nominated as member of RPSC? They asked. Congress's conduct should not be biased. The state's former CM should have nominated someone from the most neglected section of society in Rajasthan. But it is surprising that CM has not nominated even a single such person after more than six decades. There is a strong feeling that Congress government did nothing for them. Nobody can deny the problem that exists. There is also general acknowledgement of injustice to this community, as a result of which they did not even get a chance. Not only were their fundamental/human rights affected, in majority cases they are even deprived of nomination in various government bodies. There are few persons even today who have been victims of government bias.

They also expressed their resentment over almost nil or meagre representation of the Bhangi community in government bodies and asked how Bhangi community could get justice when out of 1,150 employees in the state secretariat only 53 belonged to Bhangi caste.

Table 6.1 gives distribution of different types of employees categorywise. It will be seen that all categories (from 1 to 7) put together, account for 4.60 per cent Valmiki (53 in number), while others including the general, OBC, SC and ST employees occupy the largest place with 95.40 per cent (1,150 in number).

Table 6.1

Categorywise Distribution of Employees

S. No.	*Category*	*Bhangi/Valmiki*	*Others*
1.	Peon	40	229
2.	L.D.C	2	181
3.	U.D.C	1	229
4.	Section Officer	2	NA
5.	Assistant Section officer	8	370
6.	Personal Assistant	–	62
7.	Additional Personnel Assistant	–	79
	Total	53	1,150

Source: These figures are not taken from government official record but have been gathered from Office-bearer of Valmiki Association Jaipur.

In State Assembly election 2013 and General polls, 2014 Akhil Bharatiya Valmiki Mahasabha had created a political furore by supporting 'BJP' candidates in the state and Modi for Delhi. The biggest surprise came from Akhil Bharatiya Valmiki Mahasabha. Valmikis made it a point to underline that they are supporting BJP after more than six decades of animosity to stop the march of 'Kamal'.

The number of the Bairwas, Chamars, Balais, Meghwals, Khatiks nominated by the government to the various bodies in Rajasthan are hundred times that of Bhangis. Bhangis suffered more. There are virtually no nominees in various bodies now. The affected people belong to the most vulnerable section.

Strangely, few people know that one of the states where person of a sweeper caste was nominated for the first time on a coveted position is Madhya Pradesh. It was the Chief Minister Digvijay Singh's decision in Madhya Pradesh in nominating Joharilal Sangat IAS (Retd) as a member of Madhya Pradesh Public Service Commission in March 1999.[2] The rationale was twofold. First a nomination of sweeper could be presented as empirical proof and also to demonstrate Congress government's commitment to uplift the downtrodden by acts, especially the appointment of Johari Lal Sangat as member, Madhya Pradesh

Public Service Commission. Second, to tell the sweeper community that Congress government in Madhya Pradesh could not remain indifferent about their continuing plight.

Separate Reservation: A Must for Bhangis

It is high time that Bhangis must change. The Bhangis should try to change the whole lifestyle and they should struggle to get their due share as other communities have done. But some mechanism has to be devised to give them reasonable representation in legislatures, at the centre as well as in the states. Jobs should be provided in adequate numbers. In order to achieve these aims, some 40 years ago a few state governments had paid special attention as part of its policy and took initiative on separate reservation issue of Bhangis within the framework of existing quota for SCs. For instance in 1975, for the first time in the country, it was the Punjab government which took the initiative and issued orders and fixed 50 per cent reservation for Valmiki and Mazbhi caste groups out of the quota reserved for SCs in Punjab.[3] The members of the Chamar, Adidharmi and Ramdasia castes challenged these orders in the High Court. But the High court of Punjab and Haryana upheld the government orders. An Appeal was filed before the Supreme Court of India which, too was dismissed. This is the only way the Bhangis can get redress from their grievances and can secure social justice. Then, in a similar step (1996) the Haryana government also issued the orders[4] and fixed 50 per cent reservation for them, out of the quota reserved for scheduled castes in the state. These conscious and concerted efforts by both Punjab and Haryana governments were made to increase the numbers of sweepers in government jobs. Finally, in 1998–99, the Telugu Desam Party (TDP) government in Andhra Pradesh set up a committee to examine the entire gamut of the question. One of the key findings of this committee was that benefit of reservation has reached only to certain untouchables castes or communities. It outlined the need of categories within scheduled castes. The advanced scheduled castes had to be made aware that basic philosophy behind the reservation policy was to bring them at par. Since there is still disparity in certain castes, government had to create categories within untouchables[5] and this carried no injustice against any castes or communities.

These categories will certainly be able to safeguard the interest of Bhangis, in particular, in a more substantial way. Efforts for their welfare and empowerment can now be made in a more effective manner. At another level, these legally constituted categories acquire the status of statistical entities which are used by the state for the serious treatment of social context in which these categories are rooted. Let this be tried just for 25 years. Within this period, hundreds of homes will emerge that are aware and enlightened and who are fired with ambition and enthusiasm.

Direct Caste Discrimination

Soon after coming into power at the end of 1998, the Congress formed as many as nine commissions,[6] such as Gau (Cows) Sewa Ayog, Power Regulatory Commission, OBC Commission, SCs/STs Commission, Administrative Reforms Commission, Women Commission, Consumer Commission, Human Rights Commission and the Minority Commission. This was done within the early phase between 1999 and 2002. It gave equal importance to minority, OBC, women, SCs/STs, human rights, etc. and created an impression on various segments of the society, in the social arena. But the government did not constitute a Commission for Safai Karamcharis. This again gave a setback to Bhangis in Congress rule. By ignoring their genuine demand, the Congress came to be identified as a prejudiced government. Hence, in spite of massive victory of the Congress in 1998 (155 seats), the Bhangis gained nothing and no Bhangi oriented programmes were launched during this period. The government never encouraged the Bhangis. Thus, Congress government continuously ignored them, rejected their demands and showed indifferent attitude towards their grievances.

It was only in 2001 that the Congress government vide Notification dated 29 October 2001 constituted the Rajasthan SCs/STs Commission and on 3 November 2001 Ramji Lal Kharadia[7] a sweeper from Jaipur was nominated as Vice Chairman of the Commission. This development was best seen among the Bhangi workers of Jaipur district who, since early

1947s, had been working under the influence of Congress. From 1932, a small but influential Bhangis took to education, entered local politics and began taking interest in the National Movement.[8] Barring a Vice Chairman in a Commission, things will not be much different, when the overall situation remained the same. A lot more needs to be done in this direction.

In September 2000, the author had a chitchat with the senior Congress Bhangi social worker Dau Lal Jawa. He said, that the Congress had assured to reserve 4 to 5 per cent quota for Bhangis in Rajasthan, but to date not even 1 per cent had been reserved.[9] This is the same demand which Punjab and Haryana government accepted, but was not accepted by the Congress government in Rajasthan. Thus, at present the government is determined not to make a separate reservation for Safai Karamcharis within the existing reservation for SCs and to establish separate commission for the Safai Karamcharis in the state. The community is unhappy that government has not shown concern for Bhangis. The Bhangis in Rajasthan have begun to feel that perhaps Bhangis are not a part of Congress at all. It hardly matters whether the party is in power or not, but the apathy will remain the same.

The Bhangi community is a much deprived caste. After independence, government had diverted its attention towards other castes. This community's struggle is to get social justice, while several communities who are economically and politically strong, have been given the benefits of reservation for the seats of MLAs/MPs, but the poor Bhangis are denied this benefit even today, said Dr Jagdish Chandra Jawa[10] a retired Senior Medical Officer. It is a pity that the Bhangis who are the lowest of the low, have been denied the responsibilities of nominated positions in various organisations/bodies, whereas the Chamars, Meghwals, Bairwas and Mochis and Khatiks, who are strong enough have been nominated. The Bhangis are not considered for the nomination like other scheduled castes/communities because they are politically nowhere.

It is true that even before independence, socio-educational reforms among the other untouchable communities had started because of the efforts initiated by their leaders. But the Bhangi community did not have such inspiring leaders.

The Bhangis and Congress were once inseparable. The views of other political parties in respect to Bhangis were that they were staunch supporters of the Congress. The Congress policy has for long time been oriented towards this traditional 'vote bank', the scheduled castes, but in the process, the Bhangis have been ignored. As a result, until 1990 the Congress had no definite programme towards the Bhangis. Many of the current problems are still pending with the present Congress government (1998 to 2003 and 2008–2013). The attitude of the government is not encouraging towards this community.

In 1990, Shiv Narain Valmiki, a Bhangi social worker from Jaipur, relinguished his association with Congress, accusing it of neglecting the Bhangis and patronizing Chamars, Meghwals, Khatiks, Bairwas, etc. at the cost of Bhangis.[11] Thereafter, he joined the BJP and became a pivot around which all the anti-Congress leaders of the Bhangi community flocked together and later on, other Bhangi social workers also joined him. Then, in a similar step (1999), Heeralal Parmar[12], another active Bhangi Congress leader from the Udaipur, condemned the Congress and left it. Thereafter, Parmar, well known for fighting for the Dalit cause in Udaipur, joined the BSP and was appointed General Secretary of the state unit.

During the condolence ceremony of Suresh Chanwaria (1999) Haridass Teji, a Bhangi social worker of Jodhpur who had worked for the Congress party in several Assembly and Parliamentary Elections and also for late Barkatullah Khan, the Chief Minister of Rajasthan, told me that Congress Chief Ministers and Ministers namely Jai Narain Vyas, Barkatullah Khan, Mathura Dass Mathur, Anand Singh Kachhawah, Poonam Chand Vishnoi, etc. lived amongst the Bhangis and realized the miserable conditions of the Bhangis. But the present Chief Minister Ashok Gehlot never lived amongst them which makes all the difference.[13] Till recently, the Bhangis have supported the Congress and identified themselves with its ideology. However, Gehlot's indifferent attitude towards Bhangis has frustrated them. Roshan Lal Chanwaria, another staunch supporter of Gehlot who worked during Gehlot's election 1998, told me that he had been unhappy with Gehlot for ignoring or deferring the Bhangi's issues.[14] He also said that there were no jobs for educated Bhangis and no steps had been taken for the formation of Commission for the Safai Karamcharis at the state level.

Today, the Bhangis are living in very miserable conditions. For the isolation of Bhangis, to some extent, they are themselves responsible. All other scheduled castes/communities have deserted the Congress, Chamars and Jatavas of Uttar Pradesh, Mahars of Maharashtra, Meghwals, Bairwas and Raigars of Rajasthan and Delhi, all barring the Bhangis have affiliated their respective parties to the BJP, Samata, BSP, etc. making the latter a powerful alliance of upper castes, middle class/castes and section of dalits.

In fact, many social and political workers, government servants and professionals lament privately despairing the conditions of their community.

While it is true that neglect by the Congress is certainly responsible for this kind of socio-political crisis amongst the Bhangis, it cannot be ignored that Bhangi social workers and activists also remained inactive to such kind of oppressive politics. They did not try to offer any political alternative by invoking their own authentic form of politics. Actually, they criticized Congress within limits without seeking any alliance or assistance from the radical political forces that are operating almost simultaneously.

Most Bhangi leaders, netas, social workers and activists are reluctant to expose the Congress's indifferent attitude to the Bhangi samaj, thinking this will defame the Congress and so they prefer to avoid or tolerate all this. Some think exposing Congress leaders will become the victim. But is avoidance a solution? Such toleration one day will burst.

Discrimination of Bhangis by other Untouchables

Within the untouchable communities, throughout the country, there is a major segment which is less adamant and militant in opposing the caste orders. This attitude is equally more evident among the untouchable communities in Rajasthan, such as the Chamars, Meghwals, Bhambhis, Raigars and the Khatiks.

It is not surprising that each of the major untouchable communities has developed its own caste rules and regulations, as the rivalry and distinctions among them are of long standings. It is testament to the potency and pervasiveness of the idea of caste that amongst the untouchable communities themselves the notion of the pollution and purity shape their interrelationship. Chamars consider themselves as the most 'pure' of the untouchables and thus do not dine or marry with either the Raigars or the Khatiks. The Chamars, Meghwals, Bhambis and Raigars and Khatiks, as well, consider Bhangis to be more impure of the others and have very limited interdining or commensality. The residential pattern of each of these communities are segregated, there being a Chamar Mohalla, 'Bhambhi Mohalla' as well as a 'Bhangi Mohalla' in any given town and village.

These ritual differences among these major untouchable communities are parallelled by the socio-economic differences as well. Chamars seem to have been the most economically secure. They had their own trade in shoe making and leather working which was essential to the village and which they could pursue anywhere. They also had connections with the village administration and were thus considered the village servants.[15] The advent of British rule had a positive effect on this community, as the establishment of leather factories in India improved Chamars' economy. The leather communities in general and the Chamars in particular were the most advanced communities. According to Moffatt, the principles of the hierarchy, either within the caste system or within the untouchable community, are the same. This is essentially due to the cultural consensus of untouchables to the religious principles of hierarchy-opposition and interdependency between pure and impure which defines the status of untouchables as the most inferior, and places them at a lower strata as they are inherently impure.[16]

The Bhangis are the most impure among the untouchables. The Bhangis accept the food and water from the rest of the untouchables (except Dhobies and Dholis) but they (rest of the untouchables) refuse to accept food and water from Bhangis.[17] This refusal of lowest rank can be explained by stating that every one wants to see someone below them. I look at the problems from the perspective of purity and impurity. Chamars,

Meghwals, Bhambhis, Raigars, Khatiks, etc. do have someone below them in rank. What they do not like is to be treated as inferior to someone else. In case of Rajasthan, the untouchables claim equal status in public even though the Chamars, Meghwals, Raigarh, Khatiks, etc. feel superior in the private.

The untouchables created a microcosm of the wider caste structure for themselves, and the principle of separation of caste according to ritual purity and impurity, occupation and endogamy underlies the untouchable caste system. This implies consensus of untouchables on the principles by which the castes system is constructed.[18]

The Chamars and Jatavas of Uttar Pradesh, Mahars of Maharashtra, Nadars of Tamil Nadu, Ramdasia of Punjab, Raigars of Delhi with sizeable population, now occupy a dominant caste status in the preferential scale of influential communities.

In Rajasthan, Chamars or Bhambhis or the Jatavas, Meghi or Meghwals, Balais, Thori or Nayak, Koli or Kori, Khatiks, Bairwas or Berwas are the top seven.[19] But the Bhangis with a population of nearly 3,17,779 (Census of India 1991) are nowhere in sight. The Chamars, Meglwals, Bairwas, Khatiks and Raigars who were desperate not so long ago, are at the forefront in all the spheres of life. In contrast, the Bhangis' socio-economic, educational and political condition is miserable. Chamars, Jatavas and the Bairwas, Meghwals and Khatiks, according to social scientists are a few advanced scheduled castes/communities whereas the Bhangis are the most backward.

Chamar is the first in the dominant caste list and also the first in political category. Raigar is second and has good political influence. Khatik is the next one and its political influence is the topmost. Bhangi is the last with no social, political and economic base.

For such a socio-economic plight of the community in the Rajasthan, arguments may be expressed in the following ways.

First, it is asserted that most of the members in the selection Board's/Committees are caste Hindus and dominant scheduled castes, where as most of the candidates are from dominant scheduled castes/communities and a few are sweepers. Therefore, there is a competitive conflict of interests within dominant scheduled castes candidates and sweeper caste candidates over access to a given array of opportunity like government jobs. Since identities have already been formed along caste lines, caste interest clashes occur.

Second, it is true that in most of the cases sweeper candidates are rejected. For instance, at the end of 2000, when Kavita, a Bhangi girl candidate, resident of Jodhpur was interviewed for RAS and allied services, she was rejected. Gautam, another Bhangi candidate, who obtained his MBBS degree from Sampurnanand Medical College, Jodhpur in 1998 and in 1999 he was interviewed for the post of doctors in government hospitals, Rajasthan was also rejected. Though it is important to note that later on in 2001 Dr Gautam was selected by Gujarat Public Service Commission.[20] Similarly, very recently in February 2002, when Vinod who took his MA in sociology from Jawaharlal Nehru University, New Delhi and also qualified NET examination, was interviewed for the post of Lecturership in the Government College, Rajasthan was also rejected.[21]

Third, due to government officials and dominant scheduled caste prejudices against Bhangi caste, percentage of Bhangis in the government jobs is dismal. This percentage has continued to be low because of the discrimination in jobs. Thus, it has further increased their sense of frustration. Finally, because of being politically nowhere, economically most poor and numerically thin, Bhangis cannot convert their caste identity into political pressure groups. This makes Bhangis feel isolated. An objective analysis shows that their low social status and caste-based discrimination are the main cause of the disturbed Bhangi mind.

There are many instances when Bhangi candidates have successfully cleared the written examinations conducted by the RPSC for RAS, Lecturership, Doctors, Engineers, Police Sub Inspectors and inspectors in various other departments and other jobs, but have been rejected. Thus, the present problem is a problem of both upper castes versus lower castes and dominant lower castes versus still lower castes in the hierarchical table. The political power equation is in favour of dominant untouchables castes in a democratic set-up because of their number, voting potential and better organization in asserting their rights. These views are further endorsed by Assadi, who on the basis of his analysis of caste conflicts in Karnataka, observed:

> Dalits of Karnataka are increasingly facing a new crisis – their scheduled castes/tribe brothrern are now emerging as primary oppressors in many parts of Karnataka. This has shifted the domain of rural conflicts from dominant caste dalits to dalits SCs/STs. (quoted by S.P. Srivastava in E.A. 1997–50 March 4)

Assadi's observation is to be viewed in the context of an emerging elite class amongst the Dalits for whom life is far more comfortable and free from oppression and exploitation. For the non-elite Dalits, life has not changed very much relatively, if not in absolute terms. They may have a little better quality of life today than what they had in the past. However, the educational and economic backwardness of the non-elite Dalits exposes them to exploitation and oppression both by the upper and intermediate caste people as also by their elite brothern.

The number of Bhangi employees is not in proportion with the number of dominant untouchables in the government sectors. This major proportion of representation in favour of dominant untouchable castes will continue unless government intervenes with a new policy as framed and executed by Punjab, Haryana and Andhra Pradesh governments to increase the job opportunities for the Bhangis and like other weaker communities and thus it has to be done in spite of the formidable political clout of dominant untouchable groups.

Notes

1. Office of the Rajasthan Public Service Commission, Ajmer.
2. Talk with Joharilal Sangat, Bhopal, 6 May 2002.
3. For more detailed coverage, see, Notification No. 1818–SWI-75/10451, 5 May 1975; issued by Secretary to Government Punjab, Welfare of SCs and Backward Classes Department.

4. Discussion with Mangilal Arya, Former Chairman, National Commission for Safai Karamcharis, Pali, 11 April 2002.
5. Ibid., Mangilal Arya, 11 April 2002, see also Pamphlet 'Safai Mazdoor-ka-Desh' Vyapi Andolan and letter to CM Ashok Gehlot. For details regarding their demands, especially 50 per cent reservation for Bhangis, formation of State Commission for Safai Karamchris and State Safai Karamcharis Finance and Development Corporation, published and circulated by Akhil Bharatiya Safai Mazdoor Congress, Jodhpur.
6. विभिन्न प्रकार के आयोग के गठन हेतु देखें 'कर्मचारियों व अधिकारियों के स्थानान्तरण की तिथियां' तथा Dainik Bhaskar, Jaipur, 11 April 2002.
7. Suchna Kendra, Jaipur.
8. Shyam Lal, 'Educating the Bhangis in Rajasthan during the Twentieth Century' in *Eastern Anthropologist*, Lucknow, Vol 47, No. 2, 1994.
9. Discussion with Daulal Jawa, Jodhpur, September 2000, See also 'आरक्षण नहीं दिया तो चुनाव का बहि कार' दैनिक भास्कर, जयपुर 14 नवम्बर 1999 'पृथक आरक्षण के लिए उपवास रखा' दैनिक भास्कर, जयपुर 15 नवम्बर 1999 'सफाई कार्य निजी क्षेत्र को सौंपा तो आन्दोलन'। दैनिक भास्कर, जयपुर, 13 दिसम्बर 1999, सफाई कर्मचारी आयोग और वित्त निगम गठित करने की मांग 'दैनिक भास्कर, जयपुर, 10 मई 2000 एवं 'मुख्यमंत्री को ज्ञापन' दैनिक भास्कर, जयपुर 14 मई 2002.
10. Talk with Dr Jagdish Chandra Jawa, Jaipur, January 2002.
11. As told by Ram Narain, Jaipur, 5 May 2002.
12. As told by Babu Lal Ghavri, 5 May 2002. Also see for more details 'जनहित के मुद्दों पर बसपा ने घेराव किया' दैनिक भास्कर, जयपुर, 30 दिसम्बर, 2000.
13. Talk with Haridas Teji, Jodhpur, October 1999.
14. Talk with Roshan Lal Chanwaria, Jodhpur, Oct 1999: For apprising caste anguish toward present Congress Government in the state. See, Personal and Confidential letter No. 1,178/2002, 18 May 2002. This strongly worded letter was written by Mangilal Arya himself, the working President of the All India Safai Mazdoor Congress to the Chief Minister Ashok Gehlot. Concluding the letter, Arya urged the Chief Minister, 'if you could not do our welfare, kindly do not harm us'.
15. Sato Masanori, 'The Chamar's of South-eastern Rajasthan, AD 1650–1800' in H. Kotani (ed.), *Caste System,*

Untouchability and Depressed. New Delhi, Manohar Publications, p. 32.

16. N. Sudhakar Rao, 'The Structure of South Indian Untouchables Castes: A View' in Ghanshyam Shah (ed), *Cultural Subordination and the Dalit Challenge*, Vol. 2, Dalit Identity and Politics, New Delhi, Sage Publications, 2001, p. 74.
17. Marwar Census Report, 1891, p. 582.
18. M. Sudhakar Rao, ibid., p. 78–79.
19. Census of India, 1971: Rajasthan, Series 18, p. X.
20. As told by Babulal Pandit, 6 May 2002.
21. As told by Santosh Anand, Bhilwara, 6 May 2002.

7

Demand for Community Hostel and Bhawan

State President of Akhil Valmiki Samaj Nyaya Manch (henceforth called AVSNM) Rajasthan, Mohan Lal Joad made a significant attempt to construct a building in Jodhpur under the name of 'Valmiki Hostel' in 2011. In that year, Joad submitted an application to the Chief Minister, Ashok Gehlot to allot a piece of land generously to Valmiki Samaj to build a hostel for the most neglected and educationally backward section of the society, as the state government had already allotted lands for construction of hostels to different scheduled castes/communities in Jodhpur, Udaipur and Jaipur regions.[1]

It is also true that Bhangi Samaj (community) has made very little progress in the field of higher and technical education. The contrast is all the more obvious, if one considers the progress made by Meghwal, Chamar, Bairwa, Raigar, Khatik, etc. in the field of higher education.

The Bhangis were most active in Jodhpur, as Jodhpur is the home town of the Chief Minister, Ashok Gehlot. The Bhangis of Jodhpur for this reason enjoyed a privileged position. It is interesting to note that there were social workers and social activists who were supporting Congress, and among those Tarachand Chanwaria and Bachan Pandit were very close to the Chief Minister.

On 5 December 2011,[2] Thakur Das, OSD to the Chief Minister forwarded the application of Joad to the Secretary, Jodhpur Development Authority (JDA) for perusal and necessary action. A copy of the same was endorsed to Joad.

Soon Joad, the President of AVSNM on 21 December 2011[3] sent a letter to the Secretary, JDA, Jodhpur and wanted to see him personally to seek his support for hostel land. But he was not given an opportunity. Joad in his letter of 14 March 2012[4] submitted all the required information and documents to the Secretary, JDA, Jodhpur as desired by him. Joad also sent copy of the letter to the Chief Minister. After a few months, on 30 December 2012 in his letter addressed to Secretary, JDA Jodhpur, he again wanted to see him, but in vain.

Joad made constant efforts to get a piece of land from JDA. This time, he presented the Chairman, Rajya Safai Karamchari Aayog, Rajasthan, Jaipur (henceforth called RSKAR) a memorandum stating the need for early allotment of land for Valmiki hostel. The Chairman of RSKAR showed interest in the matter as he considered it as an important social issue. In 2012, the Secretary[5], RSKAR, forwarded the Memo of Joad to the District Collector, Jodhpur. It should be noted in this connection that प्रभारी अधिकारी, अपर जिला कलेक्टर, जोधपुर, further forwarded the same to the Secretary, JDA, Jodhpur on 7 February 2013.

On 18 March 2013[6], Joad submitted another letter to the Chief Minister Ashok Gehlot, requesting him to donate a piece of land on his birthday (in the month of May 2013) to Valmiki Samaj and urged him to issue necessary directives to the Chairman, JDA, for allotment of land. The letter also contained a series of correspondence exchanged between him and JDA. Likewise, Joad presented the Chairman, RSKAR, another letter urging him the need for early grant of land. On 10 May 2013, the same was forwarded by Special Assistant to the Commissioner, JDA, Jodhpur stating to do the needful.

Jodhpur Development Authority did not show any interest in the case. Joad made a complaint against JDA, accusing them for non-cooperating in the educational development programmes of the community. JDA is working against the welfare of the most neglected and educationally backward section of the society – the Bhangis. They are ignoring the directives issued by the Chief Minister's Secretariat. There was also serious difference of opinion amongst the authority of JDA regarding the submission of documents to JDA. Having failed to gain the support of JDA, on 6 June 2013[7], Joad sent a letter to the special officer to the Chief Minister urging him to interfere in the matter. Whenever Chief Minister Ashok Gehlot visited Jodhpur during the last two years Joad personally met him. The aim of his meetings with the Chief Minister was to urge him to allot the land for construction of a hostel.

In his letter addressed to Ashok Gehlot on 15 July 2013[8], Joad narrated,

> मैं आपसे पुनःनिवेदन करता हूं कि मैं बाल्मिकि छात्रों के लिए एक छात्रावास बनवाना चाहता हूं। जिसके लिए मैं बार–बार आपसे अनुरोध करता रहा हूं कि 'बढ़ली भैरूजी' (बम्बोर के पास) जोधपुर में बाल्मिकी छात्रावास बनाने के लिए जमीन आवंटित करावें। लेकिन बड़े खेद की बात है कि लगभग दो वर्ष व्यतीत हो गए मुझे पत्राचार करते हुए और जब भी आप जोधपुर पधारे हैं, तब मैंने व्यक्तिगत रूप से आपको ज्ञापन दिये हैं। जोधपुर विकास प्राधिकरण, आपके विशेषाधिकारी और जोधपुर कलैक्टर को सैंकड़ो पत्र लिखने के बाद आज तक भी जमीन का आवंटन नहीं हुआ है। जोधपुर विकास प्राधिकरण ने बहुत सारी सूचनाएं मुझसे मांगी। सभी सूचनाएं उनको प्रेशित करने के बाद भी जमीन के आवंटन की कोई कार्यवाही नहीं हो रही है।
>
> आज आप जोधपुर में कई जगह भूमि पूजन और भवनों का शिलान्यास कर रहे हैं। कृपया इस अवसर पर बाल्मिकी छात्रावास के लिये भी जमीन आवंटन की घोषणा कर राजस्थान के बाल्मिकी समाज को एक तोहफा दिलावें। हम सदियों तक आपके आभारी रहेंगे।
>
> सधन्यवाद

JDA had treated the demand of land for Valmiki hostel with a different orientation as if they were people of lesser value. Joad reportedly sought the Chief Minister's intervention, but was cold shouldered and asked to take up the issue with JDA. Consequently, Joad tried to meet JDA. But the two sides could not make any headway. The outcome disappointed him.

The assessment of socio-educational and economic conditions of the Bhangi caste in Rajasthan no longer needs corroboration by statistics, it is a daily experience: chronic shortage of jobs in Nagar Palikas, Nagar Parishads and Nagar Nigam, an excessively privatization of jobs, graduate and post-graduate youths standing in queue for the post of sweepers and total marginization of political leadership. Decline of support by political parties, government employees (Bhangis) roaming here and there for transfer/posting, lack of recruitment due to upper caste prejudices and increasing groupism among themselves and everything pushed to the brink of collapse. Step into basti and talk to any social workers, social activists, worker leaders and common men you will know that they are victims of Congress leadership in the state. Obviously, the caste is in direct need of social repair, but its unfortunate status as 'lowest of the low untouchables' causes administrative and political negligence. As things stand today, the agglomeration of the Bhangi community maintain distance from the Congress.

The foregoing account shows that the Bhangi Samaj could not get benefit during Gehlot's regime. The Bhangi masses are feeling cheated as Congress is reluctant to act.

It is a fact that a few dominating scheduled castes have made positive progress. But an overwhelming majority of SC including the Bhangi is seen as educationally poor and economically backward.

To be honest, though, even the author was not aware what was going on until he started researching the feelings of Bhangi Samaj. To his pleasant surprise the story was quite different. It was not the story, as the author had assumed, of a community still stuck in a time warp to wallowing in self pity and paranoid about pro-Congress.

Instead, the author found a generation of young, educated, self-confident and articulate Bhangi men and women keen to shed the untouchable tag and live a respectable life. They believe that time has come for the Bhangis to stop seeing themselves as victims of external factors. Rather, they should take their destiny in their own hands. This change is particularly noticeable among young Bhangi boys and girls. Contrary to the popular notion of a typical/traditional Bhangi, they are vocal, conscious about their rights and aspirations are no different from those of any other modern Indian men.

Moreover, for the first time, there is willingness to acknowledge that many of their problems which they blame on others, are actually self-inflicted.

Today's Bhangi youths are also extremely conscious of their lowest of the low untouchable identity and shamelessly flaunts this, by becoming Doctors, Engineers, RAS, IAS, Academicians, Teachers, etc. In fact, it is perhaps the most educated generation of the Bhangi in independent India.

Having been away from Jodhpur for many years, the author is struck by the growth of socio-political consciousness among the Bhangi youths. Almost every other boy or girl you meet is educated and planning to go ahead.

Demand for Valmiki Bhawan, Dharamsala II

We shall discuss in this section the growth of Bhangi demands for Valmiki Bhawan, Dharamsala, etc. in different parts of Rajasthan. This serves two important purpose in understanding the build up of the movement. First, it brings out the diverse programmes to fight against different kinds of deprivation. *Secondly,* it enables us to analyse the nature of linkages and feedbacks between different levels of organizations – local, regional and All India in movement.

Similarly, major demand of Akhil Bharatiya Valmiki Maha Sabha (ABVM) centred round two prominent issues – demand of land for construction of Valmiki Bhawan in Bhangi basti in Jalore district and recruitment since 1982 of sweepers in Nagar Palikas, Nagar Parishads and Nagar Nigams lying vacant across the state and demand of land for construction of Dharamsala at village Ram Devra, Tehsil Pokaran, district Jaisalmer. The initiators of this demand were Narpat Solanki,[9] District President, ABVM of Jalore and Smt Sarla Devi Goyal[10] Divisional President, ABVM of Bikaner. Smt Sarla Devi Goyal realised the trouble of the yatris in staying Ram Devra during the religious fair of Baba Ram Dev and therefore on 14 June 2009 appealed to the District Collector, Jaisalmer for allotment of land to Valmiki samaj. प्रभारी अधिकारी (राजस्व) Collectorate Jaisalmer vide his letter No. Rajasva/2009/3603 dated 29 July 2009; sent 17 terms and conditions to ABVM to furnish them immediately. This was in response to an appeal made on 14 June 2009 by ABVM of Bikaner. These efforts to seek the land through the District Collector Jaisalmer were not successful.

Another problem which attracted the attention of ABVM was recruitment of sweepers in the state. The ABVM insisted on recruitment of sweepers on vacant posts since 1982 across the state, and this was enthusiastically followed by ABVM from all over Rajasthan. In pursuit of this, regional organization petitioned the authorities to initiate the process of recruitment immediately. The Bhangis of Jalore for instance under the auspice of their regional association, Jalore ABVM applied to Collector for allotment of land for construction of Valmiki Bhawan to Bhangi Samaj.

The Collector of Jalore vide his letter No. 1/Raj/2004/626 dated 20 February 2004[11] informed about the non-availability of land for construction of Valmiki Bhawan to Bhangi Samaj. This was based on the report of Tehsildar, Jalore submitted to District Collector, Jalore. The Collector also directed to approach the Deputy Director, DLB Jaipur, Rajasthan for allotment of land.

These regional associations had made the Bhangi masses aware of their mythical descent from Valmiki Rishi and necessity of exploiting modern educational and employment opportunities in order to make socio-educational progress. The District associations supported and strengthened the ABVM whose activities were to fight against socio-economic and political discrimination in the different parts of the state. This was the main means to political mobilization. In this the state machineries, bureaucrats do not support their cause. The regional associations did not get disheartened: they strengthened their support to the struggle/agitation.

Just before the State Assembly Elections 2013, the Congress government headed by Ashok Gehlot, allotted the land on token money or concessional rates to 29 Charitable Trusts including SCs/STs. Around seven months after the formation of BJP government in the state, Vasundhara Raje reviewed the policy. The past beneficiaries of land allotments were found violating the terms and conditions of allotment.

The Cabinet in its meeting held on Thursday, 5 May 2014[12] chaired by the Chief Minister Vasundhara Raje cancelled all 29 such allotments made during the last six months of the previous Congress government. The result is before us. However,

Congress government's not allotting of land for Valmiki Hostel still matters.

Notes

1. For construction of a building in Jodhpur under the name of 'Valmiki Hostel' 2011, State President of Akhil Valmiki Samaj Nyaya Manch (AVSNM) Rajasthan, Mohan Lal Joad submitted an application to the Chief Minister Ashok Gehlot to allot a piece of land generously to Valmiki Samaj. For details see, Mohan Lal Joad's letter No. 1014 dated 21 December 2011 submitted to Chief Minister Ashok Gehlot.
2. After a few weeks, Thakur Das, OSD in Chief Minister Secretariat, Government of Rajasthan forwarded the application of M.L. Joad to the Secretary, Jodhpur Development Authority (JDA) for perusal and necessary action. See, मुख्यमंत्री कार्यालय राजस्थान सरकार, पत्र कमांक मु.मं. विशेशाधिकारी (टी)/4–2/(जोध. विप्रा)/(जोध)/ ।।/97542 जयपुर, दिनांक 5 दिसंबर 2011. Also see, M.L. Joad's letter No. 11/10 dated 30 December 2012 to the Secretary, JDA Jodhpur.
3. See, Mohan Lal Joad's letter No. 1,014 dated 21 December 2011 to The Secretary, Jodhpur Development Authority.
4. The Secretary, Jodhpur Development Authority, Jodhpur vide his letter No. F. 46/ALLOT/JDA/JU/DCE/229/2012/11140 dated 8 February 2012 asked Mohan Lal Joad to submit the required documents and information as early as possible for allotment of land for Valmiki Hostel. Also see, the Secretary JDA's letter No, फ 48/वसूली/2012/65 दिनांक 18 मई 2012 to Mohan Lal Joad to furnish required documents and information. In response to the Secretary, JDA Jodhpur's letter dated 8 February 2012, Mohan Lal Joad submitted all required documents and information to the authority concerned. For more details, see, Mohanlal Joad's 2-page letter No. hos/14 dated 14 March 2012 to the Secretary, JDA Jodhpur. Also see, Mohan Lal Joad's letter No. 11/10/47 दिनांक 20 दिसंबर 2012 to the Secretary, JDA Jodhpur in response to his letter No, फ 48/वसूली/2012/65 दिनांक 18 मई 2012.
5. Mohan Lal Joad presented the Chairman, Rajya Safai Karamchari Aayog, Rajasthan, Jaipur a Memorandum stating

the need for early allotment of land for Valmiki hostel. The Secretary RSKAR vide his letter No. रा.स.क.आ./12/2721 fnukad 31&12& 2012 forwarded the Memo of Joad to the District Collector Jodhpur. After a few days प्रभारी अधिकारी, (सतर्कता) अपर जिला कलक्टर (तृतीय) जोधपुर vide his letter क्रमांक सतर्कता/2013/5333–34 दिनांक 7–2– 2013 forwarded the same to the Secretary, JDA, Jodhpur.

6. Vide his letter No. 11/10/55 dated 18 March 2013 Mohan Lal Joad submitted another letter to Chief Minister Ashok Gehlot, requesting him to donate a piece of land on his birthday to the Valmiki Samaj, Jodhpur. On 8 May 2013 Officer on Special Duty to the Chief Minister's office vide his letter No. मु. मं. विशेशाधिकारी (टी)/प–2/जोध विप्रा/जोध/13/42863, जयपुर दिनांक 8 May 2013 forwarded the same to the Commissioner, JDA, Jodhpur for necessary action. Similarly, M.L. Joad presented the Chairman, RSKAR another letter urging him the need for early grant of land. On 10 May 2013, the Special Assistant to RSKAR vide his letter No. रा.स.क.आ./12 sent the same to the Commissioner JDA, Jodhpur.
7. See, Mohan Lal Joad's letter क्रमांक 11/12/13/56 दिनांक 6 जून 2013 जव विशेषाधिकारी, मुख्यमंत्री, राजस्थान सरकार, जयपुर।
8. See, Mohan Lal Joad's 2-page letter क्रमांक 11/10 दिनांक 15 जुलाई 2013 to The Chief Minister, Government of Rajasthan, Jaipur.
9. For recruitment of sweepers in Nagar Palika, Nagar Parishads and Nagar Nigams across the state and allotment of land for construction of Valmiki Bhawan in Jalore district. Several letters and Memorandums were submitted to Chief Minister of Rajasthan, Collector Jalore (2003) Local MP Buta Singh, Ram Lal Meghwal MLA, (10 January 2012) Smt Meera 'Balu' Aggarwal, Chairman, Nagar Palika Mandal, Jalore (2003) and others. See particularly, Letter dated 7 November 2003 to The Collector, Jalore by District President, ABVM of Jalore. In response to an Appeal made on 7 November 2003, see particularly, the Collector Jalore's letter No. 1/राज/2004/626 dated 20 February 2004 informing the District President, ABVM of Jalore about non-availability of land for construction of Valmiki Bhawan to Bhangi Samaj. Also see, Sardar Buta Singh's letter to Smt Meera 'Balu' Aggarwal, Dated 26 February 2003. District Collector, Jalore's letter No. 1/Raj/2004/626 dated 20 February 2004.

10. Every year thousands of yatris from Bhangi Samaj attended the religious fair of Baba Ramdev at the village Ramdevra, Tehsil Pokran, Jaisalmer from different states of the country. Here they face a lot of staying difficulties as they belong to Bhangi Samaj. In this regard, Smt Sarla Devi Goyal, Divisional President, ABVM of Bikaner submitted an appeal on 14 June 2009 to the Collector, Jaisalmer for allotment of land for construction of Valmiki Dharamsala at Runicha. In response to an appeal made on 14 June 2009 see particularly प्रभारी अधिकारी (राजस्व) कलैक्ट्रेट जैसलमेर के Letter No. राजस्व/2009/3603 दिनांक 29 जुलाई 2009 alongwith 17 terms and conditions to Smt Sarla Devi Goyal.
11. Ibid.
12. कैबिनेट की बैठक, 29 समाजों की रियायती दर पर जमीन आवटन के आदेश निरस्त, दैनिक भास्कर, जयपुर, शुक्रवार, 6 जून, 2014 Also see, Government set to form policy for land allotment on concessional rates in *The Times of India*, Jaipur, Friday, 6 June 2014, 'गहलोत के समय 31 समाज–संस्थाओं के जमीन आबंटन निरस्त किए गए' दैनिक भास्कर, जयपुर, शुक्रवार, 8 मई, 2015.

8

Bhangis Cry for their Basic Needs

Two years before India's assembly election descended on Rajasthan, Madhya Pradesh, Delhi and Chhattisgarh's political horizon, various delegates from Jodhpur, Jaipur, Ajmer and other regions had met Ashok Gehlot, the Chief Minister of Rajasthan and submitted several memoranda requesting him to recruit sweepers in Nagar Palikas, Nagar Parishads, Nagar Nigams, Government Hospitals and in other departments as well. But he failed to salvage the situation and again turned a deaf ear to their demands.

Since 1995 there has been no recruitment in Nagar Palikas, Nagar Parishads and Nagar Nigams across the state. It was only during the past few years when agitations, protests, dharnas and rallies were organized, that the government took some last minute steps. But all of them were on paper and implementing them will still take a long time. Congress has used Bhangis' votes but neglected their rights which is a reason that their position has not changed much since independence. For instance, on Tuesday, 7 October 2014, *The Times of India*[1], Jaipur, quoting Suresh Kalyani, President, Rajasthan Mehtar Mazdoor Sangh reported:

> It's been almost 18 years now, permanent vacancies have not opened up in JMC. The last recruitment drive was in 1996 and due to shortage of manpower and resources, sanitation condition is not up to the standards.

Meanwhile, Mayor Jyoti Khandelwal said,

> The proposal to appoint sanitation workers was sent to the State Government but there has been no response till date. In 2012, during Congress government recruitment process was started but was stalled due to litigation.

With acute shortage of manpower and resources, the civic body is struggling to make the city clean. According to Roshan Saini Sanitation Committee Chairman,

> As per the high court direction, for 1,000 residents five sanitation workers should be deployed. By this standard, the city is facing shortage of 11,000 sanitation workers. There should be at least 18,000 sanitation workers in the city. At the moment, there are JMC 5,715 employees and 925 daily workers in city wards.
>
> Employing 8,000 people and spending ₹ 19 crores per month on sanitation, JMC employs 5,617 regular employees including sweepers. The total amount it spends to pay them per month stands at a staggering ₹ 12 crore. To supervise them, 300 supervisors have been hired which includes Chief Sanitary Inspectors, Sanitation Inspectors, three health officers and one Health Commissioner.

The problem which attracted the attention of Bhangi organisations was daily wages workers working in various Nagar Palikas, Nagar Parishads and Nagar Nigams across the state, because a large number of Bhangis were working there and Bhangi organisations, social activists, social workers and Bhangi netas strongly advocated their regularization. Thus, a major agitation of Bhangi Samaj in 1998 centred around two prominent issues, the abolition of daily wages work system and absorption of all of them as permanent employees across the state. The leaders of this campaign were: O.P. Jawa[2], Vishnu Sarvate and others of Jodhpur districts. They appealed to the then BJP Chief Minister Bhaironsingh Shekhawat for their regularization. The most notable leader in this period was Jabar Chand Barasha, Jodhpur.

During 1998–99 a major political change developed in the state due to state assembly election. Ashok Gehlot became the Chief Minister and was known for his sympathetic attitude to weaker sections of society in general, and Bhangis in particular, and with sincerity of purpose. He wanted to introduce a few welfare measures/programmes, such as regularization of daily wages workers and fresh recruitment too. These, he thought will provide livelihood means to the Bhangis.

Consequently, the Government of Rajasthan (local self government)[3] in GO No. 99/2509–2592 dated 28 May 1999 directed all executive officers of Nagar Palikas, Nagar Parishads and Nagar Nigams throughout the state to regularize all daily wages workers with the following terms and conditions.

1. Absorb all those daily wages workers who have completed 240 days up to 31 December 1995 and still working there.
2. They would be made regular under Rajasthan Nagar Palika Rules, 1964.
3. The concerning body will first prepare the seniority list, then send the same to Deputy Director, DLB, Jaipur for their regularization.
4. No appointment of any daily wages workers will be made further.
5. Benefit will be paid since their regularization.
6. The deadline set to achieve target was 15 July 1999.

An analysis of government order issued by Government of Rajasthan (local self government), Jaipur shows that government bodies/agencies and others who control the DLB did not show much interest in working for the Bhangi caste/community, which resulted in failure in 1999. Information collected from social workers, social activists and Bhangi netas indicates that only a few of daily wages workers were benefitted. They said, it was unfortunate that Congress brass in general, and Ashok Gehlot in particular, did not heed or understand their problems which were being faced by them. At that time O.P. Jawa, a social activist from Jodhpur, said that showing no interest by government machinery was 'a sign of the state leaderships weakness'. How long will this trend of persecution and harassment continue?

It may be noted here that on 24 April 2013, Tara Chand Meena,[4] Deputy Secretary, Government of Rajasthan (local self government) Jaipur issued a fresh 5-page notification/guidelines regarding recruitment of sweepers across the state. As a result of this, the recruitment of sweepers was increased from 11,376 to 30,000. But it was stated in the notification that it is necessary to complete the entire process in two phases at the state level. In the first phase, all the concerning authorities will recruit only 20,000 sweepers throughout the state and shall recruit remaining 10,000 sweepers in the second and last phase.

During 2008–2013, the Congress government introduced for the first time in the history of local bodies a few radical measures. For instance, in 2013 a major policy and administrative changes came with introduction of 50 per cent reservation[5] for general category (all upper castes including OBC) and 16 per cent reservation for all scheduled castes including Bhangis in recruitment on the post of sweepers. As a result, in 2013 recruitment campaign, general candidates were recruited. The recruitment of general candidates had an adverse effect on livelihood of the Bhangis. The local Bhangis which primarily used to be recruited, had been taken over by the upper castes but did not function as mainly sweeper.

After a long struggle of agitation, authorities issued an advertisement[6] No. 1/2012 dated 10 June 2012 for the recruitment of 11,376 sweepers in 183 Nagar Palikas, Nagar Parishads and Nagar Nigams and applications across the state were invited. Sources said, later on posts were increased. The Bhangi leaders considered the advertisement of government a step towards recognition of the problem and hoped for an early recruitment. The government authorities in general and the Chief Minister Ashok Gehlot in particular earned the appreciation and good will of the Bhangi caste/community. As a result of all this, thousands of Bhangi men and women applied for the posts. When this writer visited Jodhpur to see his elder brother, then Rakesh Jawa[7] said that each applicant spent at least two or three thousand rupees for completing the requirements including legal formalities. Thereafter the progress towards the recruitment was nil, the Bhangi leaders once again started agitation as noted earlier. They bitterly criticized Ashok Gehlot.

Negative Perception of Congress Government to their Demands

While tracking negative perception of Congress government, it has increasingly become clear that the Rajasthan Government has abdicated its responsibility and let wounds fester. First, it failed to protect their interest during 2009–2013. Then it failed by not nominating, adequate number of Bhangi representatives in various government organizations and party committees. And when social workers, social activists, etc. launched agitation and protested against government in the state, the Rajasthan Government responded with the drive to fulfil the sweepers' posts.

When the author asked Kanhailal Kaloshia – an eminent Bhangi activists from Ajmer, what was the attitude of Ashok Gehlot or Congress government about the Bhangi samaj/community, Kaloshia[8] said, 'he (Gehlot) was not only anti-Bhangi but anti-recruitment. The Bhangi samaj was not happy with the functioning of the government. Just to create sensation, government was issuing statement after statement on recruitment of sweepers in Nagar Palikas, Nagar Parishad, Nagar Nigams and others in the state, but the fact is that government did nothing about providing livelihood to them'.

The ties between the Congress and Bhangi leaders soured since 20 November 2012, when Bhangis blamed Ashok Gehlot for creating hurdles in the recruitment of sweepers. The Chief Minister had promised to recruit sweepers when he met with Bhangi leaders. The Bhangi samaj had suffered a lot due to breach of his promise.

As a social activist, Kanhailal Kaloshia[9], who lives in Ajmer criticized the Congress and the Chief Minister for doing nothing during the last five years and mentioned how the samaj was pushed back in terms of development. He added, the Congress claim to work for the Bhangis is, at the best, only on paper. But in fact, the schemes meant for the scheduled castes in general and Bhangis in particular, were not implemented on the ground. He claimed to have sent several letters to former chief minister to discuss the issue but there was no response. We have been supporting Congress since independence but they have done very little to improve our socio-educational and economic conditions here. Our educated youths are often rejected for government jobs because they are from Bhangi community, complained Bhangi leaders.

Sometimes, a few officials of our members are transferred from one place to another place due to caste prejudices of the officers concerned. Those who are honest and sincere in their duties are harassed, humiliated and tortured because they are from Bhangi caste group. As a result of all this, they made several attempts to seek the help of local upper caste Congress leaders, but failed. They claimed to have submitted applications to Chief Minister's office seeking his help, but there was no response.

In 1980, the Congress Ministry headed by Jagannath Paharia came into power and Mangi lal Arya became one of the ministers. The Central Government constituted the National Commission for Safai Karamcharis in 1993. Mangi Lal Arya was appointed Chairman of the Commission in 1994. Arya was also the foremost Bhangi leader of Congress party, who became the Chairman of State Safai Karamchari Aayog, Rajasthan, Jaipur in 2003. His relation with Ashok Gehlot, the then Chief Minister and Congress was good.

As a father-in-law of Smt Gayatri Arya, Mangi Lal Arya met Ashok Gehlot, the Chief Minister and submitted application requesting him for the transfer of Smt Gayatri Arya from village Reni in Alwar district to Jaipur district. But Arya could not get the success in transferring of his daughter-in-law, Smt Gayatri Arya. The response from Ashok Gehlot was not encouraging. Arya in his autobiography 'यह मेरी यादें' published in 2008, made a statement attacking the Congress Government'.[10]

> पुत्रवधू श्रीमती गायत्री देवी आर्या की पदोन्नति व्याख्याता पद से प्रधानाचार्य के पद पर होकर पदस्थापन अलवर जिले के 'रेणी' गांव में हुआ। जो जयपुर से 180 किलोमीटर दूर है। घर पर तीन छोटे–छोटे बच्चे हैं, पुत्र आनन्द कुमार आर्य सेवा में अधिकारी है। दूसराघर में कोई नहीं है। ऐसी स्थिति में गायत्री देवी आर्या को जयपुर या आस–पास कहीं नजदीक में लगवाने के लिये शिक्षा मंत्रीजी के घर दिनांक 17 से 25 (नौ दिन) तक चक्कर लगाता रहा। परन्तु केवल आश्वासन मिलता रहा, आखिर में मैने श्रीमान मुख्यमंत्री जी अशोक गहलोत को अपनी घरेलू समस्या बताकर पुत्र वधू का रैणी से जयपुर या आस–पास स्थानान्तरण करने को कहा, आनन्द कुमार आर्य और गायत्री आर्य दोनों राजकीय सेवा में हैं। तीन बच्चे छोटे–छोटे हैं। घर में रोटी बनाकर देने वाला कोई नहीं है। गायत्री प्रातः 3 बजे उठकर बच्चों व अपने लिये खाना बना करके

सवेरे पांच बजे गांधी नगर रेलवे स्टेशन जाकर ट्रेन से राजगढ़ स्टेशन पर उतर कर वहां से जीप पकड़ कर मावेडी चौराहे तक जाती है। मावेड़ी चौराहे से दूसरी जीप अलवर से रैणी के लिये आती है उससे वह दस बजे तक रैणी पहुंचती है। रैणी से शाम को वापस जीप से राजगढ़ आकर बस से दौसा पहुंचती है। दौसा से बस द्वारा रात्री 9 बजे जयपुर आती है।

माननीय मुख्यमंत्री श्री अशोक जी गहलोत ने जवाब दिया कि अभी दो माह तक स्थानान्तरण नहीं होगा, चुनाव बाद देखेंगे। मैने कहा , शिक्षा मंत्रीजी स्थानान्तरण कर रहे हैं? सुनकर मुख्यमंत्री ने जवाब नहीं दिया और नाराजगी के अन्दाज में बोले कि आपने समाचार पत्र में राज्य सफाई कर्मचारी आयोग द्वारा छपी खबर पढ़ी है क्या? उसमें लिखा है – 'आयोग, सफाई कर्मियों के प्रति सरकार के रवैये से नाखुश' आपको राजस्थान में होने वाले चुनावों का ध्यान रखना चाहिये। मुख्यमंत्रीजी के उपेक्षित रवैये को देख, मैं लौट आया। संभव है आयोग द्वारा छपे समाचारों के कारण मेरी पुत्र वधू का स्थानान्तरण नहीं हुआ'।

Similarly in another case, some of the main developments that took place due to lukewarm attitude of the government were summarized in *Jan Satta*, New Delhi (Hindi) daily newspaper, as given below.[11]

> It is a sorry tale. It is rather ridiculous that after passing the bill in Parliament in August 1993, the government took nearly one year in appointing Chairman and Members of the Commission. Further after the lapse of three months, the Commission was constituted. Not only this, the Commission is temporary, as the tenure of the Commission would expire on 31 March 1997. Thus, one-third period of Commission constituted for 43 months, was lapsed in its formation.

Describing the miserable infrastructure facilities[12], the paper stated that since its inception the Commission requested the then Prime Minister again and again, and also tried its best to procure 69 employees for its proper functioning, but it failed in its attempts. As far as budget is concerned, the government sanctioned in all, ₹ 50 lakhs for the first year 1994–95 and for the year 1995–96 government sanctioned ₹ 55 lakhs. Similarly, as a part of infrastructure facilities government provided two cars out of eight.

It should also be noted here that in order to perform their duties with sincerity and also to do something for the betterment of the community, the Commission requested the government for a suitable office building and residential accommodation for members. In this regard, in the month of January 1995,[13] necessary directions were issued from the Prime Minister's Secretariat for the allotment of residential accommodation for members. After an interval of nine months or so, a meeting was held on 11 October 1995, the government assured the Commission that by 15 October 1995, accommodation will be allotted. But this time also government failed to do so. Such was the attitude of government. The Commission cannot function in vacuum nor can it build up its machinery or infrastructure.

High and increasing expectations of AISMC. on the one hand and the lukewarm attitude of Government to provide basic requirement on the other, as discussed above, caused the tension and dissatisfaction in the AISMC.

Such attitude of the Congress government discouraged Chairman Mangi Lal Arya and his fellow members. They continued their attempts but were conscious enough not to antagonize the party in power for these reasons. First, they knew that the AISMC did not have the capacity and resources to obtain political power on its own strength. For that they have to work through a party. Second, Congress being a dominant party, was the only party capable of satisfying their demands. Finally, Buta Singh and Mangi Lal Arya, who dominated the sabha were Congressmen since the very beginning. The sabha's leader, therefore, made attempts to win over the sympathy of the Congress for the organization.

In such circumstances, the Congress minded Buta Singh, who was also an ardent champion of Bhangis cause, found himself in an embarrassing situation. He therefore, took a middle course and worked for compromise between the party and his caste brothers.

Then complaints were expressed in the meeting of Welfare Ministers, held at Delhi on 3 February 1996 to discuss and analyse the socio-economic conditions of SC, ST, Minorities and OBC, Mangi Lal Arya – Chairman, National Commission for Safai Karamchari strongly criticized the government for its step-motherly attitude towards the Commission. Though we have worked with the Congress it has failed to understand our feelings. We are being neglected, no one welcomes us. Therefore, PM said in the meeting:

> It is my humble request to all the Ministers and Senior officers to visit the Bhangi bustees at least once and observe, how they are living.[14]

In such circumstances, Arya has expressed some of the anti-Congress feelings, found it difficult to work properly. Prime Minister, P.V. Narasimha Rao, on the other hand was emotionally ready to accept the feelings of Arya. Ideologically, he felt that in the present circumstances the problems of scavengers have become the main issue of the country. By taking note of regrettable fact that State Government has taken little interest in the all-round development of the sweepers,

> Prime Minister requested to welfare ministers and Senior Government officers that they should concentrate their full energy for all round development of the sweeper class. I want to involve you in my emotions as I had to face a lot of difficulties in Constitution of this Commission particularly.[15]

The basis, for a discussion on the recruitment of sweepers at Jodhpur Nagar Nigam (JNN) is the information available regarding 270 recruited sweepers, published in *Rajasthan Patrika*,[16] Jodhpur edition, on 17 January 2014. In 2011, state government sent a formal sanction of 799 posts of sweepers to JNN. Thus, JNN which was pro-Congress, in May 2012 invited applications for recruitment. The main issue before JNN in 2012 was recruitment of sweepers. JNN started its recruitment process but soon the process was increasingly and inevitably caught up with party politics. This development should also be seen in the context of continuing rift between the Congress and JNN. As a result of all this, JNN recruited only 270, out of 799 sanctioned posts. Having seen the negligence and non-cooperative attitude of JNN authorities with respect to political dimension, the paper wrote:[17]

> राज्य सरकार ने नगर निगम में 799 सफाई कर्मचारियेां की भर्ती का पूरा मौका दिया लेकिन निगम अधिकारियों व महापौर की लापरवाही व उदासीनता के चलते सभी सफाई कर्मचारियों की भर्ती ही नहीं हो पाई। मात्र 270 सफाई कर्मचारियों की भर्ती हुई।

The paper further commented[18]

मई 2012 में सफाई कर्मचारियेां की भर्ती के लिए नगर निगम ने आवेदन भी लिये। लेकिन जानबूझ कर इस भर्ती को लटकाए रखा। हर बार आवेदनेां की छंटनी का बहाना बनाया गया। अन्त में जब राज्य विधान सभा चुनाव नजदीक आए तो निगम ने हाथ–पैर मारे , आचार संहिता लगने सेएक सप्ताह पहले साक्षात्कार लिए गए। ऐसे में 4 अक्टूबर को आचार संहिता लग गई । जिन्हें ज्वाईनिंग मिल गई उनकी नौकरी पक्की, शेश करते रहे इन्तजार।

By Jodhpur district President, Sonia Gandhi Brigade, Rakesh Kumar Jawa's[19] estimate, the Jodhpur Nagar Nigam recruited 279 widow women sweepers, out of which 263 widows were recruited exclusively from Bhangi caste and rest from other scheduled caste communities, Muslims, OBC and upper castes. The fate of other applicants is uncertain.

Similarly, State Government sanctioned 2,800 posts[20] of sweepers in Jaipur Nagar Nigam (JNN) for recruitment. JNN reacting favourably invited applications, and in all received 42,000. Out of 42,000, only 17,000 were found eligible. However, only 5,000 have been scrutinized so far. The local Bhangi netas also intensified the efforts to help the Bhangis entry in the JNN. The JNN is a major source of employment for the Bhangis. A solution to the recruitment imbroglio to Nagar Palikas, Nagar Parishads and Nagar Nigams will likely have to await the parliamentary election 2014.

Gehlot government had also failed to remove fear in many unemployed Bhangi men and women who were roaming in Government Secretariat, Jaipur. Instead, the Mayor, Jodhpur Nagar Nigam said to many Bhangi activists and leaders to get the financial sanction from State Government, if they wanted jobs in Jodhpur Nagar Nigam. This more deliberately or otherwise has heightened a sense of hurt and injustice. Ashok Gehlot, the Chief Minister of Rajasthan too had been scarce in his solidarity with Bhangis. There was scant investment in confidence building amongst the Bhangis. The failure of promises made by the Congress government changed that, rupturing political relations cemented over decades. And if relations soured, who did this? Gehlot is quick to express anguish but always stop short of taking responsibility and this is why the Bhangis are hurt.

During the talks, O.P. Jawa told that the Bhangis hate the Congress and have doubt about the credibility of Ashok Gehlot. Jawa is also said to have told his loyalists that now was the time to research a new political party to offer an alternative to the samaj. Gehlot's not fulfilling promises has disappointed the Bhangi masses.

Bhangis need solution. Bhangis are of course, sick of promises. Congress has not addressed any of the systematic solution of the problems. The Congress did no good to the common Bhangi, who aspired to getting a job in the Nagarpalika, Nagar parishads and Nagar Nigam or the common Bhangi who wanted good hostel facilities for his children's education.

Congress leaders, social workers, social activists and staunch supporters of Congress say, their leader Ashok Gehlot is a 'Marwar-ka-Gandhi'. For Congress, Gehlot is a Gandhi. It was indeed an 'idea' when Mahatma Gandhi was alive. Now, after the fake Gandhi's arrival, the Congress party has been left thinking. Gehlot behaves like anti-Dalit and indeed, he is a problem for Scheduled Castes. It is precisely for this reason that scheduled castes criticized Congress and its leadership and maintained distance from Gehlot. They call him, 'Fake Gandhi'.

The first few Chief Ministers of Congress surely knew in their hearts what their minds might refuse to admit. Ever since they first sipped power at the fountain of government in 1952, one fact has been transparently clear. The Congress brass have always been far better at politics and government. Such fact should not be underestimated in Rajasthan.

Their formula began to seem infallible. The Chief Ministers' loyal castes were rewarded with stake in power, other weaker sections of society (like Bhangis) were kept on the side with marginal benefits and the vital Bhangi vote was patched on with a debilitating concoction of illusion and fear. Gehlot's decade tenure had little to do for the betterment for the SC/ST in general and Bhangi in particular. His years in power were primarily consumed by a relentless search of sub-castes to knead into political dividend. It was vote bank politics.

Today's voter is sick to the stomach of deceptive jargons. Politics unfortunately has become a malevolent word. The youth want jobs, security and employment through economic growth. They are equally tired of the misuse of Liberalization, Privatization and Globalization (LPG).

This is why Ram Vilas Paswan, an eminent Dalit leader from Bihar, who left the BJP coalition a decade ago over riots has now become a partner in 2014 and addressed a rally alongside with Narendra Modi in Bihar. This is why Udit Raj another Dalit leader, joined BJP in the presence of Rajnath Singh. This is why BJP has been picking up new SC/ST leaders each week.

The long tenure consequences are significant. For decades SC/ST masses, social activists and workers in Rajasthan have maintained a distance from BJP. Now they compare facts. They know that Congress has always used them. BJP was successful in 2013 assembly election in winning 32 seats out of 34 reserved seats in Rajasthan.

Today, instead of being wooed, Congress has been isolated. And Gehlot, who was so certain about his repeat performance has been hit by thunderbolt from blue skies.

No party can achieve a majority in the State Assembly Election without significant support from SC/ST to form a government in Rajasthan.

Politics of Betrayal

The Bhangi community has neither learnt anything nor forgotten anything. The story is no different to previous assembly elections in the State. Congress has a history of stalwarts betraying the downtrodden section of the society in general, and Bhangis in particular, who have wholeheartedly supported the Congress since 1952. When late Sri Ram Sarvate – an eminent Bhangi leader from Jodhpur, Ramji Lal Jaipuri another staunch Congress leader from Jaipur and others demanded the Congress tickets in 1972 and 1985 respectively, two veteran leaders Barkat Ullah Khan and Hari Dev Joshi, promptly refused them. In 2013, Ashok Gehlot's assurance to J.P. Chandelia met a similar fate. The negative perception of Congress to Bhangis, serves as an eye-opener. Several Bhangi organizations, workers and social activists have bitterly criticized Gehlot for betraying the 'true loyalist' of Congress party. The Congress leaders made a negative impact on their staunch supporter's lives. Thus, the continued overlooking of the interests of Bhangi community in the state by Congress makes it amply clear that, it is time to abandon conventional political relations and think of the once, unthinkable. So long as Bhangis remain with Congress, they will not be treated fairly. 'There will be no justice done to the community by Congress' the social activist Mohan Lal Joad said,

> Ending a month long waiting for state Congress, the party President Sonia Gandhi appointed Union Minister and Ajmer MP Sachin Pilot as the new Pradesh Congress Committee (PCC) Chief.

Commenting on this, *The Times of India* stated:[21]

> The appointment of 36 a year old Union Minister at the helm of Congress affairs in the state could mark the end of Ashok Gehlot era here. The party's rout in assembly elections has equally been attributed to former chief minister Gehlot and his style of functioning, has been seen as 'divisive politics' by majority in the State Congress.

A veteran Congress leader remarked:[22]

> It would check, if not immediately end, the dominion of leaders like Ashok Gehlot, who practice conservative and divisive politics.

The former Congress's Valmiki face in Jaipur, Mukesh Valmiki blamed the veteran Congress leaders including former Chief Minister Ashok Gehlot for not grooming the Dalit leadership in general, and Bhangis in particular, in the State. But the Congress leaders crushed the emerging Dalit leadership in Rajasthan.

Kanhailal Kaloshia, the State President of Akhil Bharatiya Valmiki Mahasabha slammed the Chief Minister for not heeding to his plea to recruit on the sweeper posts, warning that not fulfilling the promise would bring no electoral gain to the party.

In a conversation, Kaloshia said,[23] 'the caste support (for Congress in Rajasthan Assembly Election, 2013) is zero'. It is going to be a death blow to Congress in Rajasthan. He (Gehlot) has not understood the problems, which were hurting us. He has not understood why we (Bhangi caste) are rebelling, in spite of being loyal Congress persons for 66 years.

Kaloshia said that during Assembly Election 2013, the workers and officials of ABVM used SMS facilities and mobiles also for quick and effective contact. They had issued SMS to more than 5,000 men and youths to convey the message 'इस सरकार को बदलो'. In other words, Bhangis would not cast their votes for Congress. 'There was no denying the fact that Congress was on a weak wicket ahead of General Assembly Election 2013'.

The Bhangi vote bank is not as secure and predictable as it used to be. Bhangis could support the Congress in large numbers provided Congress brass could win their trust; of course, wooing Bhangis is easier.

The politicians make statements like socio-educational and economic development of Bhangis. Some propose separate reservation for the Bhangis. Others talk about Bhangis representation in government organizations. These are all positive thoughts. However, Mohan Lal Joad would like Bhangis to be cautious about one thing, the real solution to Bhangis empowerment is unlikely to come from political class. The Bhangis empowerment is not a set of LPG cylinders that can be granted by the government. It can only happen when there is a change in culture. This change in culture will require Bhangi Samaj to accept, share and live with the rising power of other lower castes/communities. Since it involves a strong caste unity and organization and effective leadership. It is likely to make traditional leadership extremely uncomfortable, since these leaders supported for the current set of politicians. It is likely the Bhangi netas will go against them to empower educated persons.

Like Dalits several Muslim leaders from Uttar Pradesh, Haryana and Rajasthan had alleged that the Congress is anti-minority. For instance, very recently a prominent Mevat leader Zakir Hussain, who had remained Member of All India Congress Committee (AICC), General Secretary of Haryana Pradesh Congress Committee (HPCC), president of District Congress Committee (DCC) and State Convener of party's minority cell alleged that the Congress is anti-minority. Ex-AICC member Zakir Hussain[24] further stated:

> The Congress gets Muslim votes, but after acquiring power, it exploits them and wants to suppress them. It cheats the Muslim and the recent happening at Muzaffarnagar and Gurgaon are the latest instances.

Faheem Baig, a Unani doctor,[25] who lives in Jaffrabad in north-east Delhi protested at the inauguration ceremony of National Waqf Development Corporation on 29 January 2014. The function was chaired by Prime Minister Manmohan Singh and Congress President Sonia Gandhi. Dr Baig complained that:

> schemes meant for minorities were not being implemented on ground. He filed numerous RTI applications with the education health and several other departments to know how they were spending the money sanctioned under the 15 point programme but the answers were not satisfactory. So he decided to raise the issue the way he did.

Similarly Dalit paper *Haqdar*[26] published since 1969, from Bikaner termed the entire period of Gehlot's government in Rajasthan as 'Anti SCs/STs and Minorities'. The paper in his 16–17 February 2014 issue narrated to this thus:

> गहलोत ने अपने कार्यकाल 1998–2003 एवं 2008–2013 में इन वर्गों के साथ खुले रूप में नाइन्साफी की है। गहलोत के गत कार्यकाल को दलित एवं अल्पसंख्यक के विरोधी माना जाता है। ... राजस्थान में गोपालगढ़, भरतपुर में नमाज अदा करते हुए नमाजियों पर पुलिस ... द्वारा गोलियां चलाकर नमाजियों की हत्या किये जाने की मिसाल देश के इतिहास को कलंकित करती है ... राजस्थान में 7 करोड़ की जनसंख्या में 1.25 करोड़ अनुसूचित जाति, 98 लाख अनुसूचित जन जाति व 50 हजार अन्य एवं अल्पसंख्यक 80 लाख हैं।

The Aam Aadmi Party movement in Delhi grew steadily and in the 2013, Delhi Assembly Election won 28 seats. Between 2012–2013, a large number of retired judges, advocates, army officers, academicians, etc. joined AAP including lower caste section across the country.

A major political change came with the joining of renowned writer and thinker, Raj Mohan Gandhi, son of Devdas Gandhi and the grandson of Mahatma Gandhi. On Friday, 21 February 2014,[27] Raj Mohan Gandhi disenchanted with the

Congress joined the Aam Aadmi Party in Delhi in the presence of Arvind Kejriwal, calling '*Congress only for the Khaas Aadmi*' (special people).

When asked why he choose to join electoral politics? Raj Mohan Gandhi replied to this question, thus:[28]

> No party is perfect. But Congress today has become a party for the Khaas Aadmi, BJP for the Ameer Aadmi and only AAP is left for the Aam Aadmi.

Similarly in response to another question regarding not joining the Congress, he said:[29]

> Because I have seen the performance of the Congress ... I have been pained by it. I could not feel that I could put my heart and soul at this fairly advanced age into anything other than the AAP.

On the completion of two months, the newly elected BJP government in Rajasthan had removed the ban imposed on all kind of appointments (including recruitment of sweepers) during election, 2013. As a result of this Government of Rajasthan (local self government)[30] confirmed that letters were sent to all Executive Officers of Nagar Palikas, Nagar Parishads and Nagar Nigams across the state for releasing appointment orders of those candidates who were interviewed for the post of sweepers prior to imposing ban. The Department also communicated its decision to complete the selection procedure for remaining posts, suspended during the election period. This is a good news for Bhangi Samaj. Various caste organizations released press note of appreciating the Chief Minister for having removed the ban. Social workers, social activists and Bhangi netas said, '*We trusted the Congress party for more than 66 years and thought that they will do good to them, but they betrayed us.*'

Notes

1. See, 'Manpower shortage bogs down city's Swachh image. No recruitment of Sanitation Workers for several years' in *The Times of India*, Jaipur, Tuesday, 7 October 2014.

2. Telephonic conversation with O. P. Jawa, and others, Jodhpur, on 22 January 2014.
3. For most important discussion and regularization of 'दैनिक वेतन भोगी कर्मचारी' (The Bhangis) working in Nagar Parishads, Nagar Palikas and Nagar Nigams across the state, see, in particular राजस्थान सरकार, स्वायत्त शासन विभाग जयपुर, क्रमांक प 1 (मांगे) एसएमई / डीएलबी / 99 / 2509–2592 जयपुर, दिनांक 28 मई 1999.
4. For more detailed information see, 5-page letter from Tara Chand Meena, Deputy Secretary, स्वायत्त शासन विभाग राजस्थान सरकार, जयपुर to all Chief Executive Officers/Commissioners/and all Nagar Palikas, Nagar Parishads and Nagar Nigams across the state. See in particular कमांक प 1 (ग) का / स कर्म भ / एसएम ई / डी.एल बी / 12 / 951– 1134 जयपुर दिनांक 3 मई 2013.
5. Ibid.
6. For detailed information, see pamphlet, स्वायत्त शासन विभाग नगर निगम राजस्थान, 11,376 सफाई कर्मचारियेां की भर्ती।
7. Conversation with Rakesh Kumar Jawa, Jodhpur, in May 2012.
8. Telephonic conversation with Kanhailal Kaloshia, State President of Akhil Bharatiya Valmiki Mahasabha, Ajmer, on 8 January 2014.
9. Ibid.
10. For more details see, Mangi Lal Arya, यह मेरी यादें. पाली, अखिल भारतीय सफाई मजदूर कांग्रेस, 2008 पृ. 527, 528.
11. For more details see particularly, Shyam Lal, *The Changing Bhangis of India: A Study of Caste Association*, Jaipur, Sublime Publications, 1999, p. 173–174.
12. Ibid.
13. Ibid.
14. See, Sarkaro/Kendra shasit pradesho-ka-Samyik Kalyan, Anusuchit Jati/Janjati/Alap Sankhyak Avam pichre vargo-ke-prabhari Mantrio-ke 1–3 February 1996 Ke Nai Delhi Mai Aayojit Sammelan Me Rashtria Safai Karamchari Aayog ke Adhiksh/Shri Mangi Lal Arya ka Bhasan. Date not mentioned. Also see, Shyam Lal, *The Changing Bhangis of India*, ibid., 1999 p. 173–174.
15. For details, see, 'Dinak 3 February 1996 Ke Kalyan Mantriyon ke Sammelan Mai Pradhan Mantri ke Abhibhasan se Udhrit ansh ka Hindi rupantaran'. Date not mentioned. Also see,

Shyam Lal, *The Changing Bhangis of India*. ibid., 1999, p. 173–174.

16. For detailed information, see in particular 'बैठे बिठाए मोल ले ली आफत, अब शेष सफाई कर्मियों के लिए फिर मांगी अनुमति। मौका मिला था, फिर भी नहीं कर पाए थे भर्ती' राजस्थान पत्रिका, जोधपुर संस्करण, दिनांक 17 जनवरी 2014.
17. Ibid.
18. Ibid.
19. Talk with Jodhpur district President, Sonia Gandhi Brigade, Rakesh Kumar Jawa, Jodhpur, in September 2012. Also see, 'निगम में भर्ती के लिए सफाई कर्मचारियों के आवेदन की फिर होगी छंटनी' दैनिक भास्कर, जोधपुर, मंगलवार, 23 दिसम्बर 2014.
20. For detailed information, see in particular 'अब सफाई कर्मियों की भर्ती लौटरी से होगी' राजस्थान पत्रिका, जयपुर, बुधवार 5 फरवरी 2014.
21. See, 'Sachin Pilot appointed new PCC President' in *The Times of India*, Jaipur, Tuesday, 14 January 2014.
22. Ibid.
23. Conversation with Kanhai lal Kaloshia, Jaipur, on 8 February 2014.
24. See, 'Congress anti-Minority: Ex-AICC member' in *The Tribune*, New Delhi, Wednesday, 6 November 2013.
25. See particularly, 'Jaffrabad doctor heckles PM' in *The Times of India*, Jaipur, Thursday, 30 January 2014.
26. See particularly 'हकदार, वर्ष 46, अंक 03, 16–17 फरवरी 2014.
27. See in particular 'Bapu's grandson joins AAP' in *The Times of India*, Jaipur, Saturday, 22 February 2014. Also see, 'Gandhi's grandson now part of AAP' in *Hindustan Times*, Delhi/Rajasthan, Saturday, 22 February 2014.
28. Ibid.
29. Ibid.
30. 'See, 'प्रदेश में सफाई कर्मियों की भर्ती पर रोक हटी' दैनिक भास्कर, जयपुर, गुरुवार, 30 जनवरी 2014.

9

Bhangis and Congress Veteran Leaders

Myth and Reality

Removing of the night soil as head load is a curse on Indian culture and a crime against the fundamental rights of the poor. Even after 67 years of independence of the country, it is still in existence and practising high in many cities of the states. One or two generations ago most Congress veterans including Mahatma Gandhi, Pandit Jawahar lal Nehru, Indira Gandhi, Rajiv Gandhi and P.V. Narsimha Rao were sorry for it and hated it. Besides, they also expressed 'Lip' sympathy to the miserable conditions of the Bhangis'.

The pitiable plight of scavengers is best summed up in the following observations made by the Father of the Nation, Mahatma Gandhi in 1927:[1]

> The condition of Bhangis is extremely miserable and the betterment of this unfortunate section is one of the crying needs. When compared with the average income of the common people, the earnings of the Bhangis attached to local bodies and municipalities may not be very low. Yet the condition of these people is extremely miserable. Drinking and gambling habits, lack of education and lower standard of living are responsible for many of their ills.
>
> Socially they (Bhangis) are lepers and economically, they are worse than slaves. Religiously, they are denied entrance to places we miscall 'House of God'.

The obvious reasons are that peculiar situation exists in our country. Nowhere in the world is this occupation confined to a particular caste as in India and that the job of scavengers is considered as the meanest. In the words of Mahatma Gandhi:[2]

> 'We have reduced them to the level of beast, they earn a few coppers but only at the expense of their human dignity. The weights of oppression has crushed them. It is enough to break one's heart to see them eating their food covering under the shadow of the latrine wall'.

Extracts from Jawaharlal Nehru's[3] speech in a public meeting of sweepers held at Ramlila Maidan, on 2 January 1964:

> When you asked me to address your meeting I felt some hesitation, though I liked the invitation. I had heavy work to do which I could not easily leave behind. But I could hardly refuse to attend this special gathering of Safai Mazdoors. So here, I am before you this evening. Now it is embarrassing for me to find words for speaking to you. In fact in this matter I feel somewhat ashamed. I visited several times, several years back, the places where you live. Seeing your huts I felt unhappy and ashamed. I therefore hesitated to appear before you now and then and yet be reconciled to your miserable conditions. This is our Government and we have our own Constitution which provides that our worker comrades and those who are considered as 'low' should receive special care and protection. It is our duty to abolish this evil of high and low by birth and specially to improve the condition of those who do sanitation work.

Indira Gandhi[4] also voiced her concern and worked for their liberation from their human bondage.

> Everybody is conscious of this fact (Inhuman system of carrying and handling human excreta manually), and we have discussed this many times and there is no doubt that this is a disgrace and it should be eradicated as early as possible.

Now, the Vice-President of Congress, Rahul Gandhi[5] expresses the same sympathy. On Tuesday, 8 October 2013 speaking at the packed Talkatora Stadium, New Delhi, largely dominated by safai karamcharis families from across Delhi and neighbouring states, Rahul Gandhi came out 'to woo the Balmikis by referring to the community as the backbone of the Congress' and citing the bill to eradicate manual scavenging.

At the end of the speech, Rahul, 'offered an apology for the delayed efforts to work towards eradication of manual scavenging. In fact, they do not have strong political will except' lip sympathy. Just after a few days of historical defeat of Congress in 2013 Assembly elections Mohan Lal Joad, a retired senior manager, State Bank of Bikaner and Jaipur and also a social activist, sent a 2-page letter from Jodhpur to Ashok Gehlot, former Chief Minister of Rajasthan, Jaipur enumerating reasons of unprecedented decay. Joad[6] in his letter of 15 December 2013, said,

> श्रीमान अशोक गहलोत,
> पूर्व मुख्य मंत्री राजस्थान
> जयपुर (राज.)
>
> *राजस्थान राज्य में कांग्रेस पार्टी की हार के कारण।*
>
> महोदय जी,
>
> इस पत्र के माधयम से मैं आपको राजस्थान विधाान सभा में कांग्रेस पार्टी की हार के कारणों और उसके निराकरण के उपाय बताना चाहता हूं-
>
> 1. कांग्रेस पार्टी ने राज्य स्तर पर कुछ विशेष जातियों को जोड़ने की कोशिश की।
> 2. जाट, राजपूत और विश्नोई समाज के लोगों को सत्ता और संगठन में भागीदारी दी।
> 3. कांग्रेस पार्टी ने राज्य सत्ता या संगठन में वाल्मीकि समाज के लोगों की कोई भागीदारी नहीं दी। वाल्मीकि समाज का शिक्षित युवा वर्ग और प्रबुद्ध नागरिक नाराज हो गये और कांग्रेस से टूट गये और कांग्रेस से दूर हो गये। उन्होंने कांग्रेस को वोट नहीं दिया।
> 4. वाल्मीकि समाज को किसी भी प्रकार का सामाजिक न्याय नहीं मिला। जैसा कि श्री राहुल गांधी ने अपने दिल्ली में भगवान वाल्मीकि फाउन्डेशन महासम्मेलन में कहा था 'Whatever representation we give to Valmiki Community would be less. They are the backbone' को जोड़ा नहीं और तोड़ा।
> 5. श्री राहुल गांधी का कथन स्पष्ट और सारगर्भित था कि 'I want people of all the caste, creed and region in the Congress party. I want each one of them to have a voice in the party. The day we include everybody, the Congress will again win 360 seats.' परन्तु राजस्थान में कांग्रेस पार्टी की विचारधारा ही अलग रही। वे वाल्मीकी जो दलित में भी दलित है, उनके साथ

अपनी जड़े नहीं जमा सके। आप दलितों के घरों में रुके उनकी झोंपड़ी में खाना खाया किन्तु कांग्रेस के अन्य नेताओं ने ऐसा नहीं किया।

6. एक पार्टी अपनी जड़े कैसे जमा सकती है, यदि उसके अनुयायी स्पष्ट तौर पर यह भी नहीं जानते कि इनकी पार्टी की सैद्धान्तिक/वैचारिक लाइन में क्या फर्क है जिसका उन्हें विरोध करना है। अत: असफलता का एक कारण यह भी है कि कांग्रेस पार्टी वर्गों में सैद्धान्तिक/वैचारिक सिद्धान्त की घोषणा का उच्चारण नहीं करवा पाये।

7. पार्टी के संकीर्ण कार्यक्रम भी हार का कारण रहा। पार्टी को अच्छा नेता नहीं मिला। अच्छा संगठन नहीं मिला और राजनीतिक प्लेटफार्म भी सीमित दायरे तक रहा। पार्टी पिछले पांच सालों में तो कांग्रेस कार्यालय तक ही सिमट कर रह गई।

आपका शुभेच्छु
मोहन लाल जोड़

It is especially unfortunate that even as staunch supporters of the party, the Congress is more responsible to the miserable conditions of the Bhangis in Rajasthan. Bhangis also remained untouched by winds of change.

Rajasthan's ex-untouchables are on cusp of progress. But Bhangi community's future is critical compared to that of the dominant untouchable communities. Rajasthan's Congress stalwarts need to respond as they remained in power for longer period in the state. If Congress was so much of a well-wisher, why it failed to protect the interest of the Bhangis for decades is a big question.

Marwar Ka Gandhi: Ashok Gehlot

The idea of Mahatma Gandhi was a thrilling one because it was a clear instruction by him that the disposal of night soil should be done only by the volunteers of the Congress and not by the Bhangi. It was first implemented at Sevagram, Wardha Ashram of Mahatma Gandhi in Gujarat. He was amongst those who laid the foundation of liberation of Bhangis in India.

Ashok Gehlot's idea of Dalits in general and Bhangi in particular, on the other hand was the complete antithesis of Mahatma Gandhi. This can best be understood by some of the actions of Gehlot during his tenure, a decade ago when he was the Chief Minister of Rajasthan.

Given the inherent contradiction in Gandhi's and Gehlot's action, the calling of Gehlot as 'Marwar Ka Gandhi' by Congressmen is a sheer political cover-up.

Gehlot, who joined Youth Congress, when he was young, was deeply influenced by Gandhi's philosophy. He had stated that he imbibed the Gandhi's values. It was even more surprising that Gehlot was called an ardent follower of Gandhi. If for a moment we assume that he is ardent Gandhian, what did Gehlot do for Dalits during his tenure? For instance the establishment of 'Dr Ambedkar Foundation' honouring Ambedkar, for the first time in the socio-political history of Rajasthan, conceptualized by the then BJP Government in 2007, under the dynamic leadership of former Chief Minister Vasundhara Raje. It was made possible by generous fund from BJP Government. Gehlot who led the Rajasthan Government from 2008–2013 did not contribute a single rupee to the cause.

Where was the admiration at that time for Ambedkar? or was Ambedkar Foundation commemorating Ambedkar not an appropriate honour? Gehlot, the Chief Minister of Rajasthan has twisted the truth repeatedly stating that Ambedkar foundation was established under BJP rule.

Apart from the fundamental different ideology, Gehlot's style of administration was also intrinsically dissimilar to Gandhi's. It is known to one and all that this Rajasthan's Chief Minister believed in one man rule and autocratic style of functioning. Ambedkar Foundation having been established by BJP Government, Gehlot never showed any interest to implement welfare policies and programmes for the betterment of socio-educational and economic conditions of Dalits in Rajasthan. Since 2008–13 Ambedkar Foundation was not put into operation.

If Gehlot did truly understand Gandhi's social philosophy, the ₹ 10 crores spent on establishing Ambedkar Foundation by BJP Government, could have been used towards various schemes to benefit the downtrodden people. Gehlot's Congress Government could have then earned the appreciation from Dalit activists, social workers, Ambedkar followers, Ambedkarites, etc. but he failed.

Pretenders of Gandhi's legacy should introspect themselves. If Gehlot does desire to emulate Gandhi, he should do so in a holistic manner, and look at how Gandhi dedicated his life to Dalits, which has space for every-one, irrespective of caste, creed and most importantly religion.

Strong Caste Bias

Before independence all untouchable castes/communities including Bhangis were not admitted to the educational institutions. But after 1947, they are more educated. Now, it is not unusual to find a good number of graduate and postgraduate young Bhangi youths in the cities of Rajasthan moving here and there in search of jobs. The state has failed to provide jobs to them. As a result of this, it is highly painful to find young Bhangi youths, having graduate and postgraduate degrees applying for sweeper's jobs despite protective discrimination policy.[7] But it is in fact so. In the long list of candidates for the post of sweepers in the municipal corporations of Rajasthan, there were dozens of youth, who have graduate and post-graduate degrees. The changes among the Bhangi community over the last more than six decades have apparently been only skin deep. The socio-economic and educational impact will further deteriorate.

The old caste prejudices never go away. Rajasthan Government fares poorly in most social and economic spheres. This limits opportunities for the Bhangis and results in painfully slow progress in making their lives better. The Bhangis lag far behind the other scheduled castes/communities of the state in terms of development. Considering their genuine demands, the writer long back mooted the idea of having a separate reservation[8] for the community, based on pattern of Bihar, what is called 'Maha Dalit' and is already in use in Bihar.

It is not a question of right, wrong or more accurately, if what was right six decades ago continues to remain equally right today.

One should make a persuasive case that reservation for Dalits should remain in force for another five decades. But government should think over for the amendments that those dalits who have flourished from reservation should be excluded from further positive discrimination, so that benefits can accrue to the less fortunate among them.

A significant newspaper report which appeared on the front page of a leading English Daily newspaper, *The Times of India*,[9] on Wednesday, 12 February 2014, shows that for the first time in the history of Rajasthan, Anil Barupal, a scheduled caste applicant who applied for the post of Physical Training Instructor (PTI) in response to advertisement issued by the State Government in 2011, challenged in Rajasthan High Court, Jodhpur, the rationale of current system of SC/ST reservation and asked 'as to why the provision of creamy layer should not be made applicable in the SC/ST reservation'. The Counsel of petitioner S.P. Sharma argued that 'due to absence of this provision in SC/ST reservation, the right of the deserving person (economically weaker) was shadowed by those economically capable which was in contravention of the Constitutional Mandate'. Hearing the arguments justice G.K. Vyas, issued notices to the Union and State Government, seeking reply on 'Why the creamy layer was not made applicable in the SC/ST quota in the manner while it has been provisioned in OBC quota'.

Government sources said that it was due to the then Rajasthan Chief Minister, Vasundhara Raje that a meeting had taken place in the Government Secretariat in 2003–2008 to nominate members to Rajasthan State Human Rights Commission. The meeting was expected to be declared by the committee headed by the Chief Minister. Other members were: Leader of Opposition, Speaker, etc. B.D. Kalla, the then leader of opposition in the assembly and Senior Congress Leader was there. Kalla played a negative role and vehemently opposed the name of the present writer and turned down the name. Government had chosen my name as an eminent sociologist and University Professor.

It appears that there was a clear collusion with Ashok Gehlot to oppose my name for nomination to the commission. Terming the opposition, 'Unfortunate' the then Home Secretary, V.S. Singh,[10] said,

It was due to B.D. Kalla that writer's name had been excluded from panel.

But it was never expected that Congress known for being pro-Dalits could oppose to such an extent. Congress has been discriminating against socially and economically disadvantaged section of society. This is further confirmed by the then Principal Secretary to Governor, Umrao Salodia,[11] who said it was B.D. Kalla, who targetted writer's name. When writer asked how he came to know, he hinted about the file sent to Raj Bhawan. Veteran Congress leader buttressed the Congress's social justice credentials to stub out the slightest doubt the party's intent about the welfare of downtrodden.

Discrimination and Prejudices

In 1998–2003, when Ashok Gehlot became for the first time the Chief Minister of Rajasthan, during 2002–2003, the author was working as acting Vice-Chancellor[12] of Rajasthan University. After few months, a panel was submitted by the search committee. Writer's name was in the panel, a natural claimant for Vice Chancellorship. But the author did not get it and on 7 February 2003, K.L. Sharma became Vice-Chancellor. After two years or so Sharma resigned on 30 September 2005 and as a result of this, a new search committee was constituted. This time too the writer's name was in the panel. But, on 1 October 2005, N.K. Jain, a Deputy Secretary in UGC at Poona (now Pune) became Vice-Chancellor – leaving the author out.

The Dalit scholars, students and others had been feeling resentment against Ashok Gehlot after realizing that he was determined to avoid SCs/STs interest for Brahmin's appeasement. Congress leadership has come around to recognize that to endorse a Dalit candidate would be at a heavy cost to party's interests or a wasted one. This was nothing more than special pleading to woo Brahmins back towards Congress since Congress is a personification of caste politics.

Sources say that Congress government in the state never wanted that a Dalit and that too a toilet cleaner's son should become the Vice-Chancellor of the premier Institute of the state. So, the government hit out at him and eliminated him academically. But the author never got disheartened nor did he ever fear that Congress government's indifferent attitude towards him will end the road to his Vice-Chancellor's chance. He knew the truth behind it. After a few years, he was appointed Vice-Chancellor of Patna University, Patna, Bihar, the 7th oldest university of Indian subcontinent, established in the year 1917.

Congress Government sent out a negative message to SC/ST people of the state. SC/ST formed the backbone of Congress and Congress came into power only when this section of society was strengthened. Congress brass understand the pain of the untouchables and believe in empowering the SC/ST, while Ashok Gehlot wanted to concentrate power in his hands. Gehlot did not take the neglected section of society on the path of development and stopped them from empowerment. During a decade's tenure he did not take any measures for the welfare of this section of the society.

Past experience indicates that despite vociferous support of SCs/STs in assembly election 1998, the Congress Government headed by Ashok Gehlot took an indifferent attitude. It is difficult to understand why Gehlot government did not appoint even a single SC/ST Vice-Chancellor in more than 13 state universities.

As if all this was not enough, Ashok Gehlot came under fire for other reasons. In 2009, again Congress government led by Ashok Gehlot came into power in Rajasthan. This time it was expected that at least a few SCs/STs candidates will be appointed as Vice-Chancellor in 26 State Universities.[13] But unfortunately, no such person was appointed in his second tenure too. It was too important an issue for SCs/STs. The conduct of Ashok Gehlot government did harm the interest of the downtrodden, embarrassed, its high profile adherents and provided the established parties with enough ammunition to target it. Many high profile Dalit followers of Congress were a dispirited lot.

It should, however, be noted that frustration of SCs/STs in Rajasthan was there as the Congress government of the state did not give the SCs/STs the same benefits. The upper caste Hindus were appointed in various state-managed Universities as Vice-Chancellors, whereas even University SC/ST Professors were not appointed in the Universities and they were ignored. This situation explains why agitation among SC/ST started in Jaipur.

In the first week of January 2012,[14] Rajpal Meena, the State President of the Confederation of National Backward Classes, SCs/STs and Minority Cells, decided to hold a Press Conference on Monday, 2 January 2012 at Jaipur. He addressed the press conference and declared that the purpose of the press conference was not only to inform the State Government in general and Ashok Gehlot in particular, but to launch an agitation for appointment of SC/ST persons as Vice-Chancellors in the state universities. The attitude of the government towards SCs/STs to protect their genuine demands or rights was indifferent and this led to increasing frustration among the latter. The Congress is committed to protect the SCs/STs rights. There was a great disparity in the number of Vice-Chancellors between upper caste Hindus and Dalits. While the state had more than 13 universities, all the universities had upper caste Vice-Chancellors, not a single university had SC/ST Vice-Chancellor. In this context Ashok Gehlot did not speak for SCs/STs, he was against the downtrodden.

Thus, Ashok Gehlot's government has been ignoring the interest of the weaker section of society. Even disillusioned and socio-educationally and politically empowered Dalits also distanced themselves and had been turning to other parties.

Indirect Caste Discrimination

Recent newspaper reports show that in January 2014, the collegiums of Madras High Court,[15] headed by senior judge recommended 12 candidates for the appointment as Judges. The recommendation manifests caste prejudices and mindsets even of the so-called educated or intellectuals of the social mainstream. As soon as the details of 12 names recommended by collegiums of high court, became public, a section of Madras Bar demanded its total recall. Senior Advocate R. Gandhi filed a PIL and had also won an interim order of status quo, restraining the central and state governments from processing the list of names.

It exposes the hypocrisy of the professed progressivist judges when the proposed action touches their interest or affects their castes, the rights or interests of poor downtrodden are opposed and defeated. It also highlighted a fact that few among them are steadfast to support fair play, truth and adhere to high standards of professional rectitude. But they are in microscopic minority.

New Forms of Bhangi Assertion

Ahead of 2013 Assembly Elections, the writer visited a few districts and held conversation with the social workers, social activists and educated persons. Their observations painted a grim scenario, expressing that they were disappointed with Congress. Congress have become unpopular and they would not cast their votes to Congress. Despite long history of Bhangi support and vote to the Congress in these regions, assertion at grassroots level in 2013 is a qualitatively new phenomenon. A new political assertion coming after 67 years of independence. It is a product of deep and increasing discontent with failure of Congress government to provide means of livelihood, protection to their interest and to improve their socio-educational and economic conditions. That is why many Bhangis supported and cast their votes to BJP. The Congress leaders in general, and Ashok Gehlot in particular, failed to read all this.

Notes

1. For more detailed information, see particularly S.P. Srivastava, 'Issue in scavenging: An overview of the problem, programmes and policies' in National Seminar on Action Sociology and Liberation of Scavengers, New Delhi, 8–10 February 1992, sponsored by Indian Association of the Action Sociologists and Sulabh International, p. 13.
2. For more detailed information, see particularly Shyam Lal, 'Upliftment of the Bhangis: A National Challenge' in National Seminar on Action Sociology and Liberation of Scavengers,

New Delhi, 8–10 February 1992, sponsored by Indian Association of Action Sociologists and Sulabh International, p. 76.

3. N.R. Malkani, 'Clean People and an Unclean Country', Delhi, Harijan Sevak Sangh, Kingsway, 1965, p. 153.
4. S.P. Srivastava 'Issue in Scavenging: An overview of problem programmes and policies ' in National Seminar., New Delhi, 8–10 February 1992. p. 16.
5. See, 'I was Just being "honest" on ordinance, says Rahul, in *The Times of India*, Jaipur, Wednesday, 9 October 2013.
6. Mohan Lal Joad, a retired Senior Manager, State Bank of Bikaner & Jaipur and also a social activist sent 2 page letter from Jodhpur to former Chief Minister Ashok Gehlot, enumerating reasons of the unprecedented decay. A copy of the letter is with author. See, particularly letter dated 15 December 2013.
7. 'Graduates queue up for sweeper job in Ajmer' in *The Times of India*, Jaipur, Friday, 4 October 2013.
8. See, 'Separate Reservation: A must for sweepers' in Shyam Lal, *The Changing Bhangis of India*, Jaipur, Sublime Publications, 1999, p. 143–149.
9. See, 'High Court notice to Centre, State over creamy layer in SC/ST quota' in *The Times of India*, Jaipur, Wednesday, 12 February 2014.
10. When nominations of members in Rajasthan State Human Right Commission appeared in local news papers, the author met V.S. Singh, the then Home Secretary and wanted to know about his case. Then this information was given by Singh, who did not wish to be identified.
11. In 2004–2007, when Pratibha Patil was Governor of Rajasthan, the author sought an appointment to meet her. As a result of this, the author met and requested her to write a foreword to his book written on Scheduled Castes. She was kind enough to accept his request and asked him to hand over the manuscript to her Principal Secretary. As per directions, the author met the Principal Secretary to Governor Umrao Salodia and handed over the manuscript to brief her excellency. During table talk, information was confirmed by him from their record.
12. Information was given by the Rajasthan University.

13. See, 'Cut expenses on non-teaching staff: GUV tells RU' in *The Times of India*, Jaipur, Saturday, 8 February 2014.
14 . See, ससी/एसटी से बने कुलपति " राजस्थान पत्रिका , जयपुर, मंगलवार 3 जनवरी 2012.
15. 'H.C. Judge quits panels on caste slur' and 'Madras H.C. Judge quits 14 panels', in Sunday, *Times of India*, Jaipur, 12 January 2014.

10

Political Parties and Bhangi Community

Congress Gives One Ticket to a Bhangi for 2013 Rajasthan Legislative Assembly Election

Party Lost Chance to Win Hearts, Feels Community

As stated earlier, in December 2008, Congress party won the assembly election defeating BJP. Ashok Gehlot began his second inning as the Chief Minister of Rajasthan. It was expected that Gehlot would give tickets to some Bhangi candidates for 2013 Rajasthan Legislative Assembly polls. But it did not happen, leaving few workers, social activists and sympathizers from the Bhangi community disappointed. There are 34 scheduled castes reserved constituencies in whole of Rajasthan. But Gehlot had apparently decided to give ticket to only one Bhangi candidate from Kapasan, Chittorgarh.

Gas agency owner of Udaipur, R.D. Jawa,[1] who is one of the closest confidant and well-known person to Gehlot, was given the Congress ticket from Kapasan, Chittorgarh. When Congress announced the ticket to him, the Congress MP from Chittorgarh and Union Minister Girija Vyas did not relish it. There is a perception among a section of community that had there been Girija Vyas's well-intentioned effort, support and campaign in Kapasan, the chances would have strengthened the Congress candidate's victory. But actually, the party MP did not support and campaign for him.

After allocation of the party ticket, Jawa hoped and sought the presence of prominent Congress leaders in his constituency during the Assembly Election, but he failed. Sources said that even Chief Minister Ashok Gehlot, who pushed him, failed to reach for election meetings even once. State PCC president Chandrabhan, the state's AICC General Secretary in charge, Gurudas Kamat and other senior leaders did not visit the constituency. Consequently, R.D. Jawa lost the election. Arjun Lal Gingar of BJP was declared elected.

J.P. Chandelia, another Bhangi[2], is a retired IAS officer. After his retirement, he wanted to contest the 2013 Assembly Election from Pilani, Jhunjhunu as he himself hails from Jhunjhunu district. Chief Minister, Ashok Gehlot looking at the large presence of Dalit votes in Pilani, had assured to field him from there. But the tallest leader of the Jat community in Shekhawati region, Jhunjhunu MP and Union Minister, Sisram Ola's political manoeuvring made it sure that Chandelia did not get the Congress ticket. As the Ashok Gehlot failed to fulfil his promise, Chandelia though a die hard Congress man fought the election as an Independent candidate, but he lost the assembly election. Sundar Lal of BJP, won the election.

It should be mentioned here that after an interval of two years, former IAS officer J.P. Chandelia alongwith others joined Congress on tuesday, January 6, 2016. He was welcomed by AICC general secretary Janardan Dwivedi and PCC chief Sachin Pilot in New Delhi (*The Times of India*, Jaipur, Wednesday, January 7, 2015).

If the so-called mainstream 'Secular' parties will not address their concerns, if BJP will be seen to deny them representation, then why not turn to a politician who is openly promising to promote and protect 'Bhangi' interest. A leaderless community is now seeking refuge in their own demagogues, in the belief that they alone can offer an effective counterpoint to both majoritarian and flawed secular politics.

BJP Did Not Give Even a Single Ticket to Bhangis for 2013 Rajasthan Legislative Assembly Election

During Vasundhara Raje's first term in office (2003–2008) the Department of Personnel, Government of Rajasthan, issued the letter/notification to all District Collectors to give appointment to the candidates belonging to scavenging community having

Postgraduate degree, on contract basis on fixed emoluments against vacant posts lying in various Departments. Thus, a massive recruitment drive was launched for the first time in the state's history.[3]

This notification was welcomed and appreciated by various Bhangi organizations. Several social workers, social activists and others wrote letters to the then Chief Minister Vasundhara Raje, expressing their gratitude. The scheme had become very popular. Within a few months of issuing this order, a good number of Bhangi youths had joined various Departments across the state. When Congress came to power, after defeating BJP, the Congress Government stopped it. Those who were recruited on fixed emoluments earlier, were removed later on. The Bhangi youths, social workers and social activists were said to be shaken after hearing the news about stopping this scheme. But it should be noted here that on the eve of state assembly poll 2013, the issue of ticket allocation to Bhangi's in Rajasthan was overlooked by the BJP also.

In the light of the above description, it is clear that Congress and BJP have one thing in common. Both have said 'No' to this section of society in assembly elections. BJP's rational is obvious: the Bhangis have always been the staunch supporters and followers of Congress and so BJP is not backing the Bhangis. But why the Congress had also not given priority to them. Almost all the major and minor scheduled castes/communities already had been given tickets. The Bhangis are struggling to compete against all these odds. But let us be a little realistic.

Bhangis Have No Elected MLA[4] in the State Assembly Since 1985

The Bhangis have no elected MLA in the state assembly to voice their grievances and to protect the entire community's interest since 1985. Absence of political representation has made the community silent even on the issue of fundamental rights. Their problems and challenges remain unsolved. They also alleged that the Congress government headed by Ashok Gehlot turned a deaf ear to their genuine demands.

It is true that political reservation has made it possible for greater number of Dalit leaders to enter the state legislature and Lok Sabha. In fact, according to the latest statistics, as many as 34 of 200 member of state assembly are Dalits. But of these, there are very few who identify with the Dalit masses and try to help them out. Others have left the cry of their brothern into oblivion. In the words of Parvathamma[5]:

> Scheduled caste politicians have nearly ceased to identify themselves with the cause of scheduled castes. Like their caste Hindu brethren in politics, they are interested in enjoying the privileges that power bestows. Their immediate interests are all inward looking and they are there for personal and family prestige, to elevate themselves to become neo-Brahmins. Given the choice they are willing to identify themselves with upper castes.

Pitiable conditions of the Bhangis is the brand of Congress and Congress party should be given credit for that brand building. When the author asked the educated Bhangi youths how they could vote for Congress even after the Congress over looked their interest for several decades? They said, there was no option left before the Bhangis other than Congress to vote. They also felt that Bhangis had been betrayed by the Congress veterans.

The political representation of the Bhangis in the State Assembly has been the worst in Rajasthan. Congress has been claiming equal representation of Bhangis in the party organization and government but figures give a different story.

In the first general election in 1952, Congress gave one ticket to a Bhangi candidate and he was elected for State Assembly. During the same period 16 Scheduled Caste candidates were elected.

Similarly, in 1957 and 1962 election, Congress gave one ticket each to Bhangi candidates. Since the first general election in 1952, till 1962 only one Bhangi candidate was elected for state assembly. The scene for Bhangi MLA was bleak, During the same period 16 and 28 scheduled castes candidates were elected in the state respectively. Figures say that overall representation of Bhangis in the state assembly accounts for a very meagre representation from the Bhangi community.

The 1967 and 1972 elections saw maximum of 31 Scheduled Castes candidates winning in the state assembly. Out of 31 elected Scheduled Castes candidates, there was not a single Bhangi representative.

In 1977, general election saw a maximum of two Bhangi candidates out of 33 scheduled castes reserved seats contested for state assembly election and won. The winning candidates were Gopal Pacherwal from Keshoravpatan and Dungar Ram from T.B. Ganganagar. The two were from Janta Party.

Similarly, Janta Party and Congress in 1980 gave one ticket each to Bhangi candidates. Thus, again the highest number of Bhangi candidates who won in State Assembly Elections remained two in 1980–85.

In 12th State Assembly Election in 2003, one Bhangi candidate – Mukesh Valmiki was given ticket by Congress from Phagi reserved constituency, but he miserably failed and lost the election.

Likewise, in 13th State Assembly Elections in 2013, Congress gave one ticket to R.D. Jawa from Kapasan reserved constituency in Chittorgarh District out of 34 reserved seats in the state; he contested but lost.

Since 7th State Assembly election in 1980 till 13th in 2013 election was considered the worst period for Bhangis in Rajasthan. Figures give a different story. There have been no representation of Bhangis in politics for 34 years. The Congress was ignoring the Bhangi Samaj and not taking active interest in protecting their interests.

Long back, Mukesh Valmiki who was the then active Bhangi leader had quit Congress. The decision was not because of any sudden development. Ashok Gehlot, the then PCC President and also Chief Minister of Rajasthan was ignoring the interests of Bhangi Samaj and not involving Bhangi social activists and social workers in important party programmes. Mukesh Valmiki had been fighting for social justice for Bhangis since long. It was Gehlot who marginalized the Bhangis in state politics and did not want to give benefit to them. There was a need to fight for community interest, said Mukesh Valmiki in an informal chat with the writer. However, it is not the case that nothing has been done for them. Something has been done for the Bhangis by succeeding governments.

Mukesh Valmiki admitted that as a Bhangi neta, he himself had to fight his own battles. Some he lost, some he won, but he regrets nothing in his life.

Responding to queries on development of Bhangis, he said that scope for doing a lot exists and more should be done. Jobs, education, political representation in various political bodies, economic betterment are some of the key issues for the Bhangis in the state. Political parties, government, bureaucrats, upper caste Hindus do not want the welfare of Bhangis, he said.

Which is why the community is in desperate need of a leadership that will encourage it to push for its due space in the state mainstream. It would not happen with the Congress which promises equal opportunity but in reality offers only sops; it almost certainly would not happen with BJP which offers no guarantee of equal citizenship.

Today, if the challenge of Saffron majoritarianism is to be countered there needs to be a Bhangi leadership which does not prey on fear, but offers hope – hope of a social and economic transformation.

It is a common feeling amongst the Bhangis, that after Sri Ram Sarvate, Narsingh Dev Gujarati, Jamna Prasad Jedia, Lalita Prasad Chanwaria, Bhag Chand Umarwal, Mangi Lal Arya, Gopal Pacherwal and Madan Maharaja, the Bhangis have never had leaders, only social activists and social workers, who have nursed narrow interests. Yet in the land of Sant Naval Sahib why can there not emerge a Bhangi leader who will cast out fear and sidestep the greedy.

Crushing Defeat of the Congress

Congress Fails to Win Even One Scheduled Castes Seat, 2013

The 2013 State Assembly Election results appear to have hurt the Congress leadership deeply. The Congress, which had thrived on the vote banks of SC, ST and the minorities since 1952, for the first time got mortification to see its vote bank robbed by the BJP and others.

The Congress had won a number of electoral battles as it considered itself a party of Dalits and the downtrodden. But in the latest election, 2013 the Congress could not get a single SC seat out of the 34 reserved seats for the scheduled castes while in the last election the party had 17 SC seats.

In this election (2013), the BJP for the first time scored a thumping majority winning as many as 32 seats across the state. The two other seats were won by Zamindara party's Sona Devi of Raisinghnagar and at Sikrai by Rashtriya Jan Party's (RJP's) Geeta Verma. Thus, the RJP apart from bagging two ST seats could win an SC seat also.[6]

Quoting Suraj Khatri, PCC Secretary and a chronicler, *The Times of India*, 10 December 2013 stated, 'True it's for the first time that party has failed to get a single SC seat in the electoral history of Congress'.[7] The result itself shows that the BJP has made inroads into the traditional Congress votes. The BJP won 32 SC seats against last time's tally of 14, said Satish Chandel,[8] Chairman of BJP's SC Morcha.

The following table shows the division of seats among scheduled castes in the Assembly Election 2013. It also shows that Meghwal gained the highest of 13 seats, Bairwa/Jatav 7, Koli 6, Raigar 5 and Gingar, Garg and Bavri one seat each respectively.

Table 10.1

Party-wise and Caste/Community-wise Scheduled Caste Candidates in the State Assembly Election 2013

S. No.	Caste/ Community	Party-wise Affiliation			
		BJP	Congress	RJP	Jamindara Party
1.	Meghwal	13	–	–	–
2.	Bairwa/Jatav	7	–		–
3.	Koli	5	–	1	–
4.	Raigar	5	–	–	–
5.	Gingar	1	–	–	–
6.	Garg	1	–		
7.	Bavri	–	–	–	1
	Total	32	–	1	1

Source: The figures for 2013 Rajasthan Assembly Election are not taken from official party list but have been gleaned from different sources.

An evaluation of data further shows that BJP won 32 seats out of 34. Rashtriya Jan Party (RJP) and Jamindara party won one seat each respectively. Congress lost in all 34 constituencies. The caste-wise and party-wise seats in 2013 Assembly Election given in Table 10.1 shows an increase in number of female Dalit candidates to 11 out of 34.

Similarly, there are 25 ST reserved seats. The Congress failed here too, miserably as compared to last time (2008) when it won 17, whereas this time it could win only four seats. The Congress that won 14 seats of the STs in the Mewar and Vaagad regions could win only two seats due to Modi impact. The BJP won 18 seats in Mewar, Vaagad, Jaipur and Harauti regions and one seat in Sirohi in this category. In Karauli, Congress won three seats and two of these were the ST seats, that were won by Ghanshyam at Todabhim and Ramesh Meena at Sapotra. Ghanshyam defeated the RJP candidate, while Meena defeated the BJP candidate.

Mahendrajit Malviya, a Minister in Gehlot cabinet who contested from Bagidora in Banswara won. The other Congress winner was Heeralal Darangi at Jhadol, who defeated his BJP rival.

Arjun Meena,[9] who heads the ST Morcha of the party said that:

> It was given enormous mandate by the scheduled tribe community, as a result of which the Congress could get only four out of the 25 seats which is also an all time low of the Congress.

Thus, the SCs and STs collectively have 59 reserved seats; the BJP performed extraordinarily well, winning 52 out of 59 reserved seats. Such results are not easily attained and the party will have to ensure that massive mandate of the downtrodden are respected. In southern Rajasthan, the BJP could earlier win only two ST seats but this time won 15 seats.

Thus, the State Assembly Election in November 2013, indicated that the BJP progressively made inroads into the SCs/STs constituencies and increased its support amongst the SCs and STs, who were formerly the vote bank of Congress, thereby emerging as the most powerful party in the state.

Historical Defeat of the Congress Party in the 14th Assembly Election of 2013

Fall of Gehlot: Creating History

In December 2008, Congress party won the assembly election dethroning BJP. Ashok Gehlot began his second innings as the Chief Minister of Rajasthan on a strong ground in December 2008. He proved his political mettle by comfortably forming a Congress government even though the party was short of five seats for a majority in the state assembly. By orchestrating the merger of all six BSP MLAs into the Congress, he dashed the hopes of rival BJP that at one point of time fostered the idea of midterm elections.

Gehlot survived the strongest threat to his Chief Ministerial career in the aftermath of the Gopalgarh police firing incident of 2011 in Bharatpur district. The Congress high command steadfastly backed him even as the Muslim community began to distance itself from the party after the tragic incident.

Gehlot gradually covered up the negative fallout with his social welfare schemes, but his ministers began to fail him. In the past two years, three ministers had to leave after cases of sexual exploitation of women, while a couple of others were dropped on direct or indirect corruption charges. However, the party repeated the 'Tainted'[10] ones or nominated their relatives in assembly election. Electors gave him the worst ever defeat in the state's history as Congress struggled to win 21 seats and keep itself alive, at least as an opposition party.[11]

Unprecedented: Time to Think the Unthinkable

It is the best ever for the BJP and the worst ever for the Congress. The 2013 Assembly Election in Rajasthan has delivered the most decisive result in the history of the state. BJP has won 163 seats and the Congress has been decimated with a meagre figure of 21, worst than 1977 when they were restricted to 41, amidst post-emergency and anti-Congress wave.

In fact, BJP's tally is the highest ever by any party in the state. The previous best was the 156 by the Congress in 1998 and the Janta Party in 1977. Other than Ashok Gehlot, only two Ministers of the 27-member Congress Ministry managed to win. Gehlot won from Sardarpura in Jodhpur, Mahendrajit Singh Malviya, Bagidora, Banswara and Brijendra Ola, Jhunjhunu are Minister's who have won. PCC Chief, Chandrabhan also lost and has resigned from the party post.

The Congress has been wiped out from 17 of the state's districts. In state's 12 and 3 districts, Congress won only one and two seats respectively. Only in one district, namely Karauli, Congress won 3 seats.

About the historical defeat of Congress in both the State Assembly Election 2013 and Lok Sabha Polls 2014, no one from Scheduled Caste netas, former Dalit Minister or MLAs in Congress Government/Party has spoken anything about deserting of the 129 years old Congress. Also no one from Dalit organizations in the State and Congress supporters and followers has bothered to talk about shifting of their loyalties to BJP. Only some social activists and social workers have enumerated certain reasons for Congress defeat.

Raje Again Re-elected as House Leader

The year 2013 belonged to the BJP whether it was Vasundhara Raje who stormed her way into the state politics or the BJP party unit itself which by the end of the year was basking in the glory. The year had lot of luck in store for the Saffron Party.

While her detractors sulked and political rivals screamed from roof tops about her appearance after a prolonged absence, Raje entered the state amidst a grand welcome and took over as the party's president on 7 February 2013.

While Raje took over as the state president, Gulab Chand Kataria, who had himself objected to Raje took over as the leader of opposition in the Rajasthan assembly. Raje launched the 'Suraaj Sankalp Yatra' in April 2013 touring the state extensively for the next months.

She was also officially announced to be the party's Chief Ministerial candidate.[12] Meticulous planning backed by resolute effort by her team converted 'Suraaj Sankalp Yatra' into a perfect platform for projecting Raje as the most prominent future leader.

Rise of Raje: Basks in Glory[13]

All is well, that ends well. But for Raje, there was more on the platter than what she expected. The year began tentatively with speculations of Raje being handed over the reins of party grew stronger in January. But it ended with a crowning glory as she became the state's Chief Minister for the second time, following the party's historic win on 8 December 2013. January saw some major differences surfacing within the party with senior leaders opposing Raje's come back. They marched in protest to Delhi, only to be pacified by the party central leadership. Raje took over the reins emphasizing the fact that the party had to stay united.

Bhangi and State Assembly Elections 2013

The 2013 election was important in voicing the disillusionment of the Bhangis with the Congress and BJP for neglecting and not taking any interest in the overall development of the downtrodden Bhangi population. The 14th General Election in 2013 divided the Bhangis politically.

It is a serious concern that not a single representative has been in the State Assembly since 1985, and the gap between dominating scheduled castes and other scheduled castes has widened in political representation. This dismal statistic has declined in Rajasthan over 28 years or in the last 6 election cycles. The proportion of scheduled castes in Rajasthan Assembly, for instance, increased from 16 (1952) to 28 (1957). After a gap of one decade, it was again increased from 31 (1967) to 33 (1977), following a quota policy implemented in 1952. Scheduled castes such as Meghwal, Chamar, Bairwa, Balai, Raigar and Khatik have had similar successes with the quota system in this period.

In Rajasthan and elsewhere the cost of entering electoral politics remains prohibitively high for the Bhangi candidates compared to other scheduled castes candidates, especially when viewed in context of expenditure cost and cultural barriers. Left unaltered, the current electoral political system is unlikely to throw up Bhangi leaders. Let us take a look at the barriers to entry.

Upper Castes and Scheduled Castes Voters do not Vote for Bhangis

An analysis of state election data over the last 61 years shows that a part of this problem stems from the feudal tendency among electors. The Bhangis are unlikely to contest election in reserved constituency, where the numerical ratio is skewed against them, making them an electoral minority compared to other scheduled castes. This implies that the common voter is of upper castes and dominating scheduled castes. Bhangis depend largely on them and they are not likely to cast their votes to Bhangi candidates. Such Bhangi candidates suffers a dual isolation. Scheduled caste voters tend to distance themselves from Bhangis. At the same time Bhangis are not accepted fully by the upper castes fellow voters and politicians. An analysis of socio-political behaviour in Bihar by Sachhidananda[14] (2001) concludes that:

> There is no reason to believe that politics in reserved constituencies is any different from what it is in the general constituencies. This means in reserved constituencies where there are negligible Bhangis in electorate, the Bhangi do not seek political representation by voting and not by directly contesting election.

Upper Castes Electors Refusing to Vote For SC/ST Candidate

The percentage of electors who opted for the NOTA (None of the above) button on electronic voting machines (EVM) during the recent Lok Sabha election was less than that in the Vidhan Sabha polls that were held in December 2013. The NOTA option was introduced by the Election Commission in Vidhan Sabha elections only last year.

During the Vidhan Sabha election, a total of 1.92 per cent of the over three crore voters opted for NOTA as against 1.22 per cent in the Lok Sabha election. Moreover most voters who opted for NOTA were from SC and ST reserved constituencies.

During the State Assembly Election 2013 and Parliamentary election 2014, the local press also backed Sachchidananda's views, saying the attitude of upper castes towards SC/ST candidates is the same. For instance, on 19 May 2014, Prakash Bhandari,[15] a senior correspondent of *The Times of India*, reported,

> According to Election department's official here, more NOTA votes during the Vidhan Sabha election could be because upper castes electors refusing to vote for any SC/ST candidate ... The Number of NOTA votes during that elections range between 349 and 7,244. Interestingly, the number of NOTA in some cases was higher than the victory margin of the winner.

> Going by this logic, the lesser number of reserved constituencies could have led to less NOTA users. In the ST reserved Banswara constituency, the number of the NOTA users was the highest and figures stood at 34,404. The total number of polled votes in this Constituency was 11,68,743.
>
> In another tribal reserved seat of Udaipur, the total number of voters who opted for NOTA was 26,685. But the figures in another ST reserved seat 'Dausa', the NOTA users were only 8,410.
>
> The apathy of general caste voters is reflected in the higher number of NOTA users in Udaipur and Banswara constituencies. A large number of the general category voters, particularly the high caste like Jains, Brahmins and Banias did not think it fit to vote for any candidates.
>
> In Dausa constituency where an intense battle was witnessed among three prominent Meena candidates and where each vote counted, the electors sensibly used their options and this resulted in a lesser number of people opting for NOTA. The SC seat of Bikaner recorded the highest number of NOTA users at 13,492 followed by Ganganagar, 6,918, Bharatpur 5,935 and in Karauli, it was 5,934.

There is a widespread belief among the Bhangis that they are not getting a fair share in the political process. According to them, their community has no representation and influence in local affairs. In the world of real politics, party tickets at the election time go to those most likely to win elections. Bhangis are a minority group among the various scheduled castes. The Chamar, Meghwal, Bairwa, Raigar and Khatik are more powerful. Bhangis are marginalized in Rajasthan. They do not figure in Dalit politics. It has nurtured 'Yes Men' instead of strong leaders and organization.

The political parties exploit the caste susceptibilities of voters. This is all the more so, in the case of the reserved seats. It is generally observed that caste sentiments do play a major part in selection of candidates and in voting behaviour. In the case of reserved constituencies, candidates are selected on the basis of their vote-getting ability in their constituencies.

Bhangis have remained by and large neglected. In fact it is only the dominating scheduled castes groups, with resources of wealth and numbers, that have enjoyed the fruit of caste oriented democracy while the Bhangi caste have been, for all practical purposes, outside the political arena.

Bhangis as Independent Candidates

Reserve quota which propose 16 and 12 per cent of seats in Parliament and State Legislative Assembly for SC/ST respectively has been implemented in the state since 1952, but how many political parties field Bhangi candidates.

According to report by International Institute for Democratic and Electoral Assistance,[16] all parties play a more significant role than voters as 'Gatekeepers' to political office across political system and regimes.

In his book *Samajik Niyay Aur Dalit Rajneeti*,[17] the author analysed election commission's data on SCs candidates in Rajasthan assembly election and studied the role of political leaders within Rajasthan political parties. The study reveals that political parties had failed to nurture Bhangi leaders and their support is not reflected in either their candidate list or party apparatuses.

Since 1952 election, if we look at break up of this, we see that a few Bhangi candidates contested as independents, notably Badridas Maharaj, Babulal Pandit and Brahm Dass Gujarati,[18] 1967 while a smaller fraction contested as part of recognized political parties. Absence of Bhangis in the candidate's lists of parties has remained a consistent feature over the past election cycles. The number of Bhangis running as independent indicates that more Bhangis are willing to run but are not backed by parties.

The question of human dignity and human rights is specially important in the context of Bhangis. Without progress in the situation of Bhangis, there can be no true social development. The struggle for Bhangi's equality is part of the struggle for a better society.

Political empowerment is the need of the society, but in practice due to indifferent and negative attitude of parties, Bhangis have not been empowered politically. They are small in numbers and, therefore, in a democracy where voting numbers count, they do not have many chances. These two factors have marginalized the Bhangi community in the process of political empowerment. Although they have equal political rights, they do not participate in the political process as other scheduled castes like Chamar, Meghwal, Bairwa, Raigar and Khatik do. Bhangis are at the bottom of the society, They are the lowest among scheduled castes.

They participate in the democratic process as voters. Very few contest the elections. The reason for this is lack of caste based voting strength. In addition to this, they cannot afford the finance necessary for contesting elections. They can at the most contest Municipal ward election.

Stuck in SC's/ST's Cells

This absence is a manifestation of party apparatuses that are unsupportive to Bhangi's political representation. Across the political spectrum Bhangis are scarcely represented in party leadership position and when they are, they are confined to SC's cells.

The Congress and other political parties which censure the BJP for its ideology must know that BJP elected Bangaru Laxman, who belonged to Bhangi community from undivided Andhra Pradesh, as National President. Thus, BJP had been more successful with its internal party change introduced long back. However, this change might just be cosmetic.

Caste and Political Participation in Parliamentary Election 2014

Bhangi Candidate on General Seat

When the Bhangis understood the truth of the indifferent attitude of both Congress and BJP, who did not give a single ticket to the Bhangis, a few Bhangis contested on general seats as independent candidates. Most prominent among them is Munnadass Dabodia,[19] who contested from the Jaipur general seat dominated by upper caste Hindus. Thus, political parties by neglecting Bhangis' interest created a crisis in the Bhangis organization and led finally to a split: Members of Congress and BJP. In the process, of course, the Bhangis moved closer to the BJP.

In 2013 State Assembly Election, one Bhangi contested as an independent candidate from reserved seat. The constituency was Pilani, Jhunjhunu. Congress had fielded one Bhangi, R.D. Jawa from Kapasan reserved constituency in Chittorgarh. Both of them were defeated.

From the very beginning, the Bhangi caste as a whole had remained wholly united in its support of Congress party. A local saying which is common among the higher castes, 'Bhangiyon-ke-Vote To Congress ki Jeb Main-Hai' under line the support of community to the Congress. The sentiments within the community, however, were shifting slowly.

A point worth consideration in this respect is the fact that the frustration among the Bhangis took a positive turn when Munna Dass Dabodia of Jaipur took the lead in sabotaging the Congress and BJP candidates. Born in 1949, to a poor family of Ramkavar (in village Natwara, Tehsil Niwai, Tonk district) Dabodia brought about a new political awakening among the Bhangis of Rajasthan by fighting as an Independent candidate. He was not highly qualified. He passed Higher Secondary from Board of Secondary Education Rajasthan, Ajmer, in 1967 and in 1969 he joined as LDC, in the office of Principal Accountant General Rajasthan, Jaipur. Dabodia was not interested in studying further because of poor family conditions and he joined the government job. Dabodia was promoted to the post of Senior Auditor in 1984 and thereafter as Welfare Assistant in 1991. As a senior auditor, he earned the appreciation of his superior.[20] Thus, after serving 40 years in the office of Principal Accountant General Rajasthan, Jaipur, he retired in 2009.[21]

In State Assembly Election 2013 and Parliamentary Election 2014, when national parties did not give even a single party ticket to Bhangi community,[22] they stubbornly opposed. Dabodia with a group of Bhangis started election campaign, for which act, he was appreciated by the community. It achieved its aim to a considerable extent.

Thus, it is clear that Congress had neglected Bhangis throughout these years. The lack of political representation of the Bhangis, who are educationally and economically, the poorest, ritually lowest group among the scheduled castes in Rajasthan, was striking. This made the social and political workers uneasy, as the Congress which they (Bhangis) considered their natural ally, neglected their interest.

Before submitting his nomination papers, to Chief Election Officer as an independent candidate, he went from basti to basti, urging them to support him. Dabodia led the election campaign with his poetic talents and speeches in the various bastis, mohallas and localities. His election symbol was TV.

On 26 March 2014, Dabodia[23] submitted his nomination papers to Chief Election Officer, Jaipur. Soon after this, Dabodia exposed the indifferent attitude of Congress and BJP through his speeches.

According to Dabodia[24] in all the 8 State Assembly Constituencies namely Hawa Mahal, Adarsh Nagar, Vidyadhar Nagar, Civil Lines, Kishan Pole, Malviya Nagar, Bagru and Sanganer, which fall in Jaipur Parliamentary seat, there are 85 thousand Bhangi voters alone. Fighting the election as an independent candidate marked the efforts of community leaders to equalize by pulling up the bottom strata. It also gave wide appeal, identity and popularity.

In response to Dabodia's call for financial support, Bhangi community donated ₹ 72,000[25] to meet the election expenditure to Dabodia. A few notable leaders, who were associated with election campaign of Dabodia were: Mahendra Chauhan Advocate, Vishnu Chanwaria, Advocate, Gopal Chanwaria and many more.[26]

A few held the view that the idea of independent candidates was first mooted by Bhangi leaders such as Babu Lal Pandit, Brahm Das Gujarati and Badridas Maharaj in 1967.[27] However, it may be noted in this connection that for the first time, an attempt was made by some Bhangis to enter into electoral politics, but they lost heavily.

Out of 16 candidates (including Independent) in Jaipur Parliamentary seat, Dabodia got only 4,856 votes, but it was not enough to make any impact on the outcome of the result. Thus, he lost the election. It should be noted that all the 14 candidates (including Munnadass Dabodia) except Congress candidate (Dr Mahesh Joshi) their security money was forfeited.[28] BJP looking at the large presence of upper caste votes in the constituency had opted to field Ram Charan Bohra from there, where he faced

Dr Mahesh Joshi of Congress. Dr Mahesh Joshi who was a sitting MP from this constituency had to lose this seat (3,24,013). BJP candidate Ram Charan Bohra (8,63,358) won the election because of Modi wave.

Saffron Raj Continues

As the Modi wave gathered momentum, over a period of years the BJPs drew more and more Bhangis into the party organizations, especially after State Assembly Elections of 2013. It may be recalled that prior to 2013, different saffron organizations systematically enrolled Bhangi youths into Vishva Hindu Parishad, Seva Bharati, Bajrang Dal, Shiv Sena, ABVP, etc. Thus, since 1977, the involvement of Bhangis with saffron organizations started. Since then, the participation of Bhangis in various saffron branches also increased.

In December 2013, the BJP took the state by storm literally. From 70 seats (in 2008) to 163 seats (in 2013) in the Legislative Assembly, the BJP has come a long way. BJP netas and social workers in an attempt to establish the direct contact with SCs in general and Bhangis in particular had visited several bastis, mohallas, etc. across the state. Things started changing fast in the organization after election. In a surprise move BJP during the Municipalities' election in November 2014, gave 18 tickets to Bhangi candidates across the state. ABVM's State President and others were seen maintaining a close contact with State BJP President Ashok Parnami. The Bhangi netas were consulted during the ticket distribution process, particularly during Rajasthan Municipal Corporations polls. It should be noted here that Bhangis were ignored during the ticket distribution process particularly during State Assembly Election 2013. Such a large number of ticket's distribution to Bhangis was also a surprise move. The popularity graph of BJP among the Bhangis touched new heights during polls of 2014. On 22 November 2014, polls for 46 municipal bodies were held. After two days on Tuesday, 25 November 2014, result were declared.

The ruling BJP swept the civic poll results declared on Tuesday emerging as the single largest party in 36 of the 46 Municipal bodies. Of six Municipal Corporations among these, the BJP pocketed five, including Jaipur Municipal Corporation.

In Kota and Udaipur Municipal Corporations, Congress did not even get adequate seats to stake claims for leader of opposition. In Jodhpur and Bikaner Corporations, the BJP dominated with ease. The BJP triumph reinforced Raje's leadership in the state.

BJP Plays Bhangi Card to Corner Congress in Municipal Polls, 2014

Bhangi netas, social workers and activists thank BJP for giving tickets in municipal polls. The BJP Bhangi candidates emerged victorious from several wards across the state, indicated that traditional Congress Vote Bank has drifted into saffron party's kitty. The saffron parties bid to field maximum number of Bhangi candidates in all six divisional headquarters and 11 Municipal Councils worked in its favour.

BJP have received support from Bhangi Samaj is certainly not good news for Congress. In this power game, the Congress and Congress leadership could not do anything to prevent the Bhangis going to saffron party. The Bhangis had decided en-masse to support BJP in the Municipal polls.

BJP fielded three Bhangi candidates from Jodhpur ward No 29, 39 and 60 respectively, which witnessed the success of Pooja Gujarati and Manju Kandara (both women) and this experiment ensured saffron party's entry into Bhangi bastions.

In other Municipal Corporations like Udaipur, BJP gave tickets to one Bhangi, (Ramesh Chandel); Jaipur–2 (Rajesh Bimal and Durga Pacherwal); and Bharatpur–3 (Sher Singh, Ram Babu Gehlot and Kishan Murari).

Bhangi netas said Bhangi support to BJP is indication that they know that during Congress rule in the state they were cheated. Those who have gone with saffron party are as a result of party's liberal brigade which has taken advantage of Congress's disenchantment.

In Jaipur, though only one BJP Bhangi (Rajesh Bimal) candidate won, it, however, indicates that BJP has made inroads into the community.

ABVM's State President, Kanhai Lal Kaloshia – who played a key role in ticket distribution to Bhangi candidates, says our entry in areas which are alien to us is indicative that change is evident.

A comparison with Congress for municipalities polls shows that Congress gave priority to Bhangis as BJP did. In 2014 municipalities polls, Congress distributed 19 tickets to the Bhangi candidates.

As per latest data of victorious BJP Bhangi candidates in Rajasthan is 10, where as Congress's winner candidates is 4. Likewise, independent Bhangi winner candidate is 3. Table 10.2 gives distribution of partywise candidate in different bodies, 2014.

Another good feature is that those seats which were reserved for SC candidates are now seen with good number of men/women from Bhangi Community. Activists now feel that it is possible that Bhangi men/women will be at grassroots level of governance. Kanhai Lal Kaloshia, State President of ABVM based in Ajmer said:

> This opportunity by BJP has provided the Bhangis of having its representation in the governance. The year 2013 and 2014 has started well for the community, once known as the staunch supporter of Congress. Things have changed in Rajasthan. There is a new regime (BJP) in Rajasthan. *Zamana badal gaya hai.*

On the historic day of 25 November 2014, BJP emerged as the single largest party in 36 of 46 Municipal bodies. As it happened for the first time in the last few decades, BJP distributed more than 18 tickets to Bhangi candidates stripping the Congress of its primacy in giving tickets to Bhangis. All this was set to dilute the influence that the Congress had appropriated for itself. It has been a brilliant year for the Bhangi community and BJP's great achievement is to have broadened its appeal to bring in vast numbers of aspiring Dalits in general, and Bhangis in particular, who were uncomfortable with Congress's policy of use and throw. The mood of Bhangi electorates in 2013 and 2014 was shaped by a sense of despair that had come to grip this community. Thus, BJP has created tension in the Congress.

The local body elections held recently was the second one in just one year (2014). State Assembly Elections took place in 2013. Earlier to these years, there was no denying the fact that

Table 10.2

Partywise and Regionwise Bhangi Candidates in State Municipal Polls, 2014

S. No.	Municipal Body	Partywise Affiliation of Candidate				Party Wise Seat Won/Lost							
		BJP	Congress	Bahujan Mukti Party	Independent	BJP		Congress		Bahujan Mukti Party		Independent	
						Won	Lost	Won	Lost	Won	Lost	Won	Lost
1.	Jaipur	2	3	–	–	1	1	1	2				
2.	Jodhpur	3	2	–	1	2	1	–	2	–	–	–	1
3.	Udaipur	1	2	2	4	1	–	–	2	–	2	–	4
4.	Bikaner	1	2	–	–	–	1	1	1				
5.	Kota	–	2	–	–	–	–	–	2				
6.	Bharatpur	3	1	–	1	–	3	1				1	–
7.	Pali	1				1	–	–	–	–	–	–	–
8.	Sirohi	1	–	–	–	1	–	–					
9.	Pushkar (Ajmer)	1	–	–	–	1	–	–					
10.	Beawar (Ajmer)	1	–	–	1	1	–	–	–	–	–	–	1
11.	Nathdwara	1	1	–	–	1	–	–	1	–		–	–
12.	Kanora	–	–	–	1	–	–	–	–	–		–	1

Cont'd...

...Cont'd

13. Mount Abu	1	–	–	–	1	–	–					
14. Alwar	–	3	–	2	–	–	1	2	–		–	2
15. Suratgarh	–	1	–	–	–	–	–	1	–	–		
16. Churu	1	1	–	1	–	1	–	1	–	–	1	–
17. Chittorgarh	1	1	–	1	–	1	–	1	–	–	1	
Total	18	19	2	12	10	8	4	15	–	2	3	9

Source: 1. The figures for 2014 State Municipal Polls are not taken from official party list but have been gleaned from eminent community fellows of concerned regions, namely Mohan Lal Joad (Jodhpur), Shantilal Gavri (Udaipur), Purushottam Gehlot (Chittorgarh), Kanhai Lal Kaloshi (Ajmer), Valmiki Datwal (Beawar, Ajmer) Ram Tarun Tamboli (Alwar) Rajendra Dildania (Bikaner) Roop Narain Jedia (Jaipur), Gurudayal Singh (Kota) etc. and caste organizations, such as Akhil Bharatiya Valmiki Mahasabha. etc.

2. दैनिक भास्कर, जपुर एवं जोधपुर संस्करण, बुधवार, 26 नवंबर 2014, यह भी देखें राजस्थान पत्रिका, जयपुर एवं जोधपुर संस्करण, बुधवार, 26 नवंबर 2014

3. Also see: *The Times of India*, Jaipur, Wednesday, 26 November 2014.

Bhangi politics had witnessed the paradigm changes. The Bhangi politics in Rajasthan had revolved around Congress since 1952, when Congress Government formed for the first time. However, things have changed deeply and fast.

When Ashok Gehlot became the Chief Minister of Rajasthan for the first time in 1998 and repeated in 2009, he had clipped SC's and ST's wings in general, including Bhangis. For instance, a strong senior state Congress SC leader and the then Minister for primary education, Master Bhanwar Lal Meghwal was in 2012 dropped from Gehlot's Cabinet. Soon after dropping Meghwal a large number of SC social activists, social workers, netas and several social organizations protested against Ashok Gehlot's ignoring of Meghwal for hurting SC sentiments. In fact, many netas from SC came out in support of Meghwal and were feeling bad. People called Meghwal a good administrator but we know what was the price Meghwal had to pay? Thus, his political career was crushed. Other development also point that Gehlot had managed to marginalize the SCs/STs within the party and government. Not only this, he apparently ignored the welfare and development programmes of SCs in the state.

Municipal Councillors, 2014

The emergence of municipal councillors as political elite is crucial to the career of any caste/community, for they provide fighting force. They provide leadership roles in political mobilization by establishing contact with masses and spreading the ideology of the party. The author has already noted the growth of professional politicians at the state level. Since we have already mentioned the politicians at the state level, we may now mention few prominent regional one's who won in municipal polls.

In Jodhpur region Manju Kandara was a known sitting councillor of Ratanada ward and member of BJP. Her father Manoj Gujarati is a BJP social worker and her other family members also took interest in the BJP activities. Sources said that there are 11,000 voters in this ward. Out of this there are 8,000 Bhangi voters. Thus, Bhangi voters played a significant role in the victory of the candidate. Manju Kandara fought the election on BJP ticket and won.

Pooja Gujarati, at present, is a student of MA (previous) Dept. of History, JN Vyas University, Jodhpur. As a student she took an active part in ABVP activities during the last three years. During these three years the part played by her prompted BJP to give her ticket and she won.

Rajesh Bimal's father is a BJP social worker. His father-in-law Gopal Pacherwal is a famous regional political leader (BJP). Rajesh contested the election for the first time as BJP candidate and won.

In Chittorgarh region, Vijay Chouhan was a sitting Congress councillor of Chittorgarh Municipal body. He, as the sitting councillor took an active part in social activities and did development work in his ward. So, he was a popular councillor. This was not relished by the Congress. So Congress refused the ticket to him this time. As a result, he fought the election as an Independent and won.

In Bikaner region, Nand Lal Jawa, was a staunch supporter of the Congress and his father too was a Congress man. Earlier, he lost the election but this time he fought as a Congress candidate and won the election.

In Udaipur region, Ramesh Chandel is a retired government servant. Soon after his retirement, he came in contact with RSS. Sources said that due to RSS he was given ticket for the first time and he won the election.

In Ajmer region, Ravindra Joy belongs to Jaipur – the State Capital, but his father settled down in Beawar long back. He is a middle pass. In 1985–1986 he joined the BJP. Due to his dedication, he became Deputy President of dehat BJP once and was twice Deputy President of dehat Mandal. His son Sandeep Joy is attached with ABVP, who was also District President of ABVP. This time, Ravindra Joy fought the election as BJP candidate from Ward No 8 and won. Similarly, Prakash Parihar another Bhangi is an advocate by profession. He is famous for his piggery business in Beawar. He started his political career as a BJP worker in 2004–2005. He sought the ticket from Ward No. 31, which is dominated by Raigars. So, BJP refused the ticket.

Consequently, Prakash Parihar fought the election as Independent and was declared elected. Sukh Ram Mattu was a BJP social worker in Pushkar, Ajmer district, who contested the election earlier too, but lost. This time BJP refused the ticket. As a result of all this, he contested as independent from Ward No 1 and declared success.

In Bharatpur region, Charan Das Patania is a known social worker and also a strong Congress supporter. He actively participated in various social activities and programmes. His wife Mrs Patania too is dedicated Congress social worker. During municipal polls 2014 Congress refused to field Charan Das patania as Congress Candidate. As a result, he contested the election as Independent candidate and won the election. It should be noted that Mrs Patania fought the election on Congress ticket and won.

Shyam Lal Chanwaria was a class IV employee in Sumerpur municipality, (District Pali) and was also a social worker, who retired from service last year. After retirement, he took an active part in bringing more and more Bhangis in BJP fold. Consequently, BJP give him ticket to fight the election and he won.

Notes

1. Talk with Mohan Lal Joad, a relative of R.D. Jawa and also social worker/activist at Jodhpur, in October 2013.
2. The information was gathered from some eminent social activists, social workers and colleagues.
3. For detailed information, see particularly, 'Ambedkar Foundation: Issues and Challenges II', in Shyam Lal, Dr Ambedkar Foundation, Jaipur University Book House, Chaura Rasta, 2013, p. 55–56.
4. For more important discussion of partywise and castewise elected Scheduled Castes MLAs in Rajasthan Assembly since 1952, see in particular Shyam Lal, *Samajik Niyay Avam Dalit Rajnitee* (Hindi), Jaipur, Sublime Publications, 2004, p. 43–54.

5. See, Vivek Kumar, 'Nature and Crisis of Dalit Leadership in India: A Macro Sociological Analysis' a dissertation submitted to Centre for the study of Social Systems, School of Social Sciences, the Jawahar Lal Nehru University, New Delhi in partial fulfilment of the requirements for the award of the Degree of Master of Philosophy (unpublished) 1994, p. 104.
6. See, 'Cong fails to win even one SC seat' in *Times of India*, Jaipur, Tuesday, 10 December 2013.
7. Ibid.
8. See, 'BJP's SC/ST cells seek higher representation in Cabinet' in *Times of India*, Jaipur. Thursday, 19 December 2013.
9. Ibid.
10. See, particularly, 'Sop opera flops, Cong Bites Dust' in Sunday, *Times of India*, Jaipur, 29 December 2013.
11. Ibid.
12. Ibid.
13. Ibid.
14. Sachchidananda, *People at the Bottom: A Portrait of the Scavengers*, New Delhi, Concept Publishing Company, 2001.
15. Bhandari, Prakash, 'NOTA users less in Lok Sabha than in Assembly polls' in *The Times of India*, Jaipur, Monday, 19 May 2014.
16. See, 'Why less ladies in the Lok Sabha', in Sunday, *The Times of India*, Jaipur, 11 May 2014.
17. For more details, see, Shyam Lal, *Samajik Niyay Aur Dalit Rajneeti* (Hindi). Jaipur, Sublime publications, 2004.
18. For more details, see, Shyam Lal, *Caste and Political Mobilisation: The Bhangis*, Jaipur, Panchsheel Prakashan, 1981, p. 104.
19. Talks, with Munnadass Dabodia, at Jaipur, on Friday, 24 May 2014.
20. Ibid.
21. Ibid.
22. Ibid.
23. Ibid.
24. Ibid.
25. Ibid.

26. Ibid. Also see, pamphlets published and circulated among voters particularly 'लोक सभा क्षेत्र जयपुर (शहर) के निर्दलीय प्रत्याशी, मुन्ना दास डाबोडिया' शिक्षित बनो, संगठित रहो, संघर्ष करो : बाल्मिकी समाज का हार्दिक आभार।
27. Shyam Lal, *Caste and Political Mobilisation: The Bhangis*, Jaipur, Panchsheel Prakashan, 1981, p. 103.
28. As told by Munna Dass Dabodia, at Jaipur, on Wednesday, 28 May 2014. Also see, आपका फैसला 2014 दैनिक भास्कर, जयपुर शनिवार, 17 मई, 2014.

11

Liberation of Bhangis

Sorry State of Affairs

Ever since the freedom movement the liberation of sweepers, from their bondage to this occupation which keeps them alienated and despised, had been a high point on the agenda of social reform in the country. The father of the Nation, Mahatma Gandhi, was so moved by the agonizing social situation of the sweepers that he expressed,

> I may not be born again, but if it happens, I would like to be born in the family of sweepers so that I may relieve them of the inhuman, unhealthy and hateful practice of carrying night soil.

Gandhiji made the task of improving the lot of sweepers central to the process of liberation of Indian society from the age-old social evils. Consequently, he led a movement for the institutional abolition of bondage of sweepers from their hereditary occupation, as also for the abolition of social framework in which they get detested and dehumanized. Gandhiji not only propagated the idea of 'Bhangi Mukti' (Liberation of sweepers), but also made a pioneering contribution through his plan of action and his own deeds. The initiative taken by him proved instrumental in creating awareness about the plights of sweepers and the need for their liberation from social and occupational bondage.

Following Gandhiji, many social reformers voiced their concern on behalf of sweepers and even worked for their liberation from their human bondage. However, their efforts did not produce worthwhile results, mainly because their views and actions were initiated against the well-entrenched value of the caste-ridden society.

Manual Scavenging in Rajasthan: An Assessment

After attaining our independence and even after 67 years, the despicable practice of manual scavenging in Rajasthan state's rural and urban areas can be seen even today. The Bhangis are primarily employed as manual scavengers. They are also responsible for removing dead animals and are given ₹ 5 or food for this work. It is interesting to note here that this tradition is unique which has been in existence since centuries. A deeper probe into the working of manual scavengers reveal the existence of the despicable caste system. How scavenging work – the filthiest job is perceived by country people in rejecting this work? An indication to this came during a meeting called by the top brass Brahan Mumbai Corporation (BMC) Mumbai to stop employment to family members in the conservancy Department BMC in January 2001[1]

So when the top brass in the civil administration decided to stop an over 100-year old tradition which allow sweeper's son to clean the streets like his father once he retires or dies in the service, former Municipal Commissioner, S.S. Tinaikar remarked that,

> the nature of the job is so revolting that even if you give a lakh of rupees to the higher caste persons, he will not do this job.[2]

However, during the last few years the State Government took measures to abolish this practice in the state. Despite the efforts made by the government thousands of Bhangis are still doing manual scavenging. The government and society should realize that this blot on humanity should be removed. According to Indrajit Khanna, Chief Secretary, Government of Rajasthan, there are 11,700 manual scavengers[3] in the state. On the contrary as per the statement of Ms Asha Das, Secretary, Ministry of Social Justice and empowerment, Government of India, delivered at Jaipur on 23 May 2000, there are 21,000 manual scavengers[4] in Rajasthan. Referring to the present conditions of manual scavenging in Rajasthan, *Dainik Bhaskar*, one of the leading daily Hindi newspapers of the state published from Jaipur, reported that in more than 53 various small and big towns/cities of the state, manual scavenging is still in vogue.[5] In fact, the State Government has failed to implement in letter and spirit the schemes of abolishing manual scavenging in the state.

Besides State statistics, National statistics are also available on the manual scavenging. In a significant study made by the Sujan E. Cheplin, a foreign research scholar, working on manual scavenging among the sweepers in the country, she reported that inhuman practice continues in more than 2,500 small and big towns even after 54 years of Independence.[6]

In its efforts to ban the inhuman practice of manual scavenging in the state, the Kerala Government took strong measures. An Act banning manual scavenging promulgated long back was appreciated by the Central government as a just step towards its eradication. Banning the inhuman practice did produce the desired results. Thus, Kerala was the first state in the country to ban such bad practices in an effort to remove the stigma of inhuman practice.[7]

Besides Kerala, in a similar step, Madhya Pradesh and Andhra Pradesh governments[8] too through an Act managed to ban the inhuman practice.

What, one would like to know, is the scenario in Rajasthan? Since Independence, there had been no sincere and systematic efforts in the state. No government has considered it worth while to abolish such inhuman practice in all its ramifications. A year ago, Chief Minister Ashok Gehlot in Jaipur, admitted the seriousness of the problem. He, however announced publicly his government's intention for banning the manual practice in the state through state legislation. How much time would the State Government take is not clear.[9] Several states including Rajasthan do not have political will to ban this. And the overall condition in the state is worse.

It can be pointed out here that almost in all the states, lacs of Bhangis are doing manual scavenging. According to the report of the National Commission for Safai Karamcharis, the total number of such scavengers in the country is about 7 lacs.[10] But Asha Das's reported statement made on 23 May 2000 stated that in this country there are about six lac scavengers. She however, said that nearly two and a half lac scavengers have been rehabilitated so far.[11] On the contrary, some scholars claim that there are roughly ten lac scavengers engaged in this activity.[12] Everyone talks about the 'Upliftment' of Bhangis, but no action is ever taken.

In a significant study made by the Human Rights Watch, the World's Leading Human Rights Organization, working for prevention of violation of human rights among the weaker sections of the society, in its latest report titled 'Broken People: Caste Violence Against India's Untouchables' has indicated Gujarat government[13] on the continuing practice of manual scavenging in the state.

The 291 pages report begins by quoting a Bhangi manual scavenger of Ahmedabad district,

> When we are working, they (High Caste Hindus) ask not to come near them and when we ask for our rights from the Governments, the Municipality officials threaten to fire us.[14]

It further states:

> ... those working for Urban Municipalities in the Gujarat are paying us ₹ 30 to 40 and those working privately are paid ₹ 5 for each house, they clean ... even those working for Municipalities rarely get paid and are offered little health benefits for a job that entails many health hazards. In the cities scavengers are actually lowered into filthy gutters in order to unclog them, they are fully immersed in the human waste without any protective gear.[15]

It adds:

> Human rights watch was taken to various tea stalls to witness the separate tea tumbler system which scavengers are made to wash and handle their own tumblers so that glasses reserved for Caste Hindus are not polluted.[16]

Another such telling story comes from Sikar, Rajasthan, a district 120 km, away from state capital. In March 2001, P. Shainath's essay 'सिर पर मैला, दिल में दर्द' reported the pitiable state poignantly,[17]

> जी हां, मैं लोगों की टट्टी उठाती हूं! बदले में मुझे हर घर से हर दिन एक रोटी और हुआ तो दस रूपये हर महीने मिलते हैं। मैं हर दिन करीब पच्चीस घर साफ करती हूँ, हम लोगों का मल टोकरियों में डाल, सिर पर उठाकर फैंकने की जगह तक ले जाती हैं।

Referring to the Bhangis of Jodhpur, (Home district of CM) Shainath quoting Girjabai another Bhangan, reported:

> हमें हर घर से महीने के पांच रुपए और हर दिन एक रोटी मिलती है। इस बस्ती की एक बटा पांच औरतें मेला ढोने का काम करती है।[18]

This gives the crux of what government has done as socio-economic approach towards caste.

In a significant survey made by State Government, working on manual scavenging among the Bhangis in Rajasthan, the Government reported latest that inhuman practice continues in more than 56,000 families.[19]

Mangi Lal Arya, the National Commission for Safai Karamchari's former Chairman had, an even more amazing fact to reveal. According to Arya, Central Government allotted ₹ 8 crore to the Government of Rajasthan in regard to the execution of welfare schemes including abolition of manual scavenging for the Bhangis, but due to lack of well thought out strategy and obdurate attitude of the Government of Rajasthan, the allotted amount was not utilized. The fact is that only a small sum of ₹ 25 lac had been utilized[20] so far.

These are some of the hard core realities of the large number of illiterate and neglected Bhangis in the country's rural and urban areas. The proportion of the Bhangis who have remained powerless and without any means, despite the introduction of affirmative measures since Independence is 'alarmingly high' as the opportunity to bring caste equality and change in the social arena is yet to be translated into reality. Brandished by well-entrenched cultural and social taboos and the strong caste prejudices, these Bhangis are struggling against enormous odds.

Lessons from Gujarat and Rajasthan have now made it imperative that remedial measures should not only be carried out expeditiously, but should also be seen as such. It is a question of our political preference and a reflection of our nativity as to how much of these signs and warnings, we are able to discern and learn from.

State Government should have necessary political will and determination to implement the several socio-economic measures effectively. The district administration should be made fully accountable for any lapse in this regard, particularly with respect to abolition of manual scavenging.

There has been no structured, effective and systematic monitoring of the implementation of the several Acts and measures intended to benefit the sweepers.

Like State Human Rights Commission, State SCs and STs Commission and other Commissions, State Commission for Safai Karamcharis should be constituted immediately. This will be a legal body and would be more effective and real 'watchdog' for the progress of these people. Today the progress is tardy coupled with indifference and casual attitudes. Effective monitoring system should be in place.

There is an urgent need for the State Government to discuss the issues and problems concerning the sweepers. Otherwise, the sweepers will lose faith in the constitutional means and take to other means to shake off tyranny, injustice and oppressions. They have suffered long enough and urgent steps are required to give them total emancipation.

Besides, voluntary organisations and the others concerned about the well-being of these ignored and suppressed millions should think seriously and take concerted measures to consolidate and continue the struggle, for this struggle is a long one for human rehabilitation, human dignity and human rights.

Civic Body Recruitment of Upper Castes, OBC and Tribals as Sweepers

It is not surprising that there have been many instances about educated unemployed Bhangi youths in various towns. It is true that even deserving candidates do not get jobs because of hatred and prejudices against them. When they do not get any jobs then they have to end up either as peons or as scavengers again. This is the real issue. The crux of the matter is that the issue has generated a considerable apathetic attitude towards the education not only among the youths but also among the parents who have been sending their children for education. Hundreds of Bhangi youths are without jobs. Many a time, it has been observed that they are not only unemployed, but some employment exchanges do not send their names to the various government departments. In view of all this, what is more important for the government is to launch a special drive immediately to help the lowest of the low and poorest of the poor 'to achieve the economic progress'. This is another way to serve the most deprived section of the society.

There are numerous other ways of persecuting the sweepers. The caste hatred and inherent religious prejudices have combined in such a way that the sweepers particularly are grossly discriminated in the matter of educational and employment opportunities. The mental and psychological barriers of the caste Hindus has been a stumbling block. Most of the Bhangis are still engaged in the low level sweeping work to which others were never attracted for centuries. However, the situation took a new turn after India's independence, when some tribals, other backward classes, high caste Hindus and non-Hindus were appointed on sweeper posts by different Municipal Corporations and Municipalities in different regions of the country. For instance, it appears that in early 1952, Nagar Palika in Jodhpur (now Nagar Nigam) appointed a high caste Hindu as sweeper. From then on, eight more persons were added to the official roll.[21] In Nagaur also, a few high caste Hindus got appointment as scavengers in 1987.[22] In 1989, Northern Railway Workshop, at Jodhpur employed formally for the first time six upper castes, tribals and Muslims as sweepers.[23]

After Independence, some Adivasis were appointed as sweepers by the Ranchi Municipal Corporation (RMC) to clean the drainage and the roads. In 1994 the strength of Adivasi sweepers in the RMC was 227.[24] When the author looked at the scavengers of Patna, the state capital of Bihar, he found that in the Patna Municipal Corporation (PMC), the composition of the scavengers is different from that in Ranchi Municipal Corporation (RMC). The present strength of scavengers (Category I), under PMC is 4,209.[25] Out of this, there are 2,118 scheduled castes male and 1,225 female scavengers. Besides this, there are 9 tribal scavengers (all male), 600 Other Backward Classes scavengers (584 male and 16 female) and 226 general caste scavengers (221 male and 5 female).

It is often suggested that the high caste persons be appointed for scavenging work. According to this opinion the appointment by the different Municipal Corporations and Nagar Palikas in different regions of the country is not wrong, and indeed an act of this kind is necessary to raise the image of the scavenging work in the society. But when the attention is drawn to the fact that most of appointed high caste scavengers do not do the work in the real terms then the axe is bound to fall on the traditional Bhangis. It is not merely that they do not do the scavenging work, but more interesting and amazing is the fact that the work assigned to the high caste scavengers, is entirely performed by the traditional Bhangis in addition to their routine work and that too without being paid any extra remuneration. There is a growing apprehension among the sweepers that this process will diminish their avenues of employment.

The fact is that the Congress party has since Independence till today enjoyed the support of the Bhangis. It is Congress who ignored Bhangis and their issues at both in-party organizations and welfare programmes for weaker section of the society. The worst victims of caste system even after 67 years of Independence are the Bhangis with their inhuman practice of manual scavenging.

Notes

1. For more details see, 'Where sons follow fathers in clean sweep' in government business. *The Times of India*, New Delhi, 19 January 2001.
2. Ibid., 19 January 2001.
3. 'मैला ढोने वालों को दूसरे व्यवसायों से जोड़ा जाय' दैनिक भास्कर, जयपुर, 26 सितम्बर 2000.
4. 'राज्य में आज भी मैला ढो रहे हैं 21 हजार लोग' दैनिक भास्कर, जयपुर, 24 मई, 2000.
5. 'राज्य के 53 कस्बों में आज भी ढोया जाता है सिर पर मैला' दैनिक भास्कर, जयपुर, 23 जून 2001.

   G.K. Goswami's comprehensive and authoritative essay on the present-day scenario of manual scavenging in the country and Rajasthan in particular in *Dainik Bhaskar*, concentrates exclusively on the pitiable conditions of the Bhangi caste.

Goswami also gives excerpts and quotes from the Constitution of India, universal declaration of Human Rights, 1948, Census of India, 1961. Employment of Manual Scavengers and Construction of Dry Latrines (Prohibition) bill, 1993. I have benefitted from Goswami's essay. See 'अनेक शहरों में मैला ढोने की प्रथा '... मानव अधिकारों के बीचएक अमानवीय प्रथा' दैनिक भास्कर, जयपुर 15 फरवरी 2002.

6. पी. साईनाथ 'सिर पर मैला, दिल में दर्द' समय माजरा, जयपुर, मार्च 2001 पृ. 31.
7. वही, पृ. 30.
8. वही, पृ. 30.
9. Carrying of night soil on head to be made punishable: CM. in *HT, Jaipur, Live, Hindustan Times*, New Delhi, 23 November 2001. For more details, also see, Toilet in houses Mandatory soon? in *The Times of India*, Jaipur, Monday, 22 September 2014.
10. Shyam Lal, *The Changing Bhangis of India*, ibid., p. 143.
11. 'राज्य में आज भी मैला ढो रहे हैं 21 हजार लोग' दैनिक भास्कर, जयपुर 24 मई 2000.
12. वही, समय माजरा, जयपुर, मार्च 2001 पृ. 29 सन 1961 की जनगणनानुसार देश में मैला ढोने वालों की संख्या 8.2 लाख। विस्तृत जानकारी हेतु देखें: जी. के. गोस्वामी 'अनेक शहरों में मैला ढोने की प्रथाः मानव अधिकारों के बीचएक अमानवीय प्रथा' दैनिक भास्कर, जयपुर, 15 फरवरी 2002.
13. Gujarat Government indicted on manual scavenging, in *The Times of India*, New Delhi, 9 April 1999.
14. Ibid., 9 April 1999.
15. Ibid., 9 April 1999.
16. Ibid., 9 April 1999.
17. वही, समय माजरा, पृ. 28.
18. वही, समय माजरा, पृ. 29.
19. विस्तृत जानकारी के लिए देखें, '56,000 परिवार आज भी ढो रहे हैं मैला' राजस्थान पत्रिका, जोधपुर संस्करण, 5 अगस्त 2014। यह भी देखें 'ढ़ाई हजार महिलाओं ने कहा– अब सिर पर मैला नहीं उठाएगी' दैनिक भास्कर, जोधपुर संस्करण, 10 सितम्बर 2014.
20. Shyam Lal, *The Untold Story of a Bhangi Vice-Chancellor*, Jaipur: University Book House, 2001. p. 121.
21. Shyam Lal, *From Higher Caste to Lower Caste: The Process of Asprashyeekaran and Myth of Sanskritisation*, Jaipur, Rawat Publications, 1997, p. 113.
22. Ibid., p. 113.

23. The newspaper reporting also indicates that the sanctioned strength of the sweepers on Jaipur junction, Western Railway is 45. At present only 35 sweepers are working. Out of this there are 2 upper caste sweepers. Paper also reported that being upper castes they hesitate in sweeping and cleaning the platform. They also do not remove the human excreta. The third one is handicap: See, 'रेलवे स्टेशन की सफाई की जिम्मेदारी मात्र 34 कर्मियों पर', दैनिक भास्कर, जयपुर, 16 मई 2002.

24. Shyam Lal, *From Higher Caste to Lower Caste. The Process of Asprashyeekaran and Myth of Sanskritisation,* Jaipur, Rawat Publications, 1997, p. 45.

25. Ibid., p. 45.

12

Anna Movement and Aam Aadmi Party

Arvind Kejriwal formed Aam Aadmi Party (henceforth called AAP) in 2012, during a period of political crisis against corruption and growth of consciousness among youths in Delhi. Prior to formation of AAP, Anna Hazare launched big anti-corruption movement in Delhi. Under his leadership, protests, dharnas and rallies were organized. *This has been a peaceful political revolution of near epic proportions and we as a nation, should feel proud*[1] 2012, also witnessed decline and decay of Congress in Delhi. During an early phase between 2011–2012, Anna movement emphasized upon its distinct character, based on anticorruption movement, kept a distance from both the Congress and BJP parties and in fact, was hostile to them. This was a militant phase of mobilization of the youth as a tool to identify the corrupt politicians, breaking the existing system, pass a stronger Lokpal Bill, to investigate corruption in high places, criticism of Man Mohan Singh and main stream parties as corrupt parties by highlighting the failures of Congress regime. This was required for AAP to distinguish itself from other parties, specially Congress and BJP and to create an alternative space for itself.

AAP contested for the first time in Delhi Assembly Election, 2013 and in this election, the Congress did not perform well. Congress won only 8 out of 70 seats with 25 per cent of popular vote.[2] In Delhi Assembly Election 2013, the prestigious candidate of Congress party Chief Minister Sheila Dikshit was defeated by an AAP candidate,[3] Arvind Kejriwal.

BJP stood first and was able to gain 31 seats with 33 per cent of votes[4] in an important three-cornered contest. In the post-election phase, BJP resolved not to stake claim to form its own government or a coalition government in Delhi.

However, AAP came into prominence in Delhi Assembly Election in 2013. The scheduled castes, Muslims and, middle class voted overwhelmingly for the AAP due to anticorruption movement. It was instrumental in drawing away votes from Congress. In Delhi Assembly Election, AAP stood second, but was able to gain 28 seats with 29 per cent of votes in an important three-cornered contest. Thus, by 2013, AAP emerged as the second most important and well-known party in Delhi. It profited from the decline of Congress and made inroads into its traditional votes banks consisting of Dalits, a section of backward classes (BCs) and minorities.

Arvind Kejriwal began his first inning as Chief Minister of Delhi on December 28, 2013.[5] He proved his political mettle by comfortably forming AAP government even though the party was short of 8 seats for majority in Delhi Assembly. All the 8 Congress MLAs and one JD (U) MLA gave unconditional outside support to Kejriwal to become Chief Minister.

Data regarding Bhangi candidates fighting the Delhi Assembly Election 2013 were gleaned to examine the partywise allocation of tickets to Bhangis particularly, their goal of providing social justice to this most neglected and downtrodden section of society and its impact on politics.

The Bhangis, locally called Valmikis, are socially no-where, untouchables among untouchables, economically most backward and politically most neglected group by all parties in Rajasthan including all regions.

AAP

AAP entered the electoral arena in 2013, within a few months of its formation. In fact, our data gleaned from Delhi demonstrates that Valmikis' assertion through competitive electoral politics under the leadership of AAP, was a significant phenomenon in Delhi in 2013.

The study argues that despite staunch vote banks of a party such as Congress, they (Valmikis) find it difficult to progress. This makes it necessary to build electoral alliances and join other parties with different ideologies and policies.

AAP had given its five tickets in 2013 elections to Valmiki caste group. Other national parties, such as Congress and BJP in the Delhi Assembly Election had given it 5 and 3 tickets respectively in 2013 election to Valmiki caste candidates. BSP known as a Dalit party did not give even a single ticket to Valmiki candidates. Table 12.1 shows partywise Valmiki candidates in Delhi Assembly Election for 2013.

Table 12.1

Partywise Valmiki Candidates in Delhi Assembly Election 2013

S. No.	*Name of the Reserved Constituency*	*By Party Affiliation and Number of Candidates*			
		Congress	*BJP*	*AAP*	*Total*
1.	Trilokpuri	1	1	1	3
2.	Ambedkar Nagar	–	1	1	2
3.	Mongolpuri	–	–	1	1
4.	Sultanpuri	1	1	1	3
5.	Khikri	–	–	1	1
6.	Patel Nagar	1	–	–	1
7.	Devli	1	–	–	1
8.	Seemapuri	1	–	–	1
	Total	5	3	5	13

Source: The figures for 2013 Delhi Assembly election are not taken from official party list but have been gleaned from different sources.

An evaluation of electoral performance of AAP, Congress and BJP must take into consideration, as our analysis shows that in 2013 Assembly Election, AAP won 3 seats out of 5 allotted and lost 2 seats in Sultanpuri and Khikri. Thus, AAP was able to project itself as a party 'protecting' most lower castes, with the agenda of Dalit upliftment. During this phase Congress lost four seats and obtained one seat in Sultanpuri. The collapse of Congress was due to AAP. But the performance of BJP in Assembly Election 2013 was so poor, almost all the three Valmiki candidates lost the election miserably. Table 12.2 shows parties contesting and the election result for 2013.

Table 12.2

Reserved Assembly Seats for Scheduled Castes, Parties Contesting and Election Results For 2013 Election

S. No.	*Reserved Constituency for SC*	*Seat Won by Party*			*Seat Lost by Party*		
		Congress	*BJP*	*AAP*	*Congress*	*BJP*	*AAP*
1.	Trilokpuri	–	–	1	1	1	–
2.	Ambedkar Nagar	–	–	1	–	1	–
3.	Mongolpuri	–	–	1	–		–
4.	Sultanpuri	1	–	–	–	1	1
5.	Khikri	–	–	–	–	–	1
6.	Patel Nagar	–	–	1	–	–	
7.	Devli	–	–	–	1	–	–
8.	Seemapuri	–	–	–	1	–	–
	Total	1	–	3	4	3	2

Source: The figures for 2013 Delhi Assembly Election are not taken from Official list, but have been collected from different sources.

Kejriwal's Cabinet

On Saturday, 28 December 2013, Arvind Kejriwal took the oath of new Chief Minister of Delhi at the packed Ramlila Maidan. For him, this was a 'tryst with a destiny' moment.[6] Six legislators were inducted in Kejriwal's Cabinet on Saturday at the grand show of Kejriwal's own swearing in, at Ramlila Maidan. Six ministers[7] were administered the oath of office and secrecy by Lieutenant Governor, Najeeb Jung. They were: Manish Sisodia, Somnath Bharti, Satendra Jain, Rakhi Bidlan, Girish Soni and Sourabh Bharadwaj.

We shall discuss in brief about Rakhi Bidlan, one of the Ministers in Kejriwal's Cabinet.

Rakhi Bidlan:[8] The First Women Valmiki Minister

First time legislator from Mangolpuri constituency, Rakhi Bidlan, 26, is SC face representing Valmiki Samaj. She is one of the three Valmiki legislators of AAP. She worked with a private news channel before she quit work to join Jan Lokpal Andolan. She quit the job to contest the election from Mongolpuri and caused one of the biggest electoral upsets by beating former PWD Minister, Raj Kumar Chauhan. Her father was associated with Congress for long, but quit in 2011 to join the Jan Lokpal movement.

Soon after taking the oath of secrecy, Rakhi Bidlan became Minister of Women and Child Development, Social Welfare, Languages, Women's safety.

Notes

1. See, 'Times View' in Sunday, *Times of India*, Jaipur, 29 December 2013.
2. For more detailed information, see, particularly 'सर्वजन का उदय' इंडिया टुडे, राजस्थान विशेष, 25 दिसम्बर 2013, पृ. 18.
3. Ibid., p. 18.
4. Ibid., p. 18.
5. See, 'The Aam Aadmi Had a Party', in Sunday, *The Times of India*, Jaipur, 29 December 2013.
6. Ibid.
7. Ibid.
8. See, 'Kejri's Fire Brigade' in *The Times of India*, Jaipur, Tuesday, 24 December 2013.

13

Congress Losing the Pivot

There are only a few studies in which the voting behaviour/trend of political support to political parties amongst SC/ST has been carried out in sociological literature. One has been by Owen M. Lynch (1969)[1] and another by L.P. Vidhyarthi and K.N. Sahay[2] (1976). While the former discussed voting behaviour in relation to tribal groups of undivided Bihar, the latter discussed it to explain the genesis of social movement and social change in relation to Jatavs of Agra, Uttar Pradesh. Sudha Pai[3] analyses the political behaviour of the Chamars of Uttar Pradesh. In addition to all this, attempts have been made further by Eleanor Zelliot[4] and Hard Grave, Jr.[5] to refer to the Mahars of Maharashtra and the Nadars of Tamilnadu respectively.

The Bhangis occupy the lowest social status, characterized by disadvantages and discrimination of several kinds, and of different degrees. Attempts have not been made so far to analyse objectively the voting pattern amongst the Dalits of Rajasthan. The main purpose of this study is to get some idea of changing pattern of voting behaviour of lowest of the low untouchable castes: the Bhangis, in Rajasthan, and to bring out the impact of development during 67 years.

A Section of Bhangis Deserting Congress

In Bihar

As stated earlier a few studies on the themes are available. One such study titled, *People at the Bottom: A Portrait of the Scavengers* outside Rajasthan have been carried out by Sachchidananda (2001).[6] The main purpose of the study was to get some idea of living and working conditions of different scavenging castes in Bihar.

In Bihar, there is improvement in the working conditions of the Bhangis. The attitude of youths towards political parties has changed now. Although the political support to Congress was started by Bhangis during pre-independence period under Gandhi's influence, it suffered a great setback after Rajiv Gandhi's assassination. According to Sachchidananda, there is a widespread belief among the Bhangis that, they are not getting a fair share in the political process.[7] They feel that they are being ignored by Congress men and Congress leadership. Politically, Bhangis tend to be alienated from Congress. The Bhangis remain, by and large, neglected. The study also highlights that majority of the Bhangis of Bihar keep themselves away from Congress and prefer BJP.

The study brings out the fact that, BJP is more popular among the respondents who are in the income group of below ₹ 2,000 per month. One of the interesting findings of the study is that the influence of BSP and communists who champion the cause of Dalits is almost negligible whereas the BJP is emerging as a powerful force against Congress and RJD in traditional Congress citadel; RJD is popular among the higher group members in urban areas.[8]

In Delhi

In eight reserved seats of Delhi Assembly, which went to polls in November 2013, there were 4 Valmiki candidates out of 70 assembly seats. In comparison, as per data gleaned from unofficial sources, the number of elected Valmiki candidates were 1 Congress and 3 AAP respectively. Congress, which claims to be representative of Dalits in general, and Valmikis in particular, had fielded 5 candidates, but won only one.

Similarly, there were 5 candidates of AAP in the fray, of which 3 candidates won on AAP tickets. Thus, the drifting of Valmiki voters from Congress to AAP is quite obvious.

In Rajasthan

With the development of socio-educational and political consciousness during the last 67 years, the Bhangis across the state felt the frustration. This situation partly explains why the Bhangis discarded Congress, where the discrimination against them in the field of politics and government employment were severe. This was the first set of events of significance. The Bhangis took the courage to oppose the Congress and Bhangis in increasing number supported BJP during Assembly Election, 2013 and Parliamentary Election, 2014. In course of wandering, the author came in contact with a few highly educated persons who are considered to be social activists capable of telling the grassroot realities. If their conversation is to be believed, the Bhangis may not be going enblock, but a section is certainly opting for the saffron party as an alternative. For instance, Dr G.S. Vishnar[9] made extensive tour, propagating BJP support, visiting places in east Rajasthan and meeting fellow castemen. He visited Alwar, Bharatpur, Dausa, Bundi, Kota, Jhalawar, Baran, etc. and that he encouraged his castemen to support BJP openly.

Similarly, Purushottam Gehlot[10], a retired Principal, from PG Government College, Jaisalmer, who hails from Nathdwara and comes from Bhangi Samaj, in a telephonic conversation with the author cogently argued that this time the Bhangis drifted from the earlier active and open political support to Congress. It is a fact that a sizeable section of Bhangi Samaj in Udaipur region had allied with BJP. Purushottam Gehlot claims that a good number of young Bhangis also joined other organizations by diverting its attention from politics to social service sectors. Vishva Hindu Parishad, Shiva Sena, Bajrang Dal, RSS and other saffron front organisations are making a bid to involve Bhangis and it is because of this, that they want the Bhangis to be part of their organizations and function mainly as agents of socio-religious change and also for party propaganda. The indifferent and negative attitude of Congress towards

Bhangi community, as noted earlier, in Rajasthan is responsible for their deserting the Congress in the state.

As stated earlier, since independence all untouchable communities/castes including Bhangis have been supporting the Congress, both covertly and overtly. After independence, Dalits were told by both Dalit leaders and Congress leadership that if they wanted to improve their socio-economic and educational conditions, it was their duty to support Congress, which in real terms meant voting for 'Congress'.

In India's political lexicon, thereafter, Dalits and Congress became synonymous with 'Dalit Vote Bank'.

The socio-economic conditions of the Bhangis deteriorated after Indira Gandhi's assassination; their representation in Vidhan Sabha declined. Similarly, their recruitment in Nagar Palikas, Nagar Parishads and Nagar Nigams across the state, declined; they became economically more vulnerable. They went into a shell and their sense of victimhood forced them to withdraw from the social and political ghetto.

Congress, which claimed to be well-wisher and saviour of the Bhangis, took the services of Bhangi social workers instead of educated Bhangis to garner Bhangi votes. The social workers were more concerned with Nagar Palikas, Nagar Parishads and Nagar Nigams, recruitment of sweepers and protection of their rights in these institutions.

Realizing that Congress only cared for and promoted small leaders, even educated Bhangis started speaking the same language. Bhangis have been carrying this on their feeble shoulders for the last 67 years.

Since his student days, the author along with others of his age had been campaigning for Congress candidates. They had noticed that all meetings for Congress candidates were organized in the Bhangi bastis/mohallas. Later they realized that it was not to educate the Bhangis about socio-economic reform, but to create the fear of Jana Sangh, making Bhangi vote for Congress unquestioningly. The same game has been played over and again and gullible Bhangis, as well as their intelligentsia, have carried this as an honour and privilege since independence.

Several Congress's old Bhangi netas had been unhappy with Congress's indifferent attitude and this was seen as a conspiracy to ignore the community as the party's part and parcel policy. The criticism from both old and young party supporters assume significance as there has been a discontent brewing within common Bhangi masses and even among some senior workers over lack of positive thinking.

The Congress has been steadily losing its core vote bank. Years before Mukesh Valmiki quit the Congress, while a series of acrimonious letters between top leaders Ashok Gehlot and Mukesh Valmiki was exchanged and the distance between them within the party played a major role. Mukesh Valmiki was a great social activist, a great campaigner and a good orator also.

During the Congress rule in the state there has been less attention of political will to translate intentions into outcomes. The negative power of Congress to thwart is certainly manifest. But the positive power, the power, to do something to execute programmes and provide basic goods are 'the bread and butter' of a state's responsibility to Dalits in general, and Bhangis in particular, is still a far cry.

All Dalit communities including the Bhangis feel cheated. But Congress Government did not even intend to do something for their welfare. The sense of responsibility was missing.

Till recently, BJP had been considered as 'anti-Dalits' across the state and the country. However, the BJP is spreading its wings to the country's Dalits as senior leaders of Dalit communities are now joining it.

Now situation has changed completely. For instance, during the recent State Assembly Election held in Rajasthan (2013) 32 out of 34, SC reserved seats in the state were won by BJP. Similarly, during the April Lok Sabha polls 2014, all 4 BJP Dalit candidates from reserved constituencies in Rajasthan were declared elected.

The Bhangi's exposition is not the first and may not be the last account emerging from the inner circle shedding light on Ashok Gehlot's government. This is a story of Bhangi frailty, we can instantly understand it. The rest of it is just politics. Ashok Gehlot is hardly the first, not the last, practitioner of politics in this sense.

One of the Bhangi's allegations was that Ashok Gehlot had more control over the party and government than anyone else. There are many people to corroborate this aspect of contemporary Congress culture, that people were not encouraged to express their feelings in case Ashok Gehlot had his word. In Ashok Gehlot's days, however, it congealed into a dogma that could not be questioned. The Bhangi disenchantment with Congress reflects the break down of Bhangi Congress consensus. The Bhangi community was tired of this game and eventually pulled the rug from under Congress's feet.

Immediately after the State Assembly Elections, 2013 and Lok Sabha polls in April 2014, Congress state president, Sachin Pilot declared that party's state unit would soon ascertain the reasons of defeat and would be reorganized and revitalized.

After a few months, party veterans felt the need to invigorate the workers and check the BJP tide. Mohan Lal Joad – an active social worker said that in the first week of July 2014 a dharna was staged at Aakhliya Choraha, Jodhpur by Congress against price rise and inflation. Former Chief Minister, Ashok Gehlot too came and was staying in the circuit house, Jodhpur. The former CM, however was more interested in knowing the reasons of radical defeat of Congress. The urban local bodies elections are ahead and would once again test the Congress leadership against its arch rivals BJP. Gehlot talked about the formation of Congress board in future.

While staying at the circuit house, Gehlot met each and every Congress worker and listened to them individually. When M.L. Joad met Gehlot, he freely and frankly expressed his views/opinions on the issue. He said that the reason the party had failed to secure a better result was that its traditional supporters – Dalits in general, and Bhangis in particular, did not support the Congress and voted in large number against it. He also said that since pre-independence till date, Congress considered Bhangis as their vote bank and were viewed as being in their pockets. He further said that one pocket of Bhangi vote bank has been cut by BJP in 2013 and the second pocket was cut in 2014.

Analysis done by Bhangi netas and social workers of Congress claimed that Congress's loss in Rajasthan was due to neglect of Bhangi's interest and indifferent attitude of Congress leadership and the government. This was the prime motive behind his few minutes meeting with former CM. The former CM, Ashok Gehlot remarked, 'You are right, I will see it'.

Similarly, on 18 August 2014, the district Congress unit, Jodhpur organized a meeting at district Congress office located at Jaswant Saray. Sources said that Saran, came from Jaipur. He presided over the meeting. Others who attended it were: former Congress MLA, Jugal Kishor Kabra, former JDA Chairman Jodhpur, Rajendra Solanki, Sayed Ansari, old Congress social worker, Srimali, etc.

Mohanlal Joad was also invited to this meeting. The main purpose of the meeting was believed to ascertain the reasons of Congress defeat in 2013 and 2014 polls. Sources claimed that different views and opinions were expressed on this issue individually. But Joad, however, told different stories. Here, he reiterated the same views which he had earlier narrated before former CM, Ashok Gehlot and held that the Congress itself was responsible for the debacle.

BJP Woos Bhangis, Cashes in on Resentment Over Not Fulfilling Promises

To ensure that Dalits in general and Bhangis in particular, votes go to BJP and help in winning the Assembly Election (2013) in the western region including Jodhpur and Pali, BJP workers were seen organizing meetings and canvassing with Bhangi activists.

Through these meetings, BJP was attempting to cash in on the resentment of Bhangi community over not recruiting of sweepers in Nagar Palikas, Nagar Parishads and Nagar Nigams across the state. For many of Bhangi educated youths, non-availability of government jobs for them was a huge cause of concern. Some wanted the change and hoped that upcoming government will bring in policies to provide jobs, etc. The author, therefore, visited a few cities to know the mood of Bhangi voters.

Sources said, BJP workers met Bhangi netas and urged community members to help and vote for Narendra Modi. They assured that their genuine demands would be fulfilled and urged the people of the community to vote for Modi and BJP, a Bhangi social activist said.

O.P. Jawa[11] had reportedly told several times to community social workers, leaders and netas that during Congress regime, Bhangis were betrayed several times, despite the community favouring the then ruling party. He also said Bhangis were not benefitted, though they had been supporting Congress for years/decades. For more than 20 years, no one cared for them.

The educated Bhangi youths were also seen discussing Narendra Modi's prospects of becoming Prime Minister and their support to political parties in this election (2013). This may seem unusual. Ashok Gehlot had made several promises to Bhangi community. But he failed even to fulfil a single promise. Criticizing bitterly the negative and betraying attitude of the Congress, most Bhangi voters were gravitating towards BJP and deserted the Congress. People think Congress has done much for the Bhangis. The Congress has been beating the same drum. Actually Congress has done nothing for us, says Rakesh Kumar Jawa,[12] who is a Congress supporter. The Bhangi voters tired of the ruling Congress party supported BJP for a change. Thus, Dalits including Bhangis dumped the Congress.

The generational change in Bhangi leadership and voters is evident when educated youths and social workers from different bastis, mohallas and localities decided to teach a lesson to Congress. Kanhailal Kaloshia[13] repeated and openly levelled charges against Ashok Gehlot and the party. As a result of all this, Ashok Gehlot has got the feeling that his core base (the Bhangi) is eroding.

The Bhangis do not see any point in voting for the Congress. The Congress MLAs have built community centres, schools and other basic facilities for others and nothing for the Bhangi community. Even during campaigning, none of the Congresses candidates or his/her representatives, social workers or social activists bothered to visit their bastis, mohallas and localities. Till a few decades back Congress men used to visit and interact with them. 'Now the situation has changed after 1990', said Madan Lal Boyat,[14] an octogenarian of Bhangi community whose family is residing in Lakharon-ka Bass. No amount of transformational changes in the lives of a few Bhangi families – big houses, motor cycles, scooters and cars – broaden the views of other communities towards them. Bhangis feel a buzz here this time. The outcome is certain. This time voters are being wooed with a passion.

The Congress social workers and social activists tried to garner the support of safai karamcharis in Jodhpur Nagar Nigam by plying the Bhangis with cash and drinks ahead of voting through sanitary inspectors. In various bastis, the chant was 'Khao-pio-Sabh-ka, Vote Do Manka' (accept every one's booze and food, vote at your own will).

Mohan Lal Joad[15] said the polling pattern in Bhangi bastis, mohallas and localities reflects that they have voted against Congress. The maximum benefit of this situation was taken by BJP. Those Bhangis who voted for BJP in state assembly polls wished to keep the Congress at bay. He said the situation remained the same in parliamentary polls 2014, in Rajasthan. We are used as vote bank and Congress has not done anything for us. Meanwhile, others reap benefits. To this, Kanhailal Kaloshia said that this time we have changed our strategy and supported BJP. He makes it a point to speak about social issues. Congress made hollow promises in the name of Bhangi's welfare/empowerment. The Congress party and its leaders cry for Bhangi, in and outside Rajasthan. But do not bother about their socio-economic and political problems in the state.

Even in Jaipur – the capital of Rajasthan, the consolidation is evident. In Ajmer, the Bhangis are overwhelmingly in favour of BJP – BJP was a more popular choice than Congress. A bunch of factors – the negative and indifferent attitude of Ashok Gehlot, betraying politics of Congress and others have worked in BJP's favour. According to state president of ABVM, Kanhailal Kaloshia,[16] Ashok Gehlot is anti-Valmiki. He has not fulfilled even a single promise during his ten-year tenure. Kaloshia campaigned and voted for BJP to ensure that at least BJP forms the government in Rajasthan.

Criticizing his own community's submissive nature before the Congress party Kaloshia said,

> Submissive politics is not going to help the Samaj. There is also internal conflict within the community which was strongly visible in the community meeting held in Rajasthan.

In the 67 years between then and now a lot has happened in the Congress and Congress leaders of Rajasthan. Bhangi community which is Congress's core voters have drifted away from Congress because the Chief Minister had broken the promises made and they feel cheated by Congress. There is growing frustration amongst the Bhangis of Rajasthan.

We hear a lot about the empowerment of the Dalits in the state but do not hear much on how to improve the socio-economic and educational conditions of the poor, specially the Bhangis eke out their existence from their traditional work.

Shiv Singh, the Director of NGO 'Allarippu' wanted the author to address 'Valmiki Adhikar Samvad Sammelan' at Tehsil Kishangarh, District Alwar, Rajasthan as it would encourage the Valmiki masses and also add prestige to the socio-educational awareness campaign. As per scheduled programme the author reached Kishangarh on 22 December 2013, that is more than a month after the formation of BJP Government under Vasundhara Raje's leadership. The author addressed[17] the gathering consisting of Valmiki men, women, boys, girls and social workers extolling the virtue of education in general and for Valmikis in particular. The function was Chaired by Mohan Lal Joad. The author had detailed discussion with the gathering, NGO's officials, Meo leader Noor Mohammed, social activists and educated boys and girls about the importance of education. The participants shared their experiences: that still in schools savarna Hindus observe untouchability, that school authorities do not give admission to Valmiki children, that Valmiki boys and girls have to clean the school campus forcefully, that Valmiki children are harassed, humiliated and insulted. Thus, even after 67 years of Independence untouchability is still in practice. The author was shocked to listen to personal experiences of humiliation, harassment, untouchability and insulting Valmiki men, women, boys and girls had to face. The author was grieved to find that Valmikis are still treated as untouchables by upper caste Hindus. The author was highly amazed to hear that Valmiki youths were under the influence of BJP. The author paid attention to Noor Mohammed although the author differed from him on BJP influence.

The author cited some eminent Dalit leaders, notably Dr B.R. Amedkar, K.R. Narainan, Babu Jagjivan Ram and Meira Kumar who became Chairman of Drafting Committee of the Constitution, President of India, Deputy Prime Minister of India and First Woman Speaker of Lok Sabha respectively, because of education. Apart from these personalities, the author also presented himself as a living example of becoming Vice-Chancellor of three leading universities. Literacy is very important. We, the Valmikis do not have the power because our people are not educated. The author is very much in favour of education. In the long run, the upliftment of the Valmiki community in particular, and masses in general, will depend on the education of the community people. Mohan Lal Joad also emphasized on eradication of social evils.

It is clear from the foregoing description that Savarna Hindus still treat Valmikis as untouchables. A few caste Hindu social workers who participated in the 'Samvad' are treated as sympathizers.

In the first week of April, when Parliamentary Election, 2014 across the country were announced by the Election Commission, New Delhi, BJP once again started talking of 'Mission 25'. It may be noted here that some Bhangi leaders were in favour of the Congress but majority was against it.

In this context, the author asked Ram Tarun Tamboli,[18] a resident of Kishangarh, Alwar, social activist and also attached with an NGO working amongst the Valmikis, to brief the author about the mood of Valmikis. Tamboli pointed out that a day before the election at five parliamentary constituencies including Alwar, he convened a meeting of Valmiki youths on 23 April 2014 at Kishangarh to judge the mood, whether they were in favour of Congress or against it.

The Valmikis who are voters of Alwar Lok Sabha seat and are not much educated are now aware of the political scenario of the state and country through communication tools like electronic and print media, etc. They were quite engrossed with the election happenings around them. For them the BJP candidate was not worthy of becoming a member of Parliament from this seat, but what prompted them to support him was the party's Prime Ministerial candidate Narendra Modi. The Valmikis were for 'Modi Sarkar' at the centre.

The Valmikis were traditional vote bank of the Congress for years as noted earlier. But in 2013, they shifted their loyalties to BJP. This time the people were impressed by Modi. In other words, Narendra Modi may have got the nation chanting 'Abki baar, Modi Sarkar' – the BJP slogan for change.

Congratulation Ceremony to Vasundhara Raje

In the political history of Rajasthan, 2013 was an important year. BJP had emerged as a single largest party winning 163 seats out of 200 Assembly seats. There was a national urge, on the part of BJP to form a new government. As a result, Vasundhara Raje was administered the oath of Office and Secrecy by Margaret Alva – the Governor of Rajasthan. The oath ceremony was held at Janpath in front of State Assembly on Friday, 20 December 2013, which was attended by large number of people from different parts of the state.

At this point of time, the ABVM did not lose the opportunity. Just after a few days of oath taking ceremony, ABVM decided for 'Congratulation Ceremony' to Vasundhara Raje. ABVM also prepared 8-point Charter of demands to draw her attention to the problems of Bhangis. Thus, a delegation comprising 40 people of ABVM went to Chief Minister's official residence located in Civil Lines, Jaipur, on 27 November 2013 and ABVM under the leadership of Dr G.S. Vishnar congratulated Vasundhara Raje at her bungalow. The delegation had a brief discussion with Raje – the Chief Minister of Rajasthan.

The most significant event during the meeting with Raje was submission of Charter of demands[19] of Valmiki Samaj to solve their long pending issues. For instance, ABVM demanded for recruiting of sweepers in Nagar Palikas, Nagar Parishads and Nagar Nigams across the state. The same was also submitted to the then Chief Minister Ashok Gehlot and Congress Government, but they did not pay any attention. This was a manifestation of deep resentment of the Valmiki Samaj against the Congress Government. The leaders, (Kanhai Lal Kaloshia was no doubt the foremost) were concerned with 8 basic issues:

1. Separate reservation for the Bhangis.
2. Theka Pratha (contract system) be abolished.
3. To recruit the sweepers in Nagar Palikas, Nagar Parishads and Nagar Nigams across the state.
4. To nominate Bhangis in various bodies namely Commissions, Nagar Parishads, Nagar Nigams, etc.
5. To nominate Bhangis in Vidhan Parishad, if it is formed in the state.
6. To increase Minimum Labour Wages to ₹ 166 per day for Safai Karamcharis in rural areas, particularly village panchayat and Govt. Departments.
7. To revive the scheme, which was initially launched by Raje's government during 2007 recruiting the P.G. candidates from Bhangi Samaj on contract basis against vacant posts lying in various departments on fixed emolument.
8. To declare public holiday on Valmiki Jayanti.

The delegation was headed by ABVM's President, Dr G.S. Vishnar and Rajasthan ABVM's President, Kanhailal Kaloshia.

There were two important developments, which contributed towards the removal of frustration and political gap of Valmikis with BJP. According to Kaloshia, the meeting with Chief Minister Vasundhara Raje was held in good atmosphere and the latter had given assurance of resolving their problems on priority basis after Parliamentary elections, 2014. This changed the whole attitude of Valmikis towards BJP in general and to Raje in particular. It was considered as a victory by ABVM. Raje was highly impressed by the political support, the Valmikis had extended. Raje expressed the hope and urged that Valmikis would continue their support towards 'Mission 25' goal, which Raje had placed before them. In reply to Raje's urge, the delegation promised that they would fully support the 'Mission 25'.

Bhangi Netas from ABVM Support BJP as Next Government at Delhi

It is important to note here that a few Bhangi netas, social workers and social activists, ahead of the state assembly polls

2013, met Congress and BJP party leaders. The purpose of the meeting was seeking the tickets for assembly polls 2013, although most of them were not part of the respective party organizations. Congress and BJP denied the tickets. Through them, the negative message of political parties spread all over Rajasthan and reached the masses at city level. A heated war of words erupted over Congress and BJP's indifferent attitude to Bhangi community.

After sometimes, attempts were made by certain Bhangi netas to discuss the issues of the community. These efforts acquired the character of a movement and created widespread and spontaneous excitement. In addition to leader's efforts, the ABVM too which was already in existence and functioning in the state, assumed the task of organizing the community meeting. A few months later in September–October 2013, a meeting was called at Kota, Rajasthan. A few eminent leaders, netas and social workers participated in it. They were: Madan Maharaja former Congress MLA, Kota, Ramgopal Raja, former Congress supporter and now BJP supporter (Kota), Suresh T, Congress (Jaipur), Dr G.S. Vishnar, National President ABVM (Kota), Gopal Pacherwal, Vice President, National Morcha, BJP (Kota), Narender Chanwaria and Mahesh Bimal, both Congress (Jaipur), Suresh Valmiki, BJP (Kota), Kanhailal Kaloshia, Ajmer and a few others.

They criticized bitterly Congress and BJP's indifferent attitude towards Bhangi community and it was decided that a national convention on the issue be called immediately. Due to encouragement and cooperation of all leaders, netas and social workers, ABVM was able to convene its national convention on 16 February 2014 at Sagar, Madhya Pradesh, and a large number of people from different regions attended it.

National President of ABVM, Dr G.S. Vishnar envisaged the need for a powerful political support to reach the masses and in BJP he found it. In a move that has left the Congress red-faced, the national convention on 16 February 2014 announced publically, open support to BJP in parliamentary polls 2014. The stunning development took place at ABVM's convention ahead of Lok Sabha elections on 17 and 24 April in Rajasthan.

Dr G.S. Vishnar told the author that they supported BJP because the community was upset at the manner in which his community fellows had been treated by the Congress and its leaders.

The foregoing account of national convention's achievements shows that Dr G.S. Vishnar provided a new ideology and his charismatic leadership brought about a political regeneration and gave his community fellows self-confidence and respect. Many other Dalit communities had already deserted the Congress long back and joined BJP, but Dr G.S. Vishnar was the first Bhangi untouchable to have supported BJP openly by his intellectual abilities of comprehending socio-political scenario of the state as well as the country. Since 1947 till today the entire community was with Congress in the state and this is Dr Vishnar who pleaded for BJP and asked his community fellows to support and cast their votes to BJP which they had opposed earlier. He also thought it necessary to break the old relations with Congress. Even many so-called keepers of Valmikis causes have done little for the community other than suggestions, such as, 'Never vote BJP, always vote Congress'. This approach caused more harm than good. They must not only oppose the BJP, they must also entice with support if their conditions are met. However, taking permanent side is not profitable.

The ABVM is dedicated to community's upliftment and welfare programmes. The ABVM, which has its headquarters at New Delhi and patron's residence at Kota, Rajasthan, convened the meeting of its executive committee on 30 March 2014 for preparing statement in support of BJP. The meeting was chaired by Dr G.S. Vishnar. It was attended by a few eminent Bhangis notably – Madan Maharaja, Ramgopal Raja, Kanhai lal Kaloshia, Mahesh Bimal, Narendra Chanwaria and Suresh Valmiki. Dr G. S. Vishnar maintained close contact with BJP leaders in order to strengthen the political relation that he had brought about. Hence, ABVM (Registered in 1986 registration No. 18973/88) in April 2014 two-page pamphlet titled 'अपील : बाल्मिकी समाज का भारतीय जनता पार्टी को वोट क्यों?'[20] was published and circulated throughout the state supporting Narendra Modi as the next Indian Prime Minister. He was now actively following up on this announcement and met selected BJP leaders. His decision was widely appreciated. He exhorted his people to come forward and support them (BJP).

In an open letter/an Appeal was made in April 2014: Three leaders led by Dr G.S. Vishnar, Ramgopal Raja and Kanhai Lal Kaloshia of ABVM attacked the Congress party saying …

> 65 वर्षों में अधिकांश समय कांग्रेस की सरकार रही है। कांग्रेस सरकार ने वाल्मिकी समुदाय के लिए प्रतिबद्धता तथा समर्पण भाव से इनके जीवन को उपर उठाने का उदार मन से प्रयास नहीं किया है, परिणामस्वरूप भारतीय समुदाय में वाल्मिकी समाज आज भी अन्तिम पंक्ति का समुदाय माना जाता है।
>
> मंथन और चिंतन के पश्चात इस निष्कर्ष पर पहुंचे है कि इसके लिए कांग्रेस सरकार की रीति नीति ही जिम्मेदार है। हम समुदाय से करबद्व अपील करते हैं कि भारतीय जनता पार्टी के अल्पकालीन शासन में वाल्मिकी समुदाय के लिए जो कार्य किया है , वह अत्यन्त प्रशंसनीय रहे हैं जिनका वर्णन निम्न प्रकार से उल्लेखित है–

Why should Valmiki community support and cast their valuable votes to BJP? For this, it is significant to note that during Bhairon Singh Shekhawat and Vasundhara Raje's regime, several historical socio-political decisions were taken in political history of Rajasthan.[21] For the first time, late Sri Kishan Lal Valmiki was nominated as BJP member to Rajya Sabha, late Shri Dungar Ram Panwar was made first Zila Pramukh and later on inducted as Minister in Bhairon Singh Shekhawat Cabinet. In state assembly polls 2008, under the leadership of Vasundhara Raje, two tickets were given to Valmikis, namely Gopal Pacherwal and Smt Anjana Panwar.

Apart from all this, there was Bangaru Laxman[22] – a great social worker of Andhra Pradesh. Coming from a poor and humble Valmiki family, Bangaru Laxman was appointed BJP President by the then PM, AB Vajpayee.

Similarly, for the first time in the social history of the state, the then BJP government championed the cause of the sweeper community. On 11 June 2007,[23] the Department of Personnel vide notification No. F. 17 (3) Personnel/Ka–2/2007, issued the letter to all District Collectors to give appointment against vacant posts lying in the various Departments to candidates belonging to scavenging community having postgraduate degree, on contract basis and on fixed emolument.

These are regarded as moonlight in the dark. Thus, the local association supported BJP.

The letter/an Appeal was signed by Dr G.S. Vishnar (National President, ABVM), Ramgopal Raja (National General Secretary, ABVM) and Kanhailal Kaloshia (State President ABVM) and others. They said:

> बाल्मिकी भाइयो, गत 65 वर्षों से कांग्रेस ने दलितों और आदिवासियों को झूठे वायदे, आश्वासन व भय दिखाकर गुमराह किया और उसने हजारों वोटों की कीमत को कुछ उपहार देकर वोट बैंक के रूप में इस्तेमाल करता रहा है। हमने वोट की कीमत को नहीं पहचाना और कांग्रेस के वोट बैंक होकर समाज को कलंकित किया है। भाइयो, समाज पर जन्मजात कांग्रेसी होने का जो दाग लगा हुआ है, उसेधोने का समय आ गया है।[24]

They further add:

> अतः वाल्मिकी समुदाय से इस प्रतिवेदन के माध्यम से अपील करते हैं कि भाजपा के द्वारा विगत शासन काल में वाल्मिकी समुदाय के संदर्भ में किये गए निर्णय वास्तव में काबिले तारीफ थे। पार्टी ने इतने बड़े निर्णय लेकर यह बताने का प्रयास किया कि हैसियत, सम्मान तथा प्रशासनिक कार्यो में समुदाय की व्यापक सहभागिता देखना चाहती है। इसी परिप्रेक्ष्य में आपसे निवेदन करते हैं कि भारतीय जनता पार्टी को वोट और समर्थन देकर भारी मतों से विजयी बनायें।[25]

Anti-Congress Campaign Through SMS Message

Besides publishing and circulating pamphlets across the state, supporting BJP, leaders, netas and social activists of ABVM, Rajasthan also initiated sending their SMS message, as supporting activities of ABVM from State Assembly Election 2013. SMS message was also one of ABVM's constructive programmes and was one of the main anti-Congress programmes of ABVM, which they had initiated much earlier (i.e. State Assembly Election 2013). The SMS message was 'इस बार सरकार बदलनी है'. Like Kanhailal Kaloshia, many individual workers like Indra Kumar Lohra, Alwar and Jaswant Chanwaria, Nasirabad, Ajmer took a leading part in the campaign by disuading the Valmikis from voting for Congress. SMS message campaign had succeeded to some extent in certain parts.

Kanhaiyalal Kaloshia, as state president of ABVM, Rajasthan paid a good deal of attention to its SMS message campaign. Under his leadership SMS message became well organized and acquired the character of a wider campaign.

The SMS message campaign started by Kaloshia was re-initiated by April 2014, a few days before the commencement of Parliament polls on 17 and 24 April 2014 in Rajasthan. Dear sir 'Aabki Baar BJP ki Sarkar' says SMS circulated in Rajasthan.

Kanhailal Kaloshia's message is believed to be directed against Congress candidates across the state fighting parliamentary election, 2014. Kaloshia said we were supporting BJP as a whole, not as an individual. BJP party is our choice, Kaloshia feels what BJP under the dynamic leadership of Vasundhara Raje has done for our community, Congress who remained in power for longest duration could not have done. Kaloshia, the State President of ABVM Rajasthan said he does not agree with Congress's ideology. I support the views of BJP, I want (Narendra) Modi as PM.

With the publication and distribution of pamphlets in support of BJP across the state during the Parliamentary Elections 2014, the mild reaction erupted among the Congress supporter Bhangis. There were few Congress supporters who benefitted during the Congress Government. For instance, Prem Chand Rana, a resident of Dausa district was nominated as a counsellor to Nagar Palika/Nagar Parishad, Dausa. It was possible because of Congress government. Likewise, it is also believed that Muneem Chand Tamboli, from Nasirabad, Ajmer, had political contacts with upper caste Congress leaders and that they supported him to be nominated to Nasirabad Nagar Palika/Nagar Parishad. But the common men did not oppose these pamphlets and SMS message campaign because they were not given the jobs. With the development of education during 67 years, there was frustration among educated Bhangis because of inaccessibility to the benefit of modern education. Even the undergraduate and postgraduate candidates from the community were ready to do sweeper's jobs in Nagar Palikas, but were never given opportunity to work.

Thus, in Rajasthan, better known Bhangi organizations have withdrawn their support to Congress. In current elections, and earlier ones also, a few eminent Bhangi netas notably Gopal Pacherwal, Ramgopal Raja, and Mukesh Valmiki joined the BJP. Gopal Pacherwal contested the election on BJP ticket in 2004. This reflects the extent of Bhangi's alienation in Rajasthan. The

Bhangi community that were once thought of as natural supporters of Congress have found it difficult to support Congress. It was not just in assembly election 2013 that Congress could not win a single SC seat out of 34. The Congress did not get support of Dalit's in general and Bhangis in particular, in Parliamentary Election 2014. In Rajasthan, the open support of powerful All India Valmiki Mahasabha eventually pushed Congress to the margin. Sanjay Kumar,[26] Director, Centre for Study of Developing Societies said in his article,

> यहां तक कि मध्य प्रदेश, गुजरात, छत्तीसगढ़ या राजस्थान जैसे राज्यों में जहॉ कांग्रेस की भाजपा से सीधी टक्कर है, पार्टी ओबीसी मतों को आकर्षित नहीं कर पाई है। उसके हक मेंएक तिहाई से थोड़े ज्यादा वोट आए जबकि ज्यादातर ओबीसी वोट भाजपा को मिले हैं।
>
> सीएसडीएस की ओर से कराए अध्ययन से संकेत मिले हैं कि कांग्रेस अपने दलित समर्थक, क्षेत्रीय या प्रादेशिक दलों के हक में खो चुकी है। अब कॉग्रेस दलित वोटरों के लिए पहला विकल्प नहीं रही है।
>
> अखिल भारतीय स्तर पर देखें तो 30 फीसदी से भी कम दलित मतदाताओं ने कांग्रेस के पक्ष में मतदान किया है जिन राज्यों में कॉग्रेस की सीधी टक्कर क्षेत्रीय दलों से है, वहॉ तो दलित मतों में इसकी हिस्सेदारी 22–23 फीसदी तक गिर गई है। कॉग्रेंस के इस नुकसान का भाजपा को ज्यादा फायदा नहीं होता, क्योंकि पिछले कुछ लोक सभा चुनावों में सिर्फ 10–12 फीसदी दलितों ने ही भाजपा के पक्ष में मतदान किया है। सीएसडीएस द्वारा कराए गये सर्वे में भाजपा और क्षेत्रीय दलों के पक्ष में दलित समर्थन का कुछ झुकाव देखा गया है लेकिन कांग्रेस के लिए शायद ही कोई आकर्षण है।

It is clear from the foregoing description that: For a long time, the Congress has been in steady decline, rapidly losing its support base in one time bastion of Dalits. This has been largely due to ignoring ground realities. Cocooned in their outmoded views, they have been unable to gauge the pulse of aspirational Dalits.

Results are therefore all to see. The Congress's organizational efficacy has gradually eroded. Its state leadership needs to be held accountable for this drastic decline.

Grassroot Dalit leaders were never given a greater voice. As it is, disenchantment with Congress party's style of functioning led to Dalits (their natural supporters) deserting to BJP fold.

In Uttar Pradesh

It had happened in Bihar, Rajasthan and Delhi (2013) and now it is apparently coming true in Uttar Pradesh as well (2014). According to the *Times of India:*[27]

> The drifting of second layer of Dalit voters – Pasis, Dhobis, Valmikis, Khatiqs and Dushads to BJP is quite obvious. They may not be going enblock, but a section is certainly opting for the saffron party as an alternative. Communal Polarization of course, is one reason for this. But this is also happening of alienation of these castes.

Paper further add,

> Jatavs also called 'Chamars' are the ones who have seen maximum progress during Mayawati's rule, while others have remained virtually untouched. This is the reason for a collective enhancement among non-Jatavs.

For the first time[28] since its inception three decades back, the BSP drew a blank in the Lok Sabha Election, 2014. Besides the collapse of its Dalit-Brahmin and Dalit-Muslim social engineering formula, the results indicated that a section of the party's core Dalit supporters have voted for BJP which won all the 17 reserved seats from the state with huge margins.

J.P. Shukla,[29] a political analyst, said:

> While BSP failed to open its account, the SP was restricted to its family boroughs. The upper caste deserted Maya, the Dalits too walked away to an extent. The BJP wave broke the caste barriers which BSP and SP had built over the years.

In the first wave of social engineering, while backward caste voters moved towards BJP, their real influence remained limited. Social scientist, Christophe Jaffrelot has shown that their proportional representation in the party's national executive and that of MPs returned from Hindi belt did not change significantly in the 1990s.

What Amit Shah was now promising was a second wave of social engineering. This is what is so different about BJP this time and UP was the first test of this new thrust.

In UP in 2014, Amit Shah spearheaded a realignment which saw the projection of Modi as India's first OBC Minister, the promising of a Bharat Ratan for Kashi Ram, and a concerted effort to break the Dalit vote. This meant replicating old BSP strategies of venerating Dalit icons, except that BJP chose to focus on communities like Valmiki, Pasi, Sonkar and other non-Jatav categories that were unhappy with Jatav dominance in Mayawati's BSP. This was combined with ruthless ticket selection, a technical savvy rural communications campaign and 27 seats to OBC candidates despite strong opposition by local apparatus. The result was an unprecedented 73 seats.[30]

Notes

1. Lyunch, Owen M., *The Politics of Untouchability (Social Mobility and Social Change in City of India)*, Delhi, National Publishing House, 1974.
2. Vidhyarthi, L. P. and Sahay, K.N., *The Dynamics of Tribal Leadership in Bihar*, Allahabad, Kitab Mahal, 1976.
3. Pai, Sudha, *Dalit Assertion and the Unfinished Democratic Revolution: The Bahujan Samaj Party in Uttar Pradesh*, New Delhi, Sage Publications, 2002.
4. Zelliot, Eleanor, 'Learning the Use of Political Means: The Mahars of Maharashtra' in Rajni Kothari (ed.), *Caste in Indian Politics*, New Delhi, Orient Longman, 1970.
5. Hard Grave, Jr. 'Political Participation and Primordial Solidarity: The Nadars of Tamilnadu' in Rajni Kothari (ed.) *Caste in Indian Politics*, New Delhi, Orient Longman, 1970.
6. Sachchidananda, *People at the Bottom: A Portrait of the Scavengers*, New Delhi, Concept Publishing Company, 2001.
7. Ibid., p. 104.
8. Ibid., p. 106–107.
9. Telephonic conversation of the author with Dr G. S. Vishnar, Kota, on 6 May 2014.
10. Telephonic conversation of the author with Purushottam Gehlot, Chittorgarh, on 7 May 2014.
11. Talks with O.P. Jawa, a social activist and worker, Jodhpur on October 2013.
12. Talks with Rakesh Kumar Jawa, a Congress supporter,, Jodhpur, on October 2013.
13. Talks with Kanhailal Kaloshia, State President, ABVM, Rajasthan, Ajmer, on 15 November 2013.

14. Talks with Madan Lal Boyat, 80, Lakharon ka Bass, Jodhpur on January 2014.
15. Talks with Mohan Lal Joad, social worker, Jodhpur on December 2013 and April 2014.
16. Talks with Kanhailal Kaloshia, Jaipur, on 8 February 2014.
17. Talks with Ram Tarun Tamboli, a social activist and worker, Alwar on 4 December 2013. For more details, see, particularly, 'अशिक्षा समस्या की जड़ : बाल्मिकी अधिकार संवाद सम्मेलन' राजस्थान पत्रिका, अलवर संस्करण, रविवार, 29 दिसम्बर 2014 Also see 'अशिक्षा समस्याओं की जड़ : जेदिया' दैनिक नवज्योति, रविवार, 29 दिसम्बर 2013 'वाल्मिकी संवाद सम्मेलन का आयोजन' दैनिक भास्कर, अलवर, रविवार, 29 दिसम्बर 2013.
18. Talks with Ram Tarun Tamboli, Alwar on 26 and 30 April 2014.
19. For more details, see particularly two letters addressed to Vasundhara Raje, Chief Minister, Rajasthan by Kanhai lal Kaloshia, State President, ABVM, Rajasthan.
20. Talks with Mr G.S. Vishnar, National President, ABVM, Kota, on 6 May 2014. For more details, see particularly two-page pamphlet published and circulated by अखिल भारतीय वाल्मिकी महासभा titled वाल्मिकी समाज का भारतीय जनता पार्टी को वोट क्यों?
21. Ibid.
22. Ibid.
23. Shyam Lal, *Dr Ambedkar Foundation: Issues and Challenges*, Jaipur, University Book House, 2013, p. 56.
24. देखें, 'वाल्मिकी समाज का भारतीय जनता पार्टी को वोट क्यो?
25. Ibid.
26. For more details, see particularly Sanjay Kumar 'कांग्रेंस का आत्मघाती कदम' दैनिक भास्कर, जयपुर, मई 5, 2014.
27. For more details, see: A Section of Dalits May be Deserting Maya in *The Times of India*, Jaipur, Saturday, 10 May 2014.
28. See, Mayawati O, BSPs Social engineering 'Formula fails to work, BJP wins all 17 reserved seats' in the *Indian Express*, New Delhi, Saturday, 17 May 2014.
29. See, 'Eye on 2017, SP, BSP, move away from Congress' in *The Times of India*, Jaipur, Monday, 19 May 2014. Also see, 'Right Caste fit remains crucial to win elections' and 'The Hindi Heart Lands' Caste in stone in *The Times of India*, Monday, 19 May 2014.
30. See, 'The BJP's New Shah' in *The Times of India*, Jaipur, Monday, 11 August 2014.

Index